the
ODD
BRAIN

the ODD BRAIN

mysteries of our weird and wonderful brains explained

Dr. Stephen Juan

**Andrews McMeel
Publishing, LLC**

Kansas City

06 07 08 09 10 RR2 10 9 8 7 6 5 4 3 2 1

ISBN-13: 978-0-7407-6159-1
ISBN-10: 0-7407-6159-5

Library of Congress Control Number: 2006923126

www.andrewsmcmeel.com

ATTENTION: SCHOOLS AND BUSINESSES
Andrews McMeel books are available at quantity discounts with bulk purchase for educational, business, or sales promotional use. For information, please write to: Special Sales Department, Andrews McMeel Publishing, LLC, 4520 Main Street, Kansas City, Missouri 64111.

To Buffy with love

contents

acknowledgments

Where does one start when trying to thank all those who helped make a book possible? The dedicated and tireless scientists and researchers who investigate the human brain, mind, and body are at the top of the list. It's lonely work and often goes unrecognized. But these are the true heroes in the knowledge revolution. Some are from the medical sciences, some from the behavioral sciences, and some from elsewhere. Radio and television interviewers have said, "Dr. Juan has so much to report on so many subjects." It's flattering but embarrassing, too. Yet there would be nothing to report if researchers were not toiling in the trenches to advance our knowledge. When they come up with great discoveries, my job is easy. They do all the work; I just tell their story.

I am grateful to the following authors and publishers for permission to reproduce previously published material:

Chapter 2, S. Baron-Cohen, "An assessment of violence in a young man with Asperger's syndrome," *Journal of Child Psychology and Psychiatry*, vol. 29, pages 351–352, copyright 1988 by the Association for Child Psychology and Psychiatry. Reprinted by permission of the Association for Child Psychology and Psychiatry. E. Susman, "How to tell Asperger's from autism," *The Brown University Child and Adolescent Behavior Letter*, January 1996, pages 1 and 6, copyright 1996 by the Brown University Child and Adolescent Behavior Letter. Reprinted by permission of *The Brown University Child and Adolescent Behavior Letter*.

Chapter 3, B. McEwen and H. Schmeck, *The Hostage Brain*, pages 6–7, copyright 1994 by the Rockefeller University Press. Reprinted by permission of the Rockefeller University Press.

Chapter 4, D. Dolphin, "Porphyria, vampires, and werewolves:

age 15 years and criminality at age 24 years," *Archives of General Psychiatry*, vol. 47, page 1003, copyright 1990 by the American Medical Association. Reprinted by permission of the American Medical Association.

Chapter 11, R. Siegel, *Intoxication: Life in Pursuit of Artificial Paradise*, pages 23 and 118, copyright 1989 by Ronald K. Siegel, Ph.D., Inc. Used by permission of Dutton Signet, a division of Penguin Books USA, Inc.

Chapter 15, D. Chalmers, "The puzzle of conscious experience," *Scientific American*, December 1995, page 80, copyright 1995 by David Chalmers. Reprinted by permission of David Chalmers. M. Hettinger, "The power of positive thinking," *Your Health*, September 3, 1996, page 16, copyright 1996 by Your Health. Reprinted by permission of Your Health. P. Kramer, *Listening to Prozac*, pages 2 and 13, copyright 1993 by Peter D. Kramer. Used by permission of Viking Press, a division of Penguin Books USA, Inc.

Chapter 16, R. Willard, "Breast enlargement through visual imagery and hypnosis," *American Journal of Clinical Hypnosis*, vol. 19, pages 196–197, copyright 1977 by the American Association of Clinical Hypnosis. Reprinted by permission of the American Association of Clinical Hypnosis.

Chapter 20, B. Justice, R. Justice, and I. Kraft, "Early-warning signs of violence: Is a triad enough?," *American Journal of Psychiatry*, vol. 131, pages 457–458, copyright 1974 by the American Psychiatric Association. Reprinted by permission of the American Psychiatric Association. A. Labelle, J. Bradford, D. Bourget, B. Jones, and M. Carmichael, "Adolescent murderers," *Canadian Journal of Psychiatry*, vol. 36, pages 583 and 586, copyright 1991 by the Canadian Psychiatric Association. Reprinted by permission of the Canadian Psychiatric Association.

43–44, copyright 1987 by the Avenue Publishing Company. Reprinted by permission of the Avenue Publishing Company.

Chapter 31, K. Dillon, R. Gross-Isseroff, M. Israeli, and A. Biegon, "Autoradiographic analysis of serotonin 5-HT1A receptor binding in the human brain postmortem: Effects of age and alcohol," *Brain Research*, vol. 554, page 56, copyright 1991 by Elsevier Science. Reprinted by permission of Elsevier Science. C. Mills, "Suicides and homicides in their relation to weather changes," *American Journal of Psychiatry*, vol. 91, page 669, copyright 1934 by the American Psychiatric Association. Reprinted by permission of the American Psychiatric Association.

Chapter 33, J. Andrade, "Learning during anaesthesia: A review," *British Journal of Psychology*, vol. 86, page 479, copyright 1995 by the British Psychological Society. Reprinted by permission of the British Psychological Society.

Chapter 34, B. Raphael, *When Disaster Strikes*, page 13, copyright 1986 by Basic Books, Inc. Reprinted by permission of HarperCollins Publishers, Inc.

I also wish to thank my university students for asking questions and allowing me to digress from formal lectures and simply talk about new research discoveries.

Thanks are also due to the librarians at the University of Sydney and those at other universities and hospitals in Sydney. Thanks also to the many anonymous people who put information on the Internet.

For the creators and maintainers of MEDLINE, a special thank you. For those who don't know, MEDLINE is a medical information database accessible through the Internet. It contains research articles from thousands of medical journals. Needless to say, I'm addicted, as are thirty thousand users every day. MEDLINE is a great asset to public health education.

Thanks to Stephen Ruwe, Muriel Nellis, and Jane Roberts, my agents.

Thanks too to Jude McGee and the wonderful people at HarperCollins Australia: Geof Armstrong, Kate Chad, Mel Cox, Christine Farmer, Melissa Gabbott, Sarah Gentle, Angelo Loukakiss, and Sue Page. Special thanks to my editor, Belinda Yuille, who had a larger job to do than any of us first thought. Also thanks to the fantastic people at Andrews McMeel. These include Patty Rice, Katie Anderson, Michelle Daniel, and Christi Hoffman. Again, thanks to illustrator Rod Clement for making *The Odd Brain* as eye-catching as *The Odd Body*.

Dr. Stephen Juan

intro**duction**

The brain is so wonderful!

Have you ever wondered at how fantastic the human brain truly is? Every thought, every action, every deed relies on this incredible organ. Although we take the brain for granted, we couldn't wonder without it. We would exist, but we wouldn't be conceived.

According to the World Health Organization, the 1990s were the decade of the brain. The timing was perfect. In the 1990s we learned a great deal about the human brain, its functioning as the mind, and its relationship to the body. In fact, we've learned more about the brain in the last decade or so than in all previous centuries combined. And the rate of knowledge acquisition is increasing. Indeed, from the standpoint of brain knowledge, it's a great time to be alive. Practically every week we read of some new and exciting brain breakthrough. A new piece of the jigsaw puzzle is revealed and fitted into place. The whole picture is getting a little clearer. More so than at any other time in history, we know more about the brain itself and how it operates—and what goes wrong when it doesn't operate correctly.

Sometimes the brain doesn't work right. Physical and psychiatric problems can emerge from the brain going awry, malfunctioning in some odd way to bring about some odd behavior. Simply put, when the brain acts abnormally, we act abnormally. Behaviors resulting from the brain misfiring can be as weird as they are devastating to individuals and families. Most of us are normal (or close to it). There is a range of variation in all human societies such that no one is truly typical. It is fascinating to observe the abnormal—the fringes of humanity. And as we remember that every human is deserving of our respect, tolerance, love, and sense of humanity, we must temper our observations of the abnormal with this constant thought: "There but for the grace of God go I."

It's fun to dispel widely held myths about the brain. Sometimes evidence does not support the brain being involved in common conditions or behaviors. For example, most of us have experienced déjà vu. Have you ever been curious about what goes on in your brain when you experience déjà vu?

Sadly, for centuries generations of people have inflicted social injustice on thousands and thousands of their fellow humans. We used to blame people for their so-called moral failure when they committed antisocial acts. Kleptomania immediately comes to mind. To some extent, some of us still condemn kleptomaniacs and think the only place for them is in prison. But such condemnation and punishment would cease if people understood why kleptomaniacs compulsively steal. Science now tells us that kleptomania may have multiple causes. And one cause may be organic, having to do with the brain itself. Rather than moral failure, it is a question of brain biochemistry. Thus, it's not the person's fault. And logic and justice dictate that they should not be punished for their behavior but offered therapy.

As brain research progresses, strange, unusual, and sometimes humorous facts are uncovered. And as we look ahead, in the coming years we will see new brain truths. Human behavior is complex. We know that explaining human behavior always involves multiple factors. Perhaps someday the true relationship between the brain, the mind, the body, and society will be mapped, and we will achieve a greater understanding of what it means to be a human being.

For the delight and education of readers, we bring you here some of what we know from brain research.

The brain is wonderful! And we hope you think this book is, too.

Chapter 1
The **Antiseptic Brain:**
The Brain's Little Cleaners, Or What Ever Happened to Einstein's Brain?

Besides all the other odd things about the human brain, the brain is also the "cleanest" of all organs. In fact, compared with the skin, our largest organ, you could almost say the brain is antiseptic.

As clean, trim, strong, and fit as any athlete, the brain maintains its continuous high level of top performance by "washing" itself. It keeps itself immaculately free of the slightest

MORE ELECTRIcal impulses are generated in one day by a single human brain than by all the telephones in the world.

contaminating impurity, that is, of anything that could rob it of efficiency.

Our brain is at its largest in early adulthood, when it has approximately 100 billion neurons (brain cells). Most scientists agree that we lose between 10,000 and 100,000 neurons per day. When neurons die through old age, disease, or injury, they are rapidly consumed and digested by special glial cells attached to neurons. You might say they are the brain's wonderful little housekeepers. In addition to being cleaners, these glial cells also serve as nurses by providing sustenance to healthy neurons.

This washing process helps the brain store, along its more than 100 billion neurons, more than 100 billion items of information. This is five hundred times the amount of information in a set of encyclopedias. And the glial cells may help account for the fact that the brain is still able to send out electrical impulses thirty-seven hours after death.

Since 1985, Drs. Marian Diamond and Arnold Scheibel have theorized that the more glial cells per neuron the brain possesses, the "cleaner" and more efficient the brain becomes, and hence the greater a person's intelligence is likely to be.

They base their theory on research with twelve human brains, including the brain of the greatest of all scientists: Albert Einstein.

Albert Einstein (1879–1955) had perhaps the greatest scientific mind of all time. After his fatal heart attack in Princeton, New Jersey in 1955, Einstein's brain was surgically removed by pathologist Dr. Thomas Harvey during the autopsy at Princeton Hospital and preserved for future scientific study.

When Harvey left Princeton, he took the brain with him to the University of Kansas in Wichita and then to his home in Weston, Missouri. At first, he kept the brain in the back of his refrigerator. Then, after dissecting the brain, labeling the pieces, and storing them in glass jars filled with formaldehyde, he kept the jars in a cardboard box once used for shipping apple juice.

In 1979, almost thirty years after the autopsy, Diamond contacted Harvey and asked for enough of Einstein's brain tissue to conduct her research. After many delays, specimens finally arrived on her doorstep in 1982. The brain slices were ready for study: perfect, immaculate, and neatly sealed in plastic to avoid contamination.

Diamond and Scheibel presented their glial cell efficiency–intelligence theory in a 1985 article titled "On the Brain of a Scientist: Albert Einstein."[1]

They counted the number of glial cells per neuron in Einstein's brain and compared that figure with those from eleven other brains taken from men of presumably average intelligence.

Diamond and Scheibel found that in one particular area of the brain's left hemisphere, Einstein's brain had 73 percent more glial cells per neuron than any of the other brains. They concluded that this could help account for Einstein's great intelligence.

But critics were quick to respond. Most argued that Diamond and Scheibel erred by making hasty generalizations about the relationship between glial cells and intelligence. They pointed out that science had not established any causal link between intelligence and the quantity or quality of neurons. Others argued that no

IT IS ESTIMATED that on an average day the human brain produces 70,000 thoughts.

THE HUMAN brain weighs less than 5 pounds.

CONTRARY TO popular wisdom, the human brain does not use only 10 percent of its brain matter. Imaging techniques now dramatically illustrate that the brain uses 100 percent of its brain matter, but not all of it at all times.

firm conclusions could be drawn from only twelve cases. After all, human variation is great in most other areas, so why not in the ratio of glial cells to neurons as well? Still others claimed that such a difference between humans is meaningless—that Einstein's larger number of glial cells would have no more bearing on his intelligence than would the shape of his belly button.

Critics pointed out that some evidence suggests that as the brain grows older, the effort to keep the brain "clean" becomes greater, so the number of glial cells probably increases with age. Thus, critics reasoned, because Einstein was seventy-four when he died, his glial cell count would be high anyway. Had a young Einstein's brain been studied, the results would have been different.

But the harshest critics of all dismissed the whole affair as tasteless and tawdry. Some contended that Einstein's brain should be left alone.

In the course of this debate, it was revealed that Einstein's family had never given permission for his brain to be removed, preserved, or studied. This greatly embarrassed not only Diamond and Scheibel but also Harvey.

Respecting the family's wishes, Harvey has offered to make other samples of Einstein's brain available to serious researchers. Einstein's brain cells could still be used today to enhance scientific knowledge.

Of course, the role of glial cells gives the term "brainwashing" a new meaning. And ironically, more than forty years after his death, we are still learning from Einstein.[2]

EINSTEIN AND TELEPATHY

Albert Einstein believed mental telepathy to be a very real phenomenon. He even worked out a formula to describe mental telepathy in mathematical terms. He maintained that the intensity of the telepathic signal grows weaker as the distance between the sender and the receiver increases. This is precisely what happens to radio and television waves.[3]

THE BRAIN'S FIVE LOBES

According to Dr. Philip Whitfield, the brain's five lobes on each hemisphere of the brain—prefrontal, frontal, temporal, parietal, and occipital—are named after the five bones that cover them.[4]

THE BRAIN'S COLOR

Folklore refers to the color of the brain as gray. This is the so-called gray matter. But when they see their first brain many are surprised to find that it isn't gray. Some describe it as looking more blue, light brown, pink, or even green.

THE BRAIN'S TEXTURE

What does the brain feel like when you touch it? Some describe it as firm, others as squishy. Both are correct. The human brain is rather firm in youth, but it can become squishy in old age. Some diseases, such as Creutzfeldt–Jakob disease (spongiform encephalopathy), can make the brain lose its firmness. As *spongiform* implies, the brain takes on a spongy texture.

THE HUMAN BRAIN: NOTHING BUT THE FACTS

The human brain is 11.8 inches long, 7.9 inches wide, and 5.9 inches in depth. At birth, the brain weighs about three quarters of a pound. At its largest in early adulthood, the female brain weighs between 2.65 and 2.87 pounds, and the male brain weighs between 2.87 and 3.09 pounds. At this time it consists of approximately 100 billion neurons (brain cells) and other supportive cells. Between the ages of twenty and sixty, we lose approximately 0.04 to 0.11 ounces of brain tissue each year. After age sixty, we lose 0.11 to 0.14 ounces each year. It seems that we lose neurons at an ever-escalating rate throughout life.[4]

HOW MANY NEURONS DO WE REALLY LOSE EACH DAY?

In recent decades we've been told that we lose up to 100,000 neurons each day. But according to Dr. Larry Squire, such a high estimate of brain cell loss is "one of the great persisting myths of human neurobiology." Squire adds that the brain does indeed lose some cells daily, but not on the grand scale of 100,000 every day. He notes that, in any case, it is impossible to precisely count neurons. Counting neurons can be done only by examining brain tissue on a laboratory slide under a microscope. However, the physical task of counting is too difficult because there are simply too many for a person to count without losing count. In addition, chemicals used to preserve brain tissue for laboratory examination tend to shrink the tissue.[5]

THE BRAIN'S ADAPTIVE ABILITY

The brain's connections develop quickly in response to outside stimulation, particularly during the first three years of life. A child's experiences, good or bad, influence the wiring of the brain and the connections in the nervous system. Thus, when we snuggle a baby or talk to him or her in a singsong, undulating rhythm, we are contributing to the growth of his or her brain.

How do we know this? Research examining one of the body's stress-sensitive systems demonstrates how outside experiences shape a child's developing brain. One stress-sensitive system in particular is activated when children are faced with physical or emotional trauma. Activation of this system produces a steroid hormone called cortisol. High levels of cortisol cause the death of brain cells and reduce the number of connections between the cells in certain areas of the brain. Research in adults who have experienced chronic or intense activation of the system that produces cortisol shows shrinkage of a certain brain region that is important in learning and memory. Clearly, a link exists between physical or emotional trauma and long-term impairments to learning and development.

Nature has provided a way of buffering the negative effects of these stress systems in the brain: strong attachments between children and their parents or caregivers.

Studies measuring the levels of cortisol in children's saliva show that those who receive warm and responsive care are able to turn off this stress-sensitive response more quickly and efficiently. Babies with strong emotional bonds to their caregivers showed consistently lower levels of cortisol in their brains.

Positive and nurturing experiences can help brighten a child's future, whereas negative and non-nurturing experiences can do the opposite. Children who are emotionally neglected or abandoned early in life not only are more likely to have difficulty in learning but also have more trouble experiencing empathy, attachment, and emotional expression in general. An excess of cortisol in the brain is linked to impaired cognitive ability and difficulty in responding appropriately or productively in stressful situations. Healthy relationships during the early years of development help create a framework for interactions with others throughout life.

What are positive and nurturing experiences? For starters, the young child needs good prenatal care, warm and loving emotional attachments to the adults and other children in the home, and age-appropriate stimulation from the time of birth.[6]

Chapter 2
Asperger's Disorder:
When You Are Robbed of Empathy

It is when you are robbed of empathy. Or if you have empathy, you cannot or do not show it. Yet no one is to blame. It is called Asperger's syndrome (AS). But it is also known as Asperger's disorder or now simply Asperger's.

An extreme case of AS is that of "John and Betty." It was written by noted London child psychiatrist Dr. Simon Baron-Cohen in 1988.[1]

John, age twenty-one, regularly and brutally bashed Betty, age seventy-one, his live-in "girlfriend." Betty's screams continually brought complaints from the couple's suburban London neighbors. The police eventually took John to a psychiatric hospital. When examined, John readily and unashamedly admitted to the assaults. It was apparent that John had no understanding that his violent acts hurt Betty.

John emerges as a pathetic and deeply troubled individual. His relationship with Betty, fifty years his senior and a tortured soul herself, is as sad as it is brutal.

Baron-Cohen continues:

Referral *At the age of 21 years, John was referred by his father to the Maudsley Hospital Children's Department, London, for advice on whether his son had been or might currently be autistic. He described his son's current problems as: (1) difficulties in communicating; (2) difficulties in adapting to change; (3) obsessional interest in his jaw; (4) violence towards a particular old lady; and (5) general inability to fit into any social group. The obsession with his jaw and the violence were recent problems; the others were long-standing. The recent violence had resulted in an admission to an adult psychiatric ward, where they were finding him puzzling.*

Developmental history *The pregnancy and birth were normal. As an infant he did not seek affection. He is reported to have flapped his hands at 3 years old. His language was unremarkable in the early years, although he always had difficulty with conversational use of language (and this persists). He showed unusual ability to learn verbal material such as lists. In this respect, John's father described his son as having always been very obsessional: as a boy, he had always been able to list the "Top 40" by heart, and could similarly reel off details about cars—their engine capacities, specifications, etc. John's father called it a "staggering knowledge." John also knew the waveband of* *every radio station, and the times of each programme on the different stations. According to his father, he has always lacked an ability to know what other people are feeling. As a young child, he showed no pretend play, and did not like puzzles. He was always socially withdrawn. He liked reading and repetitive activities. He has always been physically uncoordinated. At 11 years old he would still scream and shout when upset by changes in routine. He has sometimes masturbated in public. John attended ordinary school, and coped with the academic aspects, passing 3 "O" Levels and 5 CSEs. John's father explained his son's ability to pass French and German "O" Levels as "parrot stuff," similar to his ability to commit long lists to memory. His peer relations at school were always a problem. He did not complete his "A" Levels, although his teacher thought he could pass.*

Major life events and family history John's father is successful in one of the professions, and has 4 sons, of whom John is the third. His mother was a language teacher who is reported to have worried about harming members of her family. She suffered from depression and, when John was 11 years old, she committed suicide. John apparently saw his mother dead and is reported to have shown little reaction to her death at the time, and describes his feelings about his mother's death as being "disquieted." Since then, John has had many dreams that his mother is still alive. John's father remarried when John was 15. According to his father, John's new step-mother hated him, and he regularly destroyed her property and ran away from home. At 16, he tried to jump out of a window. At 17 he was arrested after a stealing incident and sent to a remand home. Following this, he went to live with his father's sister and trained to work in a garden nursery. When his father

*visited, he smashed up his father's car and motorbike with a
hammer. He was sent to a probation hostel at age 19, and
while he was there he was reported to have displayed bizarre
behaviours such as continuous mirror-gazing and smearing
excreta on the walls. He then went to live with his aunt but
after a short period moved in with an acquaintance of hers,
Betty, a 71-year-old lady whom he describes as his girlfriend.
Since then, over the 4 years they have lived together, he has
attacked her frequently, and this has resulted in two admis-
sions to his local psychiatric hospital, where he is at present.
He has recently expressed the belief that he looks like a werewolf, and this may be related to his obsession with his jaw.*[1]

Baron-Cohen ends the case study on the note that John
and Betty's destructive relationship has ended, that Betty is safe
and no longer being beaten, and that John is continuing to
receive treatment.

Baron-Cohen argues that many criminals may actually be
suffering from AS. He claims that they are not willfully antisocial. It is just how their brains operate. Therefore, instead of
being incarcerated as criminals who committed crimes based
on criminal motivations, they should be treated as psychiatric
patients. Indeed, we should think of such sufferers in the same
way as we view kleptomaniacs and pyromaniacs: criminals by
acts but not by intentions. And certainly no
one is to blame.

THE HUMAN
brain makes up
about 2.5 percent
of the average
person's body
weight.

Furthermore, Baron-Cohen argues
that we have probably underestimated the
numbers of people with Asperger's in the
community:

> *Many people who come to the attention of secure units because of violence may have Asperger's syndrome. A study of the prevalence of such cases in prisons and secure units would be worthwhile.* [1]

Besides being unable to show empathy in the normal sense, those suffering from Asperger's have difficulty forming friendships.

For people with Asperger's, social interaction is one-sided, naive, and inappropriate. As Dr. Edward Susman says, "Indeed, one of the markers of Asperger's Disorder is severely impaired social functioning." [2] This may lead to destructive behaviors such as arson. [3]

Starting in early childhood, AS sufferers often exhibit poor speech and nonverbal communication skills (for example, not responding to the facial expressions of other human beings), clumsiness, poor physical coordination, and often an odd posture. [4] In addition, they are notably lacking in imaginative skills and often have an intense absorption in certain subjects, such as the memorizing of bus and railway timetables or the compiling of unusual lists. As Susman explains,

> *The salient feature of the disorder is the child's preoccupation with a favorite subject—such as dinosaurs, genealogy and sometimes violent and sexual themes—and will talk about it, often in a monotone or in strangely affected speech patterns, at great length and at inappropriate times. Nor will the child detect, understand or heed attempts by others to stop. He or she will often avoid making eye contact with others, but will have a vast, detailed interest in the environment. The child can memorize numerous facts and understand what they mean.* [2]

Such self-absorption can have its advantages. It can often result in an individual gaining an exceptional skill or talent in a specific area. They have even been referred to as "little professors" as children. But they may be easily bullied or teased due to their social ineptitude and their naiveté concerning the rules of society. AS sufferers have a profound inability to deal with changing social situations. They prefer sameness, are particularly unaware of body language, and often cannot maintain socially appropriate distance. They are often overly sensitive to sounds, tastes, smells, and sights. Comfortable with routine, AS sufferers can be easily diagnosed as obsessive-compulsives.

AS is a neurobiological problem first recognized in the 1940s by a Viennese child psychiatrist named Hans Asperger. Dr. Asperger described a pattern of behaviors in several young boys who, although they had normal intelligence, also showed behaviors that were strangely similar to another mysterious disorder—autism. The boys had few or no social skills. Since then, AS and autism have been conceptually linked by those wanting to understand both. Autistic symptoms usually appear earlier than symptoms of AS.

The prevalence of Asperger's is unknown. But males seem to be much more likely to be affected than females. Estimates place this ratio at somewhere between four and nine males to one female.

Some authorities, including the late Dr. Asperger himself, speculate that the condition is genetically inherited from the father. Others maintain that evidence for this conclusion is lacking. Researchers at McGill University in Montreal have presented evidence that people with Asperger's have organic brain abnormalities in the right hemisphere.[5]

Asperger's disorder is sometimes confused with alexithymia, a cognitive–affective disturbance characteristic of people who cannot describe their feelings. Whereas Asperger's is characteristic of those whose ability to interpret others' feelings is impaired, alexithymia is characteristic of those who cannot express feeling for others. Alexithymia is believed to be caused by a brain problem in the thymus, hence the *thy* in *alexithymia*.[6]

WHAT'S A SIMple test of sanity? According to some psychiatrists, it's as simple as this: You're sane if you are able to take another person's point of view.

Dr. Asperger believed that sufferers could become productive citizens if given proper care, and many people with AS do have successful careers and family relationships. However, people with Asperger's often exhibit extreme anxiety and depression. When this surfaces in early adulthood, it makes employment and normal social functioning difficult.

Current forms of treatment often include the use of methylphenidate (Ritalin), which is a central nervous system stimulant, or fluoxetine (Prozac), which is an antidepressant.[2]

To sum up, although the degree of impairment varies, the typical AS sufferer is perhaps best described as having limited interests or preoccupation with a subject to the exclusion of other activities, the tendency to exhibit repetitive behaviors, peculiarities of language, socially and emotionally inappropriate behavior and interpersonal interaction, problems with nonverbal communication, and an overall clumsiness and lack of coordination.

Whatever the odd, unusual, or strange behaviors shown by the AS sufferer, such behaviors are not intentional. They are a reaction to a neurological abnormality that is no one's fault. [7]

THE FAMOUS WITH AS?

There are several prominent individuals who may have suffered from AS. These include Sir Isaac Newton, Albert Einstein, Ludwig Wittgenstein, Stanley Kubrick, and Satoshi Tajiri—the creator of Pokémon. Such individuals may have the dual diagnosis of AS and "high-functioning autism."

WHO IS MENTALLY ILL, ANYWAY?

Psychiatrists such as the late R. D. Laing and Thomas Szasz have claimed that mental illness is a myth. They argue that anyone allegedly suffering from mental illness is simply behaving in ways that deviate from what is expected. Such behavior is defined by society as deviant, and a semipermanent label is placed on the person concerned. Although most in the mental health field reject this notion, Dr. David Rosenhan is not among them. He conducted an experiment involving 193 psychiatric patients.[8] After suggesting to the hospital staff that some patients were frauds and had no mental illness, he found that the staff could not always tell who was mentally ill and who was not. He concluded, "It is clear that we cannot distinguish the sane from the insane in psychiatric hospitals."

The line between mental illness and mental health may be a fine one.[9]

Chapter 3
Body Dysmorphic Disorder: When You Are Obsessed with an Imaginary Body Flaw

Even if the brain is housed in a drop-dead beautiful body, behavior can still be bizarre.

Most of us are somewhat dissatisfied with some part of our body. It could be our nose, ears, breasts—or a part of the body that few people see. But when this dissatisfaction becomes so severe that it blocks normal social functioning, stifles happiness, and dominates our life, we are in the throes of a disabling obsession called body dysmorphic disorder (BDD).

BDD occurs when a person of normal appearance is

A PERSON WITH dyslexia is twelve times more likely to be left-handed.

overly preoccupied with an imagined physical defect. It can also occur when a person has some slight body flaw, but he or she grossly exaggerates its importance.

According to Dr. Katharine Phillips, BDD is more common than we previously thought. Although the public and the medical profession still know little about it, BDD rivals anorexia nervosa, bulimia, and obsessive–compulsive disorder in the number of sufferers. One study suggests that 70 percent of us have some body part "dissatisfaction," 46 percent of us are "preoccupied" by it, and 28 percent of us seem "to meet all criteria of the disorder."[1]

People with BDD often regard their imagined body flaw with loathing, shame, and repugnance. Sometimes they describe being tortured by their concern and rendered unable to think of anything else. Some are unable to pass by a mirror without stopping to check themselves and observe their imagined flaw. Others exhibit a morbid avoidance of mirrors, which would only remind them of their defect.[2]

Tragically, all too often a person's self-confidence is devastated, and his or her overall sense of self-worth is destroyed. When one hates a part of oneself so much, it is easy to hate the rest.

The distress caused by BDD can be so serious that severe depression and suicide may result.[2] Despite reassurances from friends and family that a body flaw is just imagined, people with BDD continue to exaggerate the importance of the alleged imperfection, not just to themselves but to everyone else. People with BDD report a perception that "everyone is looking at my _____ all the time." Often this is followed by, "But they're pretending not to."

However, one difference between BDD and the more

widely known obsessive–compulsive disorder is that with BDD, the sufferer admits that his or her concern with a body flaw is at least a little unusual.

Most commonly, BDD complaints involve supposed facial flaws such as wrinkles, spots, scars, blood vessel marks, paleness or redness of the complexion, swelling, excessive or insufficient hair, or perceived misalignment of features. Other common preoccupations deal with some aspect of the nose, eyes, eyelids, eyebrows, ears, mouth, lips, teeth, jaw, chin, or cheeks or the entire head. But any other body part can be the focus of concern: breasts, genitals, buttocks, abdomen, arms, hands, legs, feet, hips, shoulders, spine, or skin.

> SCIENTISTS DO not yet know how much information can be stored in the human brain.

Interestingly, the imagined body flaw can shift over time. There are cases in which a person is preoccupied with one imagined body flaw in his or her twenties and another in his or her forties.

In Western nations, women seem to suffer from BDD slightly more often than do men. There are 1.3 women for every 1 man who consults a psychiatrist about BDD.

According to Phillips, social, marital, and occupational difficulties often are associated with BDD. Many people stay indoors for most of the day out of self-loathing and the fear of being seen. Others are entirely housebound. In one case, a young woman's imagined facial swelling caused her to withdraw from school to avoid being looked at by peers. In another case, a man who worked from home refused to accept a far better-paying job outside his home because it meant working with others, who would observe his "ugly complexion."[2]

With BDD, impairment can take other forms. One woman spent some eight hours a day cutting her hair to make it perfectly symmetrical. Another spent nearly all of her waking hours examining her face with a magnifying glass for "excessive" facial hair. A young man dated only petite women, thinking that his "small" penis would not be so noticeable to a woman of smaller build.

Several experts suggest that people with BDD tend to share other personality traits. Some are overly perfectionistic, self-critical, insecure, sensitive, shy, or reserved. Other experts argue that BDD may run in families.

South Carolina researchers found that BDD was common in patients with social phobia (with 11 percent having BDD) or with obsessive–compulsive disorder (8 percent) but was less common in patients with panic disorder (2 percent) and not seen in those with generalized anxiety disorder.[3]

In another study, Phillips reports that compulsive skin picking was seen in 97 percent of patients with BDD. People with BDD also engage in frequent reassurance seeking.[4]

Not surprisingly, people with BDD often are willing candidates for all forms of unnecessary plastic surgery. It has been estimated that at least one in fifty plastic surgery patients suffers from BDD. Furthermore, those with BDD often seek out dermatologists and internal medicine specialists, requesting treatments such as electrolysis or hair and skin transplants.

THE BRAIN constitutes 2.5 percent of your body weight, but the brain consumes about 20 percent of the body's energy.

However, as Phillips warns, because people with BDD have a psychological problem and not a physical one, "they are rarely reassured by normal physical examination results and rarely satisfied with [cosmetic] treatment."[1]

Phillips also notes that "psychiatrists

probably see only a small fraction of patients with this disorder, most of whom consult dermatologists, internists, or plastic surgeons."[1] But counseling is what people with BDD need most.

> ONLY 20 percent of the brain's functioning is devoted to thinking.

Fortunately, BDD can be treated successfully through psychotherapy, behavioral therapy, and medical therapy (often using antidepressant drugs).

Cognitive–behavioral treatment is one promising and popular therapy for BDD. This involves the patient thinking through problems, solving them, and adopting coping behaviors. One study also showed a "clinically meaningful improvement in overall levels of depression and anxiety."[5]

BDD cuts across class, ethnic, and national boundaries. Interestingly, approximately 85 percent of sufferers are unmarried. The first recognizable symptoms usually emerge in early adolescence through the late twenties. It persists throughout life or it may cease, especially if treated.

What causes BDD? Some experts suspect that BDD stems from an as yet unspecified brain disturbance that also contributes to obsessive–compulsive disorder, social phobia, and perhaps major depression. According to Dr. Eric Hollander, the brain chemicals serotonin and dopamine probably play an important role.[6]

Case Study: Karen

She has a body women would kill for and men would die for. She is one of the most beautiful women in Australia, a nation famous for its gorgeous women.

Yet Karen believes she is ugly. She imagines, of all things, that her feet are horribly misshapen. As a consequence, she

IT HAS BEEN estimated that thinking for an hour burns about one fifteenth of a gram of fat.

wears boots or other nonrevealing shoes at all times, even during the summer. She refuses to go to the beach, although she loves to swim. She wears socks while making love. She will not allow even her lover to see her feet. Karen says, "As long as I can remember, my feet have always been ugly."

She hopes to become a model and actress but has turned down numerous opportunities to do both for fear that people will notice her feet on stage or on camera. She works as a receptionist and is currently in therapy for BDD.[7]

Case Study: BDD and the Death of Margaux Hemingway

Ironically, those widely regarded as physically beautiful by current cultural standards are not immune to BDD. In fact, they may even be more susceptible. It is not unheard of for successful models or actors to think they have a flaw that renders them ugly.

After the death of Margaux Hemingway, the link between suicide, BDD, and "the beautiful people" produced speculation that undiagnosed BDD may have played a role in the actor's alleged suicide by contributing to her depression. Known for her famous eyebrows ("But I don't *need* any ID, I have my *eyebrows*," she once said), Hemingway frequently expressed her feeling that her mouth was ugly, according to friends. Hemingway came from a family with a long history of mental illness and suicide. And she suffered from epilepsy, dyslexia, bulimia, depression, and drug dependency. Whether BDD played a role in her death, only she would know. [8]

Beauty may see a beauty or a beast in the mirror. It's all in the eye of the beholder.[7]

THE HOSTAGE BRAIN

Who knows what the human brain could be capable of if it were not held hostage in the body? Research shows that, for example, if one becomes an alcoholic the brain becomes hostage to, and ultimately damaged by, the substance.

According to Dr. Bruce McEwen and Harold Schmeck,

> The human brain has an agenda of its own as it confronts and adapts to a changing world. It changes in chemistry and even in architecture day by day, possibly even minute by minute, reshaping itself continually to cope with experience. It is obvious that the brain must change if it is to perform in the incredible fashion we take so much for granted, but the changes go deeper and are more pervasive than scientists had realized until now. Brain cells take on new duties when needs or opportunities arise. Just how they do this is still a mystery. . . . The ever changing brain seems a far-fetched concept only to people who persist in thinking the "mind" is somehow distinct from the brain and that the brain just sits there, running the whole show, aloof and inviolate on top of the backbone. In fact the brain is the whole show.[9]

SEEING THE THINKING AND LEARNING BRAIN IN ACTION

Scientists can now see the changes that occur in the brain when we think and learn. In many cases, we are able to pinpoint which brain pathways and chemicals correspond to different mental tasks through the use of new imaging techniques and devices. Such technology allows scientists to look at the active areas of healthy and diseased brains in a noninvasive manner.

Seeing the thinking and learning brain in action has resulted in the finding that approximately 10 percent of children are not able to adequately process the rapidly changing sounds of speech. As Dr. Michael Merzenich explains, "Speech is unclear to them, just like the vision of a child is unclear without glasses. A higher percentage of these children go on to be reading-impaired."[10]

Chapter 4
The **Brain of the Vampire,** the Madness of King George, or When You Can't Get It out of Your Blood

Here's a real brain teaser: What do vampire myths, King George III of England, madness, and a blood disease have in common? Read on.

In the mid-1980s, police in the state of Virginia arrested twenty-year-old Jeffery Wainwright for murder. The victim, Charles Brownell, was a forty-three-year-old brick mason and self-proclaimed vampire. It was a bizarre twist.

ACCORDING TO authorities on IQ measurement, most people have an IQ in the 90 to 110 range. You're considered a genius if your IQ is 132 or above.

Although Brownell called himself a vampire throughout his adult life, few took him seriously.

After he disappeared for two weeks, neighbors became suspicious when a trail of blood was found outside his apartment. Inside, police discovered human organs, tissue, and more blood. Police first suspected that Brownell had murdered someone and then fled. But scientific analysis proved otherwise. The remains were those of Brownell himself.

Most intriguing of all, tests of the victim's liver showed that Brownell suffered from porphyria, a rare genetic disease that occurs in only one of every thirty thousand people.

According to Dr. David Dolphin, a world authority on porphyrias and other liver disorders, people thought to be vampires or werewolves may have only been suffering from this rare liver disease.[1]

The porphyrias are a class of genetically based liver malfunctions in which heme (the red pigment of the blood) is not properly biosynthesized. There are eight enzymatic steps in heme biosynthesis, and a problem with any of them can cause porphyria.

Dolphin maintains that the effects of exposure to even mild sunlight can be devastating to a porphyriac. Lesions of the skin can be so severe that the nose and fingers are destroyed. Although the teeth become no larger, the lips and gums recede dramatically. Indeed, this creates a fanglike appearance. In addition, porphyriacs may become exceedingly hairy. Dolphin says,

*Imagine, if you will, the manner in which an individual in
the Middle Ages would have been received if they only went
out at night and when they were seen had an animal look
about them being hairy, large of tooth and badly disfigured.
It has been suggested, and it seems more than likely that
such people might well have been considered werewolves.[2]*

Dolphin argues that blood–drinking vampires were porphyria
victims "trying to alleviate the symptoms of their dreadful disease."[2] If a large amount of blood were drunk, the heme in it
would supply the missing heme caused by the malfunctioning
biosynthesis and alleviate disease symptoms by switching off the
malfunction itself. Although heme can pass into the bloodstream
via the stomach wall, this is not very efficient.

Today, porphyriacs often are treated with heme injections.
However, in the Middle Ages injections were impossible, so
drinking large amounts of blood would have been the only
way of getting the necessary supply of heme.

There must have been desperation in the porphyriac's
blood-seeking efforts because death can result from heme
insufficiency. It is no wonder, then, that personality changes and
dementia are psychiatric symptoms common in porphyriacs.

Moreover, the genetic nature of the porphyrias is consistent
with the folklore that victims of a vampire bite become vampires themselves. On this point, Dolphin
notes that there are many examples today
of siblings sharing the same defective gene,
with only one showing disease symptoms.
And it is also clear that a strain on the system, such as the sudden and major loss of
blood, can trigger the disease in a person

WHEN WE
touch something,
we send a mes-
sage to our brain
at 120 miles per
hour.

A PART OF THE brain is called the island of Reil. Sometimes called the insula, it is located near the center of the brain.

already genetically predisposed. As Dolphin says, "The likelihood then of one porphyria victim biting another and initiating the disease, could have been high."[2]

Furthermore, because the porphyrias are genetic, it seems likely that local pockets of porphyria might have developed in medieval Europe. Travel was rare and intermarriage common, especially in inaccessible areas. This could explain the folkloric home of vampires: mountainous, isolated Transylvania.

According to legend, garlic wards off vampires. Dolphin contends that many of the drugs and chemicals that destroy heme have a feature in common with the principal constituent of garlic (dialkyl disulfide). He adds that this "suggests that garlic might increase the severity of an attack of porphyria. Hence it might well act to keep vampires away."[2]

A 1994 study from Norway suggests that vampire bats may be attracted to garlic smeared on the hands. The researchers concluded (somewhat tongue-in-cheek),

> *The traditional belief that garlic has prophylactic properties is probably wrong. The reverse may in fact be true. This study indicates that garlic possibly attracts vampires. Therefore to avoid a Balkan-like development in Norway, restrictions on the use of garlic should be considered.*[3]

What's all of this got to do with King George III? Some medical experts argue that King George III suffered from porphyria. In the marvelous 1994 film *The Madness of King George*, the physical and mental decline of this hapless British monarch is painfully portrayed. A note at the end of the film states that it is believed King George suffered from porphyria. Yet this diagnosis cannot be proved today without DNA testing of his remains. If he had porphyria, he probably recovered from each bout through better diet and fluid intake. Although his behavior was indeed bizarre during the more awful bouts with the disease, there is no evidence that King George exhibited vampire-like behaviors.

THE AVERAGE human brain has between 100 and 200 billion nerve cells.

WOMEN'S brains are smaller than men's brains by an average of about 12 percent.

Symptoms of porphyria, a name derived from the Greek word for "purple" (the color of a porphyriac's urine), usually begin to appear in late adolescence.

Today, the prognosis for survival and symptom relief is good. Early diagnosis, proper fluid and dietary therapy, and avoidance of contraindicated drugs are essential. Deaths that occur nowadays usually are attributable to delays in diagnosis, absence of treatment, or failure to remain under the close care of a physician.[4]

Why have the vampire legends remained for so long in our culture? Of course, there are many possible explanations. One theory holds that such legends and the fantasies that surround them help the living deal with death and the loss of loved ones:

Vampires are, after all, persons who have died but who are nonetheless immortal or "undead." . . . An important function of vampire mythology may have been to allow the grief-stricken to believe in the continued existence of their loved ones. Likewise, in the clinical analytic situation, and especially with the transference, the appearance of fantasy material related to vampire legends may signal bereavement, especially transference bereavement.[5]

Clinical vampirism is another matter. Some people behave in a manner akin to the excesses seen in the vampire myths. Others actually believe they are vampires and often are proud of it. Indeed, there are more than a few vampire Web pages on the Internet.

According to two Swiss psychiatrists, Drs. P. D. Jaffe and F. DiCataldo, clinical vampirism is "a rare condition described in the forensic literature covering some of humanity's most shocking behaviors. Definitions of vampirism involve aspects of necrophilia, sadism, cannibalism, and a fascination with blood."[6] It can be intricately associated with schizophrenia, depression, low self-esteem, or other conditions. They add that the cause of clinical vampirism is complex and may involve "the complex mother–child dyad's blood ties running amok."[6]

This last point recalls the classic case of "auto-vampirism" in a young man who was unloved, was denied breast- and bottle-feeding as an infant and early emotional nurturance, and as an adult turned to the most horrific vampire behaviors.

Why? It was from one of the simplest and, for most of us, one of the easiest needs to satisfy: an insatiable infantile desire to suck.[7]

A PART OF THE brain is called the convolutions of Broca. It is located in the left frontal region.

Case Study: W.T.

W.T., a lesbian, apparently believed herself to be a vampire—a member of the undead. For years she shunned mirrors and sunlight and took blood collected from butcher shops as her only form of nourishment.

W.T.'s lover, P.L., donated blood to her partner on a regular basis, but W.T. wanted more. Over time, she and P.L. recruited two more disciples for their lesbian vampire cult. They all were convinced that W.T. possessed supernatural powers, including the ability to vanish at will, leaving only the eyes of a cat suspended in air. The cult members also believed that W.T. "needed strength" to work such "miracles."

In October 1989 the foursome murdered a man, luring him with offers of sex, and then slashed his throat so that W.T. could drink his blood. At the trial, W.T. pleaded guilty and was sentenced to life imprisonment. The other three cult members took their chances with the jury. Two were convicted and sentenced to prison, and the third was freed on the grounds that she had been completely under W.T.'s control.[8]

THE HUMAN brain is the most protected organ in the body. It consists of 100 to 200 billion cells guarded by three different layers. The first is the scalp. The second is the skull. The third is the meninges, membranes that envelop the brain and spinal cord.

ANOTHER VIEW OF DRACULA

A team of researchers in Philadelphia believes that the Dracula story illustrates the symptoms of borderline personality:

> It has been proposed that Bram Stoker's novel *Dracula* can best be understood as a dramatic, hyperbolic, and fantastic expression of themes consistent with contemporary psychoanalytic conceptions of borderline personality disorder

organization. Such an understanding may, in turn, shed further light on the nature of the intrapsychic world and experiences of borderline patients. Excerpts from the novel can be used to support the conceptualization of recent contributions to object relations theory and the understanding of borderline personality organization. It is uncanny how consistent Dracula's characteristics are to the generally seen complaints of patients suffering from this disorder.[9]

Is this too far-fetched? Maybe, maybe not. According to the American Psychiatric Association, the symptoms of borderline personality disorder include "frantic efforts to avoid real or imagined abandonment," "identity disturbance: markedly and persistently unstable self-image or sense of self," "chronic feelings of emptiness," and "transient, stress-related paranoid ideation or severe dissociative symptoms."[10] Clearly, these symptoms are rather general. Dracula could be seen as having borderline personality disorder—and so could a lot of other famous characters from literature.

Chapter 5
The **Brain of the Werewolf**

In rare circumstances, the human brain allows one to believe that one can be turned into, or turn oneself into, a ferocious animal. This is the psychiatric origin of the belief in werewolves.

Hollywood has immortalized the belief in werewolves, perpetuated such legends, and even encouraged them. The first werewolf film was *Werewolf of London* in 1935. Pretty tame by today's gory standards, this film left audiences gripped in fright but fascinated, wanting more. Universal Studios made a fortune in the 1930s and 1940s exploiting the public's thirst. Actor Lon Chaney Jr. became a star portraying a werewolf in several pictures.

But it was not only the werewolf that was the subject of the Hollywood treatment. People were turned into cats, snakes, flies, spiders, and other animals. Even the Disney studios got into the act with *The Shaggy Dog* in 1959. *Birdy*, a 1984 film based on the novel by William Wharton, portrays a young man who believes he is a predatory bird.

A long-running Australian television commercial shows a young man transform into a howling wolf while driving his car. He ignores his attractive female passenger, taking far more pleasure in driving. She looks on in embarrassed disbelief and jeers, "And my mother thinks he's cute!" The message: Driving this car is better than sex.

THE HUMAN brain has two types of cells: neurons and neuroglia. Neurons are responsible for transmitting information throughout the brain. Each neuron consists of an axon that sends information and a dendrite that receives information. Neuroglia are ten times more abundant than neurons and act as protective layers for neurons.

In various forms, lycanthropy lives on.

Lycanthropy is the psychiatric term for the delusion that one has been transformed into an animal, particularly a wolf. It is one of the oldest delusions known. In fact, cases are still reported in the medical literature from time to time.

Historians trace the origins of lycanthropy to the Greek myth in which Zeus transforms the devious Lycaon into a wolf as revenge for attempting to trick him into an act of cannibalism. The Bible's Book of Daniel is the source of the legend that the great king of Babylon, Nebuchadnezzar II, suffered for seven years from what today would be called a lycanthropic state. Lycanthropy is reflected in numerous legends and fairy tales throughout the world. Widespread belief in the existence of satyrs and other half-human, half-animal creatures persisted well into the nineteenth century. According to Irish legend, Veneticus, the king of Gallia, was turned into a wolf by St. Patrick. And there are legends in which reverse lycanthropy occurs. The French fairy tale "Beauty and the Beast" is a notable example.

Until the twentieth century, when the population grew bigger and the forest grew smaller, wolves were the most fearsome predators in Europe. It is little wonder that a common delusion in mental illness would be that one had been turned into a wolf. For the weak, oppressed, and downtrodden, such a transformation promises immediate power. Pent-up aggression and violent behavior could be expressed through the animal persona.

In the past, continually fearing and occasionally observing people suffering from lycanthropy undoubtedly gave rise to periodic bouts of werewolf hysteria and to persecutions of those with mental illnesses. Fears that such people would attack and eat human victims led to the widespread slaughter of the mentally ill. In medieval Europe, the burning at the stake of "animal humans" was institutionalized by ecclesiastical courts during the Spanish Inquisition.

Reports of lycanthropy are nearly universal in human societies. Besides Europe, lycanthropy is known throughout China, India, Africa, and both North and South America. Although it is the wolf that dominates as the object of delusion, other animals involved include the lion, tiger, hyena, bear,

THROUGHOUT a person's life span, brain cells continue to be lost gradually. Yet the brain is quite adaptable. The brain's plasticity helps it deal with such cell loss. The brain compensates for aging or even injury by changing its very structure. Typically, it's the number and efficiency of connections between neurons that change.

shark, and crocodile. Invariably, it is an animal at or near the top of the food chain. Thus, it is an object both of fear and of physical and sexual potency.

THE HUMAN brain probably contains more than 10^{14} synapses. There are simply not enough genes to account for this complexity. Neuroscientists have highlighted how extragenetic factors—including neuronal activity, contact with other cells, radiation, and chemical factors—influence brain circuitry, especially while the brain is growing and developing. Thus, in computer terms, our brains are constantly reprogramming themselves in response to internal and external forces.

Descriptions of lycanthropy and how to treat it are found in the earliest medical writings. Greek physician Paulus Aegineta spoke of it in the seventh century. He even suggested bloodletting as an effective treatment. Sixteenth-century French physician Jean Fernel reflected a common medical opinion of the day that human beings could be transformed into werewolves by the forces of evil, often by the Devil himself.

Two cases of lycanthropy in the psychiatric literature are mentioned most prominently. Of these, probably the more famous is one reported by Carl Jung.[1] Jung's patient, a devoted mother, had three daughters who loved her very much. However, at times they used to dream of her as a dangerous animal. Years later, the mother exhibited lycanthropic behaviors in which she crawled about on all fours, imitating the grunting of pigs, the barking of dogs, and the growling of bears. Why this behavior occurred puzzled Jung. But he used this case to illustrate the great sensitivity of children to the unconscious conflicts of parents.

The other classic lycanthropy case was reported by Karl Jaspers.[2] This case is memorable because the patient, believing he was a werewolf and highly suicidal, demanded to be killed by a silver bullet through the heart, just like in the movies.

Every lycanthropy case is somewhat different. The common feature is the transformation into an animal. Nevertheless, such people usually retain some knowledge of their human identity. For example, they will answer to their own name.

Certainly rarer now than in the past, lycanthropy still occurs. A 1985 study from Ireland reported on the intriguing case of a sixty-six-year-old widow who "had become aggressive towards some members of the family for no apparent reason. This was associated on a number of occasions with animal-like behavior, during which she would go down on her hands and knees and 'bark like a dog.'"[3]

In 1988, psychiatrists from Harvard reported that twelve patients with lycanthropy were admitted in fourteen years to just one psychiatric hospital. Of one case, they said,

DESPITE COMmon misconceptions, older adults experience only a small change in brain operation. The severity of change varies according to the part of the brain in which neurons are lost. For instance, if cell loss occurs in the hippocampus (an elongated ridge atop the ventricles), then memory loss can occur as well.

A 24-year-old single male presented to McLean Hospital [Belmont, Massachusetts] with a history of major depression, a brief period of alcohol abuse, and the belief that he was a cat trapped inside a human body. This belief has persisted without interruption for 13 years. The patient stated that he had known that he was a cat since this secret was imparted to him by the family cat, who subsequently taught

him "cat language." Though gainfully employed, the patient
continued to spend virtually all of his spare time in feline
activities. He lived with cats, had sexual activity with them,
hunted with them, and frequented cat night spots in prefer-
ence to their human equivalents. His greatest—but unre-
quited—love was for a tigress in a local zoo. He hoped one
day to release her. The patient's lycanthropic delusions
remained refractory to treatment with haloperidol, tricyclic
antidepressants, carbamazepine, and six years of insight-ori-
ented psychotherapy.[4]

In lycanthropy, the delusion may be permanent or, strangely,
may last for only an hour or so.

A brief episode of lycanthropy is evident in the 1990 case
of a German patient:

Mr R.M., a 33-year-old black student . . . was euphoric
on index admission and a few days later he suddenly
became excited, very aggressive, dropped to the floor, started
behaving like a dog, barking and running around the ward
on all fours. He claimed he was a dog while retaining his
awareness of his identity as R.M. Moreover, he was also
convinced of being possessed by the dog and that this dog
was in reality the Devil. There was no disturbance of consciousness. His lycanthropy lasted about an hour and was
terminated when an intravenous dose of an antipsychotic
was given.[5]

Of course the big question is, What causes lycanthropy? An
unknown problem in brain biochemistry has been put forward
as one possible explanation.[6] But there is little evidence to sus-

tain this view. Some in the field maintain that no one knows for sure and that many theories abound.[3] Four examples of the onset of lycanthropy show it to be precipitated by sexual intercourse in two cases, drug abuse in another, and physical brain damage in yet another.[3]

A group of Harvard psychiatrists argue that, although of unknown cause, the syndrome seems to be "generally associated with severe psychosis, but not with any specific psychiatric diagnosis or neurological findings, or with any particular outcome."[4]

Why is lycanthropy far less common today? This seems to be easier to answer: "It is speculated that the rarity of the [lycanthropy] syndrome in Europe now is due partly to the virtual extinction of wolves in Europe."[3]

IT HAS BEEN estimated that the combined weight of the brains of the 535 members of the U.S. Congress is 1,605 pounds. The number of African bull elephants that it would take to get the equivalent brain weight is 321.

As for treatment, because the cause of lycanthropy is difficult to determine, often so is the treatment. In the case of R.M., a drug was administered, and the symptoms subsided. But in the old days or in the Hollywood movies, it might have been a silver bullet through the heart.[7]

WHERE WEREWOLVES?

According to the *Weekly World News,* the first chapter of Werewolves Anonymous opened in 1996, in Baton Rouge, Louisiana. It is a self-help organization modeled after Alcoholics Anonymous. Dr. Mason Grumler, a psychologist and consultant to the organization, says that he has treated more than 200 people with what he calls organically caused lycanthropy. Grumler adds, "They suffer from a hormonal imbalance that affects both brain and body at certain times of the month."[8]

THE DICE BRAIN

Can the human mind somehow muster its power to alter physical objects? Perhaps the roll of dice? As surprising as it may seem, evidence suggests that dice can be affected by the mind, although the effect is tiny. Psychometric researchers analyzed 148 previous studies looking at this effect. Such studies go back to 1937. The researchers found that the dice thrower can influence the dice with his or her thoughts, but not very often—certainly not enough to beat the house at Monte Carlo. Put simply, chance would predict that "6" would come up once every six throws of a die. In 1,000 throws, "6" would come up 166.6 times. But data from the studies, taken together, show that "6" comes up 169.2 times—a small but measurable increase over chance. The researchers write, "We conclude that this data base provides weak cumulative evidence for a genuine relation-ship between mental intention and the fall of the dice."[9,10]

Chapter 6
Cacodemonomania:
When You Believe You Are Possessed by a Demon or Devil or Don't Know "Witch"

What causes the brain to stimulate the delusion that one is possessed by a demon? We don't really know the solution, but we have some insights into the problem.

The psychiatric term for the delusion of being possessed is *cacodemonomania* or sometimes simply *possession state*.

Cacodemonomania is one of the oldest delusional states known and the most widespread. We have accounts of

THE BRAIN IS highly specialized. For instance, certain brain areas deal only with the names of your friends. Other areas deal with the manner in which you twiddle your thumbs.

cacodemonomania from the beginnings of history and from all corners of the globe. It is known as *dojo* in Japan,[1] *embrujada* in Mexico,[2] and *kubandwa* in Rwanda.[3] But whatever the name, the belief in demonic possession is essentially the same whenever and wherever it is found: Demons, devils, spirits, or other foreign bodies are believed to inhabit and control a person.[4]

In the West, interest in demonic possession was rekindled in 1973 by the film *The Exorcist*. In fact, this film may have been responsible for some degree of public hysteria and "copycat neuroses." One report cited four cases of "cinematic neurosis" that developed after people saw the film.[5]

A 1975 United Kingdom report described an attempted exorcism by a religious group, allegedly delaying psychiatric intervention and ultimately resulting in a husband killing his wife.[6] A 1993 Australian case involved the death of a woman on her kitchen floor as the result of exorcism actions by two men, one of whom was her husband. Both men were later acquitted of homicide.

Although it is not widely reported, occasionally a mental health professional argues for the limited use of exorcism in psychiatric therapy, as in "intractable cases" of "demonosis."[7] Psychiatrists at Vanderbilt University reported that one of their deeply disturbed psychiatric patients recovered only after an exorcism was performed by a fundamentalist minister acting under their auspices.[8]

It was argued that if a delusional patient's religious conviction (for example, holding a belief in being possessed by the

Devil) blocked the success of normal clinical approaches to treating that patient, then a religious activity such as an exorcism could be used as an adjunct to that treatment by overcoming the blockage. Needless to say, this practice is highly controversial.

In 1923, Freud explained cacodemonomania as an individual's neurosis creating the demons. The demons resulted from unacceptable repressed wishes projected onto the external world.[9]

Freud's most famous cacodemonomania patient was Christoph Haizmann. Haizmann was a successful painter, but his career was hindered by the emergence of his delusion of being possessed by the Devil. Freud explained that Haizmann's delusion was merely an imagined image of his own recently deceased father, a terrifying figure who, Haizmann fantasized, wanted to rape and then castrate him. To Freud, the basis of Haizmann's delusion came from the failure to successfully resolve the Oedipal conflict. That is, Haizmann had wanted to continue a relationship with his mother and therefore resented the father for being in the way.

Freud did not personally examine Haizmann. Haizmann was born in Bavaria and grew up during the Thirty Years' War (1618–1648). Freud merely based his diagnosis on information gathered on Haizmann by others.

Drs. Sally Hill and Jean Goodwin argue that Freud's analysis of Haizmann is wrong.[10] Their argument is causing many to rethink all aspects of cacodemonomania, including the question of why people who exhibited

IF YOU ARE typical, when you are twenty your brain is heavier than it ever was or ever will be. Of course, the weight of your brain is less important than the weight of what's in it.

"possession" symptoms at certain historical times often were burned at the stake as witches.

Hill and Goodwin claim that Haizmann's "Devil" was indeed an image of his father—a man who may have severely abused Haizmann as a child—but also that Haizmann was the victim of other severe childhood traumas, a fact that Freud might have discovered had he looked at the evidence more carefully.

Apart from Freud's view, "another possibility, based on contemporary experience with patients who consider themselves possessed by demons, would be that Christoph Haizmann had experienced severe sadistic abuse. Such survivors often cannot give a direct account of their extreme abuse because terror and amnesia block internal narration and verbalization."[10]

They go on to describe the real nightmares that Haizmann would have encountered growing up in Bavaria during the Thirty Years' War. Death, destruction, murder, public executions, rape, pillaging, torture, starvation, and even cannibalism were common. (This period of German history provided the backdrop for Bertolt Brecht's 1941 play *Mother Courage and Her Children*, whose main character is the ultimate survivor.)

ZOOPSIA IS THE condition wherein a person sees terrifying animals in hallucinations. Examples might include flame-spitting snakes or flying, two-headed crocodiles.

Hill and Goodwin argue that all of this contributed to Haizmann's childhood trauma. It was so intense that he buried it deep in the innermost recesses of his mind. It resurfaced again years later in the form of a devil that wanted to destroy him, just as his father had nearly done.

Thus, Haizmann's cacodemonomania was a reflection of a violent, traumatic childhood environment. And cacodemonomania emerges as yet another manifestation of a child's attempt to cope with a brutal world.

Historians might well ask whether violence and trauma in childhood can help explain cacodemonomania's long history. If the supposedly "possessed" witches who burned at the stake were merely victims of child abuse, then witch burnings are a classic instance of victim blaming.

AN AUTOMATISM is any of the learned actions you do without conscious thought. Starting your car could be one of these.

And does this help to explain cases of cacodemonomania today? Perhaps so. Another Vanderbilt University study examined five demonic possession cases involving children.[11] Most intriguingly, they all have a common thread: severe childhood trauma in a violent family.[12]

DOES THE BRAIN HAVE THE POWER TO MOVE OBJECTS?

Yes, Virginia, it seems that the human brain can learn to move objects with its own sheer power. Although we may not be able to move mountains by just thinking about it, there's some evidence that it's possible to harness our brain waves at least enough to move a cursor around a computer screen.

Fascinating experiments by the New York State Department of Health involved attaching electrodes to the scalps of fifty subjects, who were then asked to concentrate on a video screen and move the cursor from one corner to the other. The electrodes picked up faint electromagnetic signals from the brain, which were then boosted and sent to a computer, which then moved the cursor. Some of the subjects hit the target 75 percent of the time.[13]

This research has exciting implications for those who are paralyzed and certainly stimulates the imagination.

Science fiction come true?

G.Y. SEES IT FAST OR NOT AT ALL

Here's another strange one. Researchers have long believed that visual information passes first through the primary visual cortex in the brain before being parceled out to specialized brain centers for perception of color or motion. But a blind man in his thirties, G.Y., is forcing scientists to scratch their heads and reexamine this belief. Although completely blind in almost every sense of the word, G.Y. sees objects in rapid motion but does not see them when they're standing still. Examinations confirm G.Y.'s odd vision. Experts would say that the brain doesn't work that way, but clearly, something is happening. It has been suggested that there may be a "separate consciousness for different attributes." In G.Y.'s case, the primary visual cortex may be bypassed.[14]

Chapter 7
Capgras's Syndrome:
When You Believe You Have an Identical Double

Capgras's syndrome is bizarre, strange, and weird. But it also shows how diverse, intricate, and very odd the human brain can be.

Capgras's syndrome is the psychiatric condition in which a person believes that he or she has an identical double. A variation of this is the belief that a significant person in one's life has been replaced by an identical double.

In 1923, Drs. Jean Marie Joseph Capgras and Jean Reboul-Lachaux wrote the first article on Capgras's syndrome to appear in the psychiatric literature.[1] They described the case of a fifty-three-year-old woman who displayed what they called *l'illusion des sosies*: the delusion that people in her life had been replaced by identical doubles. In fact, the patient herself used the word *sosies*, the French word for "doubles."

Sosies derives from the name of a character in the classic Roman play *Amphitryon*, by Plautus. The play involves disguises, deception, switched identities, and seduction. In the ancient Greek myth, the god Zeus becomes infatuated with Alcmena, wife of Amphitryon. Zeus takes the form of Amphitryon. The god Mercury takes the form of Amphitryon's servant, Sosia. They fool Alcmena, who sleeps with Zeus, thinking he is her husband. Alcmena conceives twins by two fathers: Hercules (fathered by Zeus) and Iphicles (fathered by the real Amphitryon).

Mirroring such a deception, Capgras and Reboul-Lachaux's patient believed that many people in her life were replaced by identical doubles. These included her husband, her children, neighbors, even the police who investigated her somewhat bizarre behaviors, which eventually resulted in her hospitalization. She also believed that her double was conspiring with all the other doubles to rob her of her property and inheritance.

There is a tragedy for anyone with Capgras's syndrome. The frightening identity confusion caused by perceived identical doubles renders a basic human need—simple human trust—impossible to achieve.

YOUR BRAIN uses ten times more oxygen than all other parts of your body combined.

Capgras's syndrome has two types: autoscopic, in which the patient believes he or she has seen the double, and Capgras, in which the double remains unseen.[2] Furthermore, there are at least five syndromes within Capgras's syndrome:

Fregoli syndrome: The patient believes that a previously familiar person has assumed the physical appearance of someone else.

Reverse Fregoli syndrome: The patient believes that others are misidentifying him or her.

Intermetamorphosis syndrome: The patient believes that both the physical appearance and the psychological make-up of the familiar person have been altered.

Subjective doubles syndrome: The patient believes that he or she has been duplicated.

Reverse subjective syndrome: The patient believes that he or she has been replaced by an impostor.[2]

Who is likely to suffer from Capgras's syndrome? Fortunately, the syndrome usually is associated with only a minority of people suffering from psychosis, affective disorders, or schizophrenia.

Capgras's syndrome is more common in women than in men. But it is unclear why this is so.

Although Capgras's syndrome may have its origin in childhood (but this too is unknown), generally it does not show itself before the age of thirty. However, two rare adolescent cases were reported in 1992 by researchers from the University of Michigan.[3]

In one case, W., a sixteen-year-old boy, developed the delusion that both his mother and his sister had been replaced by impostors. In fact, several duplicates existed of each. W. began to experience these delusions after a tragic death of a girlfriend for which W. blamed himself. Perhaps the delusion was some form of coping with this loss.

IF YOU ARE LEFT-handed, chances are your mother was also left-handed but your father was right-handed.

In the other case, N., a fifteen-year-old girl, developed the delusion after first believing that her father and brother had drugged her food while the family was eating at a restaurant. Sadly, her condition rapidly declined to the point at which she exhibited incoherent speech, auditory hallucinations (hearing nonexistent voices), and numerous delusions, including misidentification delusions. Among these delusions was her belief that

> *her mother had been replaced by an impostor, that one of the male night nurses was really her father assuming the nurse's identity so he could hurt her and that another patient on the unit was really a friend from home who had changed into this other person.*[3]

Although Capgras himself argued that the syndrome that bears his name is rare, this has been challenged by two psychiatrists in the United Kingdom. In describing three Capgras cases from their hospital, they conclude that "the traditional assumption that this is a rare syndrome is challenged." Indeed, the true incidence in the psychiatric population may be several times more than what Capgras originally estimated.[4]

Sadly, Capgras's syndrome can also lead to violence. A University of Parma study argues that people with Capgras's syndrome may easily turn violent if their delusion causes them to be fearful or threatened, as a form of self-defense. The study claims that Capgras's syndrome is very much underestimated in the population and suggests that the possibility of Capgras's syndrome should be considered in any investigation of homicide within a family: "Capgras' syndrome could lie at the

YOUR BRAIN IS almost, but not quite, its full size on your seventh birthday.

base of aggressive and homicidal acts directed towards family members during psychotic breakdowns."[5]

Fortunately, Capgras's syndrome can be treated. In fact, N. became symptom free after only ten weeks of antiepileptic drug therapy,[3] and nine patients in Panama underwent therapy for two to eleven years.[6]

Debate continues as to what causes Capgras's syndrome. Links with all sorts of physical and psychological conditions have been proposed. One prominent theory of late is that illness or injury causes a problem with the brain's visual nerve circuitry responsible for facial recognition.

RESEARCHERS have repeatedly found that if you have trouble making up your mind about something, you'll probably get tired as soon as you finally decide. Problems fraught with doubt can be exhausting.

One French study argues that people with Capgras's syndrome are unable to identify a certain person who *does not* look like them. The problem is not one of awareness of a double but an unawareness that someone is *not* a double. Furthermore, "the basic phenomenon of unawareness may be due to sensory deprivation."[7] But many dispute this notion.

Thus, the cause of Capgras's syndrome itself—this strange identity problem—still awaits proper identification.[8]

THE BOY WITH HALF A BRAIN PROVES THE BRAIN MAY REMAIN PLASTIC FOR LANGUAGE UNTIL PUBERTY

Alex was born with a disorder called Sturge–Weber syndrome, which interfered with the blood supply to the left hemisphere of his brain. Suffering regular epileptic seizures, by the time he was eight Alex was able to utter only a few indistinct sounds and one word: "Mama." Doctors decided that the seizures would cease only if the damaged hemisphere was surgically removed (hemispherectomy). Astonishingly, within two years of the surgery, Alex was speaking like a normal eight-year-old. Now Alex is a teenager, and his language is not quite up to that of an adult. However, according to Dr. Mortimer Mishkin, a neuropsychologist at the U.S. National Institute of Mental Health in Washington, D.C., Alex's language ability "exceeds what you would expect from his IQ." Dr. Mishkin argues that Alex's case suggests that the brain may remain plastic for language until puberty.[9, 10]

BRAIN ATTACKS

A stroke is a "brain attack." Just as a heart attack is caused by a blockage in a blood vessel in the heart, a stroke is most commonly caused by a blockage in a blood vessel in the brain. In both attacks, the clogged blood vessel deprives nearby tissues of vital oxygen and nutrients, causing cells to die.[11]

Chapter 8
Cotard's Syndrome:
When You Believe You Don't Exist

The brain sometimes works to deny itself. Indeed, it could be called the ultimate self-denial.

People with the rare psychiatric disorder called Cotard's syndrome believe that they do not exist, that a body part does not exist, or that they are dead. They suffer from an extreme form of nihilistic delusion (*le délire de négation*). Just as they are sure they do not exist, they may be convinced that no one else exists either—that the world does not exist, indeed, that nothing exists.

Sometimes people with Cotard's syndrome believe that major body parts are missing, such as the heart or brain. Yet

WHAT IS TRAN-
sient global amne-
sia (TGA)? This is
a sudden loss of
memory. It is
profound but tem-
porary. The person
suffering TGA
does not lose con-
sciousness. Mem-
ory gradually
returns to normal
within a few hours.
A TGA attack sup-
posedly happens
only once to a
person. There is
some evidence
that TGA may be
related to hyper-
tension. And other
evidence suggests
that it's related to
overexertion in
sexual activity by
those not used to
such strains and
stresses.

they may also suffer delusions of enormous body size (*le délire d'énormité*), the belief that their body is as large as the sky or the entire universe. Although it is common for people with Cotard's syndrome to have suicidal tendencies, ironically, they may also believe they are immortal.

It is common for people with Cotard's syndrome to test their own immortality by taking great risks or continually attempting suicide. In any case, those with Cotard's syndrome have an intense preoccupation with death and may frequently request to be killed. In one classic case, a man was obsessed day and night by a voice reading him his death warrant and describing the tortures in store for him.

Cotard's syndrome often is associated with depressive illnesses, illusions, hallucinations, and memory loss. Sometimes it involves schizophrenia.

Cotard's syndrome is named after French psychiatrist Jules Cotard, who first described patients with the syndrome at the 1880 meeting of the Société Médico-Psychologique in Paris and later wrote about them in his book *Maladies Cerebrales et Mentales* in 1891.[1] He described the condition as having various degrees of severity from mild to severe. In mild states, there are merely feelings of despair and self-loathing. But as the disorder becomes more severe, the sufferer experiences feelings of change both within and without. Cotard maintained that it is in the most severe state that the denial of the very existence of the self occurs.

Although Cotard's syndrome can occur almost at any age, the condition usually is recognized only in middle age. And it is more common in women than in men, although no satisfactory explanation has been given for this difference. The onset of Cotard's often is sudden, with no previous history of any psychiatric disorder. The patient often has an entirely normal childhood as far as anyone can tell. However, before symptoms emerge, typically there is a period of initial anxiety, which can vary in length from a few weeks to several years. Yet even this is perplexing. This initial anxiety often is vague and diffuse, and often an associated irritability is all that is shown outwardly. In denying the existence of body parts, one patient stated,

> *I used to have a heart. I have something which beats in its place. . . . I have no stomach, I never feel hungry. When I eat I get the taste of food, but once past my gullet I feel nothing. It seems that food falls in a hole.[2]*

According to Drs. M. David Enoch and William H. Trethowan,

> *Subsequently [the Cotard's patient] may proceed to deny her very existence, even dispensing altogether with the use of the personal pronoun "I." One patient even called herself "Madam Zero" in order to emphasize her non-existence. One of Anderson's patients said, referring to herself, "It's no use. Wrap it up and throw 'it' in the dustbin."[3]*

Enoch and Trethowan agree that a person with Cotard's can reach such a state of despair that he or she professes an overriding desire not to exist,

> *Yet paradoxically the possibility of death may seem impossible, leading to the development of ideas of immortality. This, then, becomes the greatest despair of all—wishing to [die] but condemned to live forever in the state of nihilism, a state reminiscent of Kierkegaard's living hell.*[3]

Indeed, Enoch and Trethowan add that other patients with Cotard's may have self-mutilation and self-destruction urges, suicide ideation, and hallucinations. For example, hallucinations may involve taste and smell. Patients have been known to be convinced that they

> *are rotting away, that their food is completely changed, or that they are being offered filth, faecal matter or human flesh. Herein is another paradox, for although they believe they are dead, or that they can never die, they still try to destroy themselves.*[3]

Since 1880, psychiatrists have debated whether Cotard's syndrome should be accorded the status of a true syndrome. Some claim that the clinical presentation does not warrant this. Instead, they argue that it should be considered merely as a subtype of depression or even as a specific delusion.

Cotard's syndrome is believed to be caused by many things. Among suggested causes are structural problems in the brain itself and toxic or metabolic diseases. Such things as diffuse brain disease of various sorts, basal ganglia atrophy (at the base of the brain), and lesions of the parietal lobe (at the middle and upper rear of the brain) have all been implicated.

However, computed tomography imaging has shown that people with Cotard's syndrome do not have problems with the parietal lobe but instead have "multifocal brain atrophy and medial frontal lobe disease" in which brain fissures are enlarged.[4]

Japanese researchers claim that problems with beta-endorphins play a role in Cotard's syndrome. Beta-endorphins are believed to be integral to the body's pain management, behavior modulation, and regulation of hormone secretions.[5]

One study detailed the case of a twenty-seven-year-old man who somehow developed "psychiatric manifestations" of Cotard's syndrome as a result of contracting typhoid fever.[6]

Conventional wisdom is that Cotard's syndrome is rare. One Hong Kong study of 349 psychiatric patients found that 0.57 percent suffered from Cotard's.[7]

A Cambridge University review of 100 cases found that, not surprisingly, nearly all the patients with Cotard's were diagnosable as clinically depressive psychotics. Interestingly, 86 percent also had nihilistic delusions about their body, 69 percent denied they existed at all, and 55 percent had delusions of immortality. Much anxiety and guilt also plagued these people.[8]

But regardless of the cause of Cotard's syndrome, one thing is clear: It is the ultimate self-denial.[9]

THE HUMAN brain makes up about 2.5 percent of the average person's body weight. By contrast, the squirrel monkey's brain makes up about 5 percent of its body weight. This is the largest brain-to-body weight ratio of any animal.

Case Study: Neil

The case of Neil, age twenty-six, is almost certainly an instance of Cotard's syndrome.

Neil, an only child, apparently enjoyed a fairly normal childhood. But when he was twenty, his parents were killed in a small plane accident. Neil was deeply religious, and this tragedy devastated and embittered him. Blaming his own actions for the deaths of his parents, Neil became reclusive and retreated from all relationships and activities. He failed at university studies, experimented with hard drugs, and generally made only half-hearted attempts at doing anything. For a brief time, Neil became interested in spiritualism, particularly in the subject of reincarnation. He was able to live a virtual hermit's life because of the estate of his wealthy late parents.

Neil was eventually convinced by his long-time family physician to seek psychiatric help. He presented to his psychiatrist with a delusion of "having no body at all." Neil refused to acknowledge that he had height, weight, head, torso, limbs, or any physical features at all. He denied that he ate, drank, urinated, or defecated and also failed to offer an explanation for why he dressed for his rare trips outside his home. At one stage of therapy, Neil was asked to drink a glass of water, which he did. He was then asked to explain where the water went. Neil replied that it "evaporated." When pressed to explain these and other inconsistencies, Neil usually either gave no

BENIGN COITAL headache syndrome occurs when a sexual orgasm brings on a migraine-like headache. It occurs three times more often in men than in women. So it's not usually "Not tonight, Harry, I have a headache." It's more likely to be Harry's headache.

answer or merely said, "I don't know." He seemed to find no inconsistency or problem with his answers. Neil is continuing psychotherapy.

A GLASS OF water often halts the effects of a headache.

A COTARD'S SYNDROME FANTASY?

Cotard's syndrome—type fantasies sometimes are depicted in films and literature. For example, the 1957 classic science fiction film *The Incredible Shrinking Man* (from a novel and screenplay by Richard Matheson) portrays a man who mysteriously continues to shrink in size. This dramatically alters his view of himself and his world. Continuing to shrink to the size of an atom, he reflects, "When you become so small, you become as large as the universe."

THE NARCISSISTIC BRAIN

If Cotard's syndrome has its opposite, it is certainly narcissism, extreme self-love.

According to Greek mythology, Narcissus gazed at his reflection in a pond and found true, tragic love. He could not leave his alluring image long enough even to eat and so died of starvation.

According to Dr. Oliver John, real-life narcissists take inspiration from their mythological namesake. A number of experiments have demonstrated that such self-ordained sources of excellence report even more admiration of their personal qualities after viewing videotapes of themselves. Moreover, narcissists seek out and enjoy situations, such as looking in the mirror, in which they can focus attention on themselves and sustain their overblown sense of self-regard.[10]

In one experiment, 51 of 130 university students tested high on a measure of narcissism. Unlike their non-narcissistic peers, narcissists preferred to watch themselves rather than others on a videotape and enjoyed looking in mirrors as a way to feel better. In another experiment, after sixty-two narcissists and sixty-two non-narcissists each completed a simple task, neutral observers judged that there was little or no difference between the performance levels of individuals from either group. However, narcissists evaluated their own performance as being far better than the non-narcissists evaluated their own performance. As John says, "Narcissists definitely have an inflated view of themselves that few others agree with."[11]

Narcissists feed on the attention they get from others and from themselves. John adds, "The motive to enhance self-esteem is stronger and more easily activated in narcissistic individuals because of their heightened sensitivity to threats to their grandiose self-views."[11] Thus, allowing narcissists to see themselves from the outside may swell their personal evaluations beyond already distended levels.[11]

THE ARISTOCRATIC BRAIN

According to the legendary neurologist of nineteenth-century Spain, Santiago Ramón y Cajal, the cells of the human brain are "the aristocrats among the structures of the body." Like aristocrats, they are grand users of resources. Although the human brain accounts for only 2 percent of body weight, at any given moment it bathes in about 15 percent of the blood and consumes 20 percent of oxygen and nutrients. However, unlike aristocrats of old, who were mere parasites on society, brain cells work very hard to keep the body functioning.[12]

BORNA BRAIN?

Can you catch a mental illness from someone the same way you can catch the common cold? For generations we've believed that mental illness is not "catching." But a group of German biologists suggest that some types of mental illness may be caused by a virus. A microbe, the Borna virus, has long been linked to behavioral abnormalities in animals. Over the last year or so, the same virus has been found in humans. Researchers isolated the Borna virus in three people suffering from mood disorders. When the virus was injected into laboratory animals, it caused the animals to develop behavioral problems. Earlier studies found that the Borna virus evolved into distinct strains for each species it infects. The human Borna virus has also been proven to be distinct. This suggests that the people in the German study were infected with a Borna virus that circulates in the human population. The researchers say, "These findings open up a new area of investigation of mental disorders."[13]

Chapter 9
The **Craving Brain**

Why do we crave things? It could be a cigarette, a glass of beer, or the most craveable culinary delight of all: chocolate.

Why do so many of us crave chocolate? The answer may lie in our brain's biochemistry.

Research shows that chocolate contains the chemical phenylethylamine (PEA). PEA is produced naturally in the brain and is both stimulating and mood elevating. PEA is "the same chemical the brain produces when people fall in love. The chemical causes a happy, slightly dreamy feeling by stepping up heart rate and the body's energy levels. One study has shown that people frequently crave chocolate after breaking up with a lover."[1]

Two New York psychiatrists have theorized that craving chocolate is an unconscious attempt to raise PEA levels and reproduce emotional elation and "the lover's high." In reply to this theory, a Chicago psychologist has said, "Clearly it is not the lovelorn sufferer who seeks solace in chocolate, but rather the chocolate-deprived individual who, desperate, seeks in mere love a pale approximation of bitter-sweet euphoria."[2]

But this debate may be irrelevant, according to Drs. Robert Ornstein and David Sobel: "Unfortunately, PEA in food doesn't make it to the brain." In arguing that "perhaps it's the flavor of chocolate itself that explains our obsession," they say that cocoa, the basis of chocolate, "is a complex blend of over five hundred flavor components—more than twice as many as are found in the simpler treats of strawberry or lemon." They point out that chocolate is also rich in volatile compounds "that waft up the back of the throat to tickle the nose with fruity, earthy, malty, and floral scents. And then there's the velvety, melt-in-your-mouth feeling of chocolate as it transforms from a solid to liquid at just body temperature."[3]

To investigate possible personality differences in chocolate addicts, researchers at the University of California at Los Angeles studied those attending a chocolate convention, of whom 53 percent were "self-proclaimed chocoholics." They then compared this group with a randomly selected control group. In all, they found that chocoholics were "psychologically normal." However, it was discovered that chocoholics "did share some traits with 'hysteroid dysphorics'— clinically depressed patients, usually women, who spend inordinate amounts of time searching for romantic attention and

HOSPITALIZED mental patients rarely complain of headaches.

AN ASPIRIN tablet is 40 percent more effective if taken with a cup of hot chocolate rather than a glass of water.

WHY DO SO many people crave chocolate so much? Chocolate has a major effect on the brain. Chocolate contains phenylethylamine (PEA), which is the same mood-lifting chemical produced by the brain when you fall in love. Subsequent research has shown that salami contains three times as much PEA as chocolate. However, salami is unlikely to replace chocolate as a romantic gift.

approval, suffer repeated episodes of depression due to rejection, and when depressed, overeat and crave sweets."[4]

Ornstein and Sobel note that chocolate is another "healthy pleasure" in which we ought to indulge freely and without guilt. They suggest that guilt is more destructive to health than chocolate and that chocolate is not nearly as bad for us as we once believed. For example, they claim that chocolate has been shown not to cause tooth decay. In fact, quite the opposite: "Chocolate contains substances that appear to protect tooth enamel and help prevent tooth decay."[3]

Despite this view, chocolate may have a dark side: It may trigger migraines. In a survey of 550 clinicians in the United States and Britain, it was found that there was "a widespread clinical belief that foods trigger much of the pain among the people, mainly women, who suffer from the one-sided headaches called migraines." The most commonly clinically cited culprit: chocolate.[5]

Could chocolate act in the brain similarly to marijuana? Cannabinoids give marijuana its psychoactive powers. It seems that related cannabinoids are in chocolate. Both chocolate and cocoa powder contain anandamide, a substance that might set off some of the same neurons in the brain that are sensitive to the cannabinoids in marijuana. However, there is so little anandamide in chocolate that one would have to eat twenty to forty kilograms at one sitting to get a marijuana-like high.[6]

The ancient Aztecs believed that chocolate was a gift from the gods. Why we crave it is still a sweet mystery of life.

Those chocolate Easter bunnies haven't got a chance.[7]

MORE PEOPLE get migraines when the sun is out than under rainy, overcast skies.

ONE WAY TO relieve a migraine headache is to soak the hands in hot water.

THE ROD THROUGH HIS BRAIN

In 1848, Phineas Gage, a twenty-five-year-old railroad worker in the U.S. state of Vermont, was working with a tamping rod more than three feet long and four inches wide when an explosive charge unexpectedly detonated. The explosion propelled the rod, like a spear, into Gage's cheek, into his brain behind his eye, and through his skull, where it lodged. Miraculously, Gage did not die. His coworkers cut off the ends of the rod until it protruded about four inches out of his cheek and four inches out of the top of his skull. Doctors were unable to remove the rod. Gage lived for thirteen more years with the rod through his brain.[8]

THE PIZZAS IN YOUR HEAD

The cerebral cortex of the human brain is a thin sheet of tissue with a very large surface area: "Flatten it out and you would have the equivalent of two 12-inch pizzas, one on each side of the brain."[9] Each "pizza" has six thin layers, composed of stacks of cells lined up in an orderly fashion— but no anchovies!

SEE AND TOUCH

It is a common belief that the loss of one sense increases the strength of the others. But a team of Japanese researchers has demonstrated that in blind people, the visual cortex (a part of the brain that normally processes visual information) is instead given over to touch. In experiments involving positron emission tomography in the blind, neurons normally reserved for vision were simply adjusted to process information from the fingertips. There was no increase in sensory ability—merely a shift in it.[10]

Chapter 10
The **Criminal Brain**

Is there such a thing as a criminal brain? Is the brain of a criminal somehow different from that of a normal, law-abiding person? Surprisingly, the answer may be "yes."

Research shows that in the brain of a criminal there may exist a mechanism known as the criminal high. That is, in certain people crime produces a subdued physiological arousal. They unconsciously seek to boost their level of arousal by performing criminal acts just as mountain climbers, skydivers, or other thrill seekers seek their high through their dangerous acts.

According to the theory, all individuals differ in their levels of arousal; some are higher and some lower. Arousal level may be measured, and it remains constant throughout one's lifetime. As a group, criminals have much lower levels of arousal than noncriminals. Therefore, the theory goes, measuring a person's arousal level in adolescence helps to predict whether

DO TRUTH serums work? Most experts now agree that so-called truth serums don't work or at least don't work reliably enough often enough. Under the influence of a truth serum, normal people often can stick to their lies. And neurotic people sometimes confess to crimes they couldn't have committed. True psychopaths are totally unpredictable.

he or she is more likely to become a criminal later on.

This theory has many "ifs." But significant evidence supporting the theory has emerged from a team of researchers at the University of Southern California (USC) in Los Angeles.

In 1990 the USC team reported its follow-up research on 101 British schoolboys spanning ten years. They found that three physiological markers indicating arousal level helped predict criminal behavior among young men a decade after these markers were measured.[1-5]

How the team was able to come to this conclusion is interesting in itself. In 1978, the team obtained physiological measurements of all 101 boys when they were still in school. The boys were aged fourteen. In 1988, the team searched the British government's computerized record of serious criminal offenses and found that 17 of the 101 subjects, then twenty-four years old, had at some time committed a crime. The most common crimes were burglary and theft, with five of the seventeen having spent time in prison.

The team then checked the earlier physiological markers of these seventeen boys. Just as the theory predicted, they found that these boys had lower levels of arousal than the eighty-four noncriminal boys when all were measured a decade before. Specifically, the seventeen boys had significantly lower physiological measurements in the markers of heart rate, electrical activity in the skin, and electrical activity in the brain.[1,2]

However, as seductive as the theory might seem, the USC researchers add that environmental factors, not just the brain or the body itself, probably are very important in explaining crime:

> *These psychophysiological differences between criminals and noncriminals do not appear to be mediated by social and demographic differences since all relationships between these variables and arousal measures were small and non-significant. Nevertheless, other environmental factors not measured in this study may mediate the relationship between crime and arousal, since there is evidence from other studies that social factors (e.g., social class) interact with biological factors in the development of antisocial behaviour.*[1]

The idea that the brains of criminals are different has profound implications for the justice system and for rehabilitation efforts. Cognitive remediation has been found to help brain-injured patients recover lost function. If such therapy is able to help criminals fortify their brains to compensate for an under-active prefrontal cortex, the changes may show up on a brain scan. Positron emission tomography may provide the most compelling evidence at a parole hearing.[3-5]

Other research shows that other, more mundane factors may act on the brain to cause criminal behavior. For example, research shows that the body's inability to cope with lead and cadmium may overload and damage the brain and thus play a role in criminality. In fact, McGill University researchers argue that a high concentration of lead and cadmium in the blood can predict criminal behavior, particularly violent criminal behavior. They have observed that high but nontoxic levels of lead and cadmium, either acting independently or interacting together, have long been implicated in learning and behavioral problems.[6]

The McGill researchers studied forty-nine men between the ages of nineteen and forty-eight who were incarcerated in an institution for psychiatrically disturbed criminals. Staff at the institutions classified each as high or low in terms of overall aggressiveness, based on both the nature of previous criminal history and the present behavior exhibited in the institution. Those high in aggression were designated as the violent group, and those low in aggression became the nonviolent group. Of the forty-nine subjects, thirty were in the violent group and nineteen in the nonviolent group.

The thirty violent subjects, all of whom were also violent in the institutions, included those guilty of murder, attempted murder, assault, armed robbery, and violent rape. Although they too had extensive criminal histories, the nineteen nonviolent subjects were all involved in nonviolent burglary or less severe crimes and were seldom or never violent in the institutions.

The McGill team analyzed the lead and cadmium levels in the blood of both groups and compared them. They also investigated whether tobacco use, amphetamine use, or any other factor came into play.

They found that both lead and cadmium "were significantly higher in the violent group." Furthermore, no other variables interfered with this relationship.[6]

From this, the researchers conclude that both lead and cadmium are related to aggressiveness such that if the level of both is high in a criminal, he is likely to be a violent criminal as well.

Thus, when a person commits a crime, the brain and the body may share the blame.[6,7]

A CAR ANTENNA THROUGH HIS BRAIN

In 1996, a man who bumped into the tip of his car's antenna drove the metal rod up his nose and into his brain. "It's the weirdest thing you've ever heard of," said Troy Harding, who managed to pull himself free. Harding, a nineteen-year-old from Portland, Oregon, told doctors he was turning away from his car when he lost balance. His head aimed in the direction of the car's radio antenna. About 3.5 inches of the antenna on his 1984 Fiero poked into his nose. The antenna, with the little metal ball at the tip, pierced his sinus, entered his brain, and hit his pituitary gland. He lost about a pint of blood. Harding was confined to hospital for about three weeks and then released. According to his neurosurgeon, Dr. Ray Grewe, "He's lucky not to have wiped anything out."[8]

DR. STRANGELOVE SYNDROME

Do you remember the classic World War III black humor film of 1964, *Dr. Strangelove?* The character in the title role, played by Peter Sellers, could not keep his artificial arm from giving a Nazi salute. Once again, life imitates art. Dr. Strangelove syndrome is psychiatrically known as alien hand syndrome. It is a weird neurological disorder that afflicts thousands of people throughout the world. It is caused by brain damage that results in one hand acting independently of the other. One hand may be controllable, but the other hand "misbehaves." For example, if a person is tying a knot, one hand may be tying while the other is untying. Sometimes the misbehaving hand may become aggressive, pinching, slapping, or punching the sufferer. In one case, the misbehaving hand attempted to strangle its owner. Whatever the person may do to try to stop the "alien" hand, it acts up almost as if it had a mind of its own.[9]

USE IT OR LOSE IT (AGAIN)

The "use it or lose it" phenomenon in brain development has been confirmed by studies of children with cataracts. Dr. Carla Shatz says that even when the cataracts were removed, the children were blind, unlike adults who have cataracts removed, because the brain pathways necessary to see were never developed in those children.[10]

IS IT A QUAIL OR A CHICKEN?

Groundbreaking experiments have shown that some instinctual behavior can be transferred from one animal to another by transplantation of brain cells. According to Dr. Evan Balaban, researchers transferred some chicken behaviors to quail and vice versa by extracting bits of nervous system tissue from very early chicken embryos and implanting them among nerve cells in quail embryos of the same age. The behaviors that were transferred were very specific noises and head motions produced by each species during crowing. Although the birds died fourteen days after they were born, there was enough time to determine that they had picked up the crowing style of the other species.[11]

Chapter 11
The **Euphoric Brain**

Why do humans take drugs to get high?

A controversial answer is that we seek mind-altering states for the same reasons as we seek food, drink, and sex. As unstoppable as our three primary drives of hunger, thirst, and sex are, a desire for drug-induced highs constitutes a fourth drive.

This radical view is put forward by psychopharmacologist Dr. Ronald Siegel, who argues that the pursuit of drugs by humans is both "universal and inescapable."[1]

Siegel claims that we learned our drug-taking behaviors from other animals and that all animal species and all cultures in all corners of the world have had their "drugs of choice" and their "favored hallucinogens." Indeed, taking drugs to achieve mind-altering states has been a part of human behavior ever since humans became humans. Whether these drugs are illegal substances such as cocaine, opium, and marijuana or legal ones such

ONE THEORY about why alcohol affects us the way it does and not in some other way holds that alcohol stimulates the right side of the brain. This hemisphere is responsible for imagination, visualization, and creativity. Furthermore, alcohol numbs the left side of the brain. This hemisphere is responsible for memory, detail, and responsibility.

as alcohol, nicotine, and caffeine, drug usage "is to be found across time and species."

According to Siegel, countless animal species from beetles to elephants seek out plants that give them various highs. He says, for example,

> Birds fall for alcohol and many have been captured and murdered in traps baited with alcohol. . . . Many people who have kept starlings for pets have observed their attraction to wines and other alcoholic drinks. . . . Raccoons have been known to seek out the alcohol readily and eagerly if only provided with the opportunity to do so. They will even open bottles and pull out corks for themselves.[1]

The pig's passion for truffles is based on the fact that truffles contain a steroid, androstenol, which is synthesized in the testes of the boar and transferred to the salivary gland, from which it is secreted during pre-mating behavior. Androstenol makes boars more sexually active and tends to immobilize the sow in a mating stance.

Koalas are dependent on the potentially dangerous chemicals contained in gum leaves. Gum leaves contain a mix of toxic prussic and hydrocyanic acids. These have anesthetic and germicidal properties, which Aboriginal Australians long have known, and also can increase or decrease body temperature. In cold climates, koalas "choose leaves with phellandrene, a compound that increases body temperature, but in warmer environments they pick leaves with cineole, the oil that decreases temperature."[1]

Siegel notes that apes, monkeys, and other nonhuman primates in the wild seek out plants that give them highs. Even Charles Darwin noted that monkeys can become addicted to nicotine in the same way we do. Siegel observes that nonhuman primates

> *will show a remarkable drive to intoxicate themselves even in a roomy laboratory cage. Whether for reasons of exploration, curiosity, stimulation, tranquillization, dispelling boredom, or depression laboratory primates have willingly pursued a vast array of intoxicants when given the opportunity.*[1]

Siegel contends that human drug taking probably began as the earliest humans struggled for food. When unsuccessful, humans often experienced times of near starvation. During such periods, humans discovered what other animals already knew: that consuming the products of certain plants can give temporary relief from hunger pangs. These plants, though yielding no real nutrients, did produce other highly desirable effects: relaxation, stimulation, escape, pleasure, joy, ecstasy, self-understanding, altered states of consciousness, mystical revelations, "or just a different feeling."[1] Thus, for a near-starving human, taking a mind-altering drug was an attractive proposition indeed. If nothing else, a drug-based high could help get a person through the day or night and provided a means to relieve what could be a drab and boring existence.

CHINESE MEDIcine used to prescribe marijuana for absentmindedness.

DOCTORS NOW recognize that many coffee drinkers appear to use caffeine to medicate them-selves against depression.

Siegel maintains that humans have always been highly motivated to seek such effects. Indeed, these effects

are the same internal urges, wishes, wants, and aspirations that give rise to much of our behavior. Plant drugs and other psychoactive substances have been employed as natural tools for satisfying such motives.

Our three primary drives to satisfy needs of hunger, thirst, and sex motivate us to perform certain goal-directed behaviors: hunting, agriculture, and warfare (to preserve access to water supplies, territory, or mates). However, Siegel contends that the need to attain additional effects motivates us to pursue drug-taking behavior, even at the risk of our physical and mental health, loss of freedom due to imprisonment, or, in some countries, the death penalty. Indeed, the zeal to satisfy this fourth drive may help explain why risk taking is so common among illegal drug takers.

To satisfy the fourth drive, heroin addicts risk using contaminated needles, inject perhaps poorly cut and dangerously adulterated heroin, interact with ruthless criminals to obtain the drug, and pay great amounts to sustain the habit.

Siegel argues that

the pursuit of intoxication is no more abnormal than the pursuit of love, social attachments, thrills, power, or any number of other acquired motives. Man's primary biological needs may be body-bound, but his acquired addictions soar beyond these needs. . . .

The lessons gleaned from animals show that we can make peace with the fourth drive, understand that drugs are a kind of medication needed to change how we feel, and use the technology and education that is our human distinction to design safe intoxicants.[1]

Siegel admits that, unfortunately, humans sometimes take their intoxicating behaviors to extremes. In their quest for a drug-based high, humans can become addicted, and this leads to impairment. Addiction threatens communities by interfering with the person's ability to perform more socially useful pursuits. Thus, in Siegel's view, human history highlights a constant "struggle between this natural drive" toward drug-taking behavior and "societal law" toward controlling such behavior. Furthermore, today's so-called "War on Drugs" is merely the latest example of the community's effort to regulate the behavior of individuals for its own survival. The intoxication of one can be a threat to all.

It seems that biology impels, but society compels.[2]

THE WOMAN WITH THREE BRAINS

Steve Martin starred in the 1983 comedy film *The Man with Two Brains*, but now according to the *Weekly World News*, a Chicago woman has gone one step better: She has three brains. Shirley Germaine, aged twenty-one, believed that she was normal until magnetic resonance imaging tests revealed she had three small but fully formed and functioning brains in her skull. She lives a normal life as a bakery clerk.[3]

WHY IS THE HUMAN BRAIN WRINKLED?

The human brain has an odd, wrinkly look about it. In fact, the brain looks pretty strange. As do most of the other organs of the body. How did the brain get its wrinkles? The main part of the brain is the dome-shaped cerebrum. The surface of the cerebrum is the cerebral cortex. This is where most of the brain's information is stored. This thin mantle of brain cells, vital to and responsible for vision, hearing, thinking, reasoning, and other higher-order cognitive operations, is nonetheless dense with folds, convolutions, ridges, and valleys. Folded up, the cerebral cortex constitutes 50 percent of the brain's total volume. But when the spongy surface of the brain is observed, 66 percent of the cerebral cortex is hidden from view. Research reveals the reason for the folds. As animals such as humans became smarter, nature had to find a way to fit a rapidly growing cortex (a thin sheet) into a confined space (the human skull). The solution was to create folds, furrows, crumples, and crinkles and generally squash the cerebral cortex into desired patterns. Thus, each human brain is folded into distinct maps and areas. It is theorized that the folds form when slender extensions of nerve cells (axons) that link nerve cells together create different degrees of mechanical tension in the developing brain.[4]

Chapter 12
The **Fearful Brain**

No matter how well the human brain functions, we humans can be deathly afraid of just about anything.

Although most of us think we have a phobia, probably only about 10 percent of us actually have a true phobia. Some phobias may be caused by organic brain damage, but probably most are not.[1]

A phobia is a neurotic disorder involving the presence of a persistent, irrational, unreasonable, and exaggerated fear. The fear concerns either animate or inanimate objects, situations, or conditions. The most prominent feature of a phobia is anxiety. Symptoms include heart palpitations, sweating, rapid breathing, shortness of breath, and even fainting. These can occur whenever a person is faced with the cause of the phobia.

The suffering brought about by fear is "all out of proportion to the actual threat, but this suffering is very real," according to the Anxiety Disorders Association of America (ADAA), located in Rockville, Maryland. The ADAA is attempting to boost the public understanding of phobias around the world.

A phobia is not a delusion, nor is the phobic mad. Phobics are fully aware of what frightens them, become scared only when exposed to the phobia source, and know how to protect themselves from contact with that source. Understandably, phobics go to great lengths to avoid the phobia source, even though their lives may become very restricted.

People often confuse fears and phobias. Basically, a fear is reasonable, but a phobia is unreasonable. The difference can be illustrated as follows. Imagine you are jogging in a public park. Suddenly, a huge, barking, snarling German shepherd races toward you, sharp teeth at the ready. You would probably become fearful. This is a fear because it is reasonable: There is a real chance that you may be harmed. But if you are terrified to enter a house where a tiny, newborn German shepherd puppy is sleeping in a closet, you have crossed the line into phobia. In fact, this particular phobia has two names, *cynophobia* and *caninephobia:* fear of dogs.

THE HUMAN brain has doubled in size over the last 2 million years. Humans can demonstrate that they've grown smarter. The brains of some other species have also grown, but they cannot demonstrate that they too have grown smarter.

Phobics should never be ashamed or embarrassed by their phobia. This is sometimes difficult because they know full well that most other people are not afraid in the same way. Nor should others poke fun at a phobic when the phobia is revealed. No one deserves ridicule, and no one is to blame.

The cause of a phobia often is difficult to determine. Phobias usually begin in early childhood. However, they have been known to occur at any age.

Research suggests that three brain structures play important roles in the phobic response. First, the brain's amygdala

> THE HUMAN brain can store perhaps 10 trillion bytes of memory.

functions as a central switchboard in the emotional reactions of fear. The amygdala, which sits at the top of the brain stem, relays crucial nerve signals related to emotions and stress. Second, the hippocampus, the sea horse–shaped cell cluster located close to the amygdala, functions as a conditioning memory bank holding the brain's library of unpleasant stimulus–response reactions. Finally, the bed nucleus of the terminal stria and the hypothalamus in the brain stem trigger the nervous system to fight, flee, or freeze.[2]

Children of both sexes are equally vulnerable. Like most other diseases, phobias occur with varying degrees of severity.[3]

Phobics as a group are no different from nonphobics. Apart from the phobias themselves, the only difference seems to be that phobics have more vivid imaginations.

Fortunately, all phobias are amenable to treatment. Usually, this begins with behavioral or talk therapy. The therapist helps the patient gradually increase his or her confidence when exposed to the phobic source. In fact, this is called exposure therapy and involves various components called desensitization, habituation, and flooding.

Drugs are not usually advised or necessary. The patient probably would have to take such drugs the rest of his or her life. In fact, some drugs may intensify or even cause phobias. Dr. Samuel Cohen of the London Hospital Medical College warned that benzodiazepines (a class of antianxiety drugs) could bring about phobias in older adults.[4]

Nevertheless, there are alternative therapies for phobias. For example, Dr. Douglas Hunt argues that "nutritional adjustment" can greatly reduce phobias.[5] And anecdotal evidence indicates that he's right. The ADAA lists sixteen drug-free ways to cope with phobias. Space does not allow a full description of them, but here they are:

Change your diet.
Center yourself.
Reach out and touch someone.
Relax.
Breathe deeply.
Distract yourself.
Snap out of it.
Write it down.
Talk to yourself.
Fantasize constructively.
Move.
Face your fear.
Imagine the worst.
Repeat, "This too shall pass."
Try support groups.
Know when to seek help.[6]

Help is available throughout the industrialized world. People with phobias should first speak with a general practitioner. They can then obtain a referral to a specialist if necessary.

At last count, there were 267 recognized phobias, all of which have technical names. Some of the more common phobias in adults are fear of open, public places (agoraphobia); social scrutiny (social phobia); enclosed places (claustrophobia); heights (acrophobia); darkness (achluophobia); lightning (astraphobia); thunder (brontophobia or keraunophobia); spiders (arachnophobia); snakes (ophidiophobia); rats and mice (rottephobia and musophobia); flying (aviophobia); and going to the dentist (dental phobia).

But we can also be horribly afraid of almost anything. Phgonophobia is the fear of beards. Clinophobia is the fear of beds. Autophobia is the fear of being alone. Kenophobia is the fear of empty rooms. Bibliophobia is the fear of books. Pediophobia is the fear of children. Levophobia is the fear of the left side. Phonophobia is the fear of the telephone. Homichlophobia is the fear of fog. Eisoptrophobia is the fear of mirrors. Chrometophobia is the fear of money. The list goes on.

Ironically, we can even be afraid of everything (pantophobia) or even fear itself (phobophobia).[7]

Case Study: Adrienne, A Fever Phobic

Adrienne, thirty-two, suffers from fever phobia. She has a morbid dread of fevers in herself and her son. For the past ten years or so she has continually taken her own temperature, usually about six times a day, including in the middle of the night. During hot weather, she panics. She says that she cannot tell whether she is getting a fever or "it's just hot." She takes her temperature more often during summer "just to be safe." At the sign of even a mildly high temperature, she immediately goes to the doctor. Adrienne explains that her fear of fever stems from the time in adolescence when she almost died of pneumonia. She is a university graduate with a career in communication. Her phobia has forced her to miss work and probably has hurt her career.

Adrienne is separated from her husband and has custody of

their five-year-old son, Jonathan. Since he was born, Adrienne has continually taken Jonathan to the doctor whenever he too is "warmish." Between them, they average three visits to the doctor per week.

Whenever Jonathan has a real fever due to a cold or flu, Adrienne panics. She is not dissuaded by the knowledge that a fever is normal in children and adults as part of a healthy immune response to disease.

Whereas most mothers greet their children with a smile and a hug, Adrienne greets Jonathan with a worried look and a feel of his forehead. When Jonathan comes in from play and is hot and sweaty, Adrienne becomes very concerned, and sometimes she takes him to the doctor. Often, by the time they arrive at the clinic, Jonathan has cooled down, and Adrienne takes him home again.

She takes Jonathan's temperature as often as she takes her own. This annoys Jonathan, especially because now that he is older and sees that he is treated differently from the way his friends are treated. This is not doing the mother–son relationship any good. Adrienne has expressed concern that, once Jonathan starts school, she will be unable to take Jonathan's temperature as often as before.

Fever phobia in oneself is related to nosophobia (fear of disease or illness). Parental fever phobia was first described in the medical literature in 1980, occurs across all social classes, and sometimes is caused inadvertently by doctors in what they say to parents about a sick child. Drs. Ariane May and Howard Bauchner of the Boston University Medical School claim that doctors may be contributing to parental fever phobia by giving mixed messages to parents about the dangers of fevers.[8]

Recognized Phobias

The list of phobias continues to grow. The list is 265 at present:

TYPE OF FEAR	NAME OF PHOBIA
AIDS	AIDS phobia
Air currents	Aerophobia
Animals	Zoophobia
Bacteria	Bacteriophobia
Beards	Phgonophobia
Beds	Clinophobia
Bees	Apiphobia
Being afraid	Phobophobia
Being alone	Autophobia
Being beaten	Rhabdophobia
Being bound	Merinthophobia
Being buried alive	Taphephobia
Being dirty	Automysophobia
Being egotistical	Autophobia
Being poisoned	Toxicophobia
Being scratched	Amychophobia
Being stared at	Scopophobia
Birds	Ornithophobia
Black people	Negrophobia
Blood	Hematophobia
Blushing	Erythrophobia
Body odors	Osphresiophobia
Books	Bibliophobia
Cancer	Cancerophobia
Cats	Ailurophobia or gatophobia
Certain names	Onomatophobia
Changes	Tropophobia

TYPE OF FEAR	NAME OF PHOBIA
Childbirth	Tocophobia
China	Sinophobia
Choking	Pnigophobia
Cholera	Cholerophobia
Churches	Ecclesiaphobia
Clothing	Vestiophobia
Clouds	Nephophobia
Cold	Psychrophobia
Colors	Chromatophobia
Corpses	Necrophobia
Crossing bridges	Gephyrophobia
Crossing streets	Agyiophobia
Crowds	Ochlophobia
Crystals	Crystallophobia
Dampness	Hygrophobia
Darkness	Achluophobia
Dawn	Eosophobia
Daylight	Phengophobia
Death	Thanatophobia
Deformity	Dysmorphophobia
Demons	Demonophobia
Dentist	Dental phobia
Depths	Bathophobia
Dirt	Mysophobia
Disease	Nosophobia
Disorder	Ataxiophobia
Doctors	Iatrophobia
Dogs	Cynophobia
Dolls	Pediophobia
Drafts	Anemophobia

TYPE OF FEAR	NAME OF PHOBIA
Dreams	Oncirophobia
Drink	Potophobia
Drinking	Dipsophobia
Drugs	Pharmacophobia
Duration	Chronophobia
Dust	Amathophobia
Electricity	Electrophobia
Empty rooms	Kenophobia
Enclosed spaces	Claustrophobia
England	Anglophobia
Erotic actions	Erotophobia
Everything	Pantophobia
Eyes	Ommatophobia
Failure	Kakorraphiaphobia
Falsehoods	Mythophobia
Fatigue	Ponophobia
Fears	Phobophobia
Feces	Coprophobia
Fevers	Fever phobia
Fire	Pyrophobia
Fish	Ichthyophobia
Flashes	Selaphobia
Floggings	Mastigophobia
Floods	Antlophobia
Flowers	Anthophobia
Flutes	Aulophobia
Flying	Aviophobia
Fog	Homichlophobia
Food	Sitophobia
Foreigners	Xenophobia

TYPE OF FEAR	NAME OF PHOBIA
France	Gallophobia
Frost	Cryophobia
Fur	Doraphobia
Gaiety	Cherophobia
Germany	Germanophobia
Germs	Spermaphobia
Ghosts	Phasmophobia
Glass	Crystallophobia
God	Theophobia
Going to bed	Clinophobia
Graves	Taphophobia
Gravity	Barophobia
Hair	Trichophobia or chaetophobia
Heart disease	Cardiophobia
Heat	Thermophobia
Heaven	Uranophobia
Heights	Acrophobia
Heredity	Patriophobia
Home	Domatophobia
Home confinement	Domatophobia
Home surroundings	Ecophobia
Homosexuals	Homophobia
Horses	Hippophobia or equinophobia
Human beings	Anthropophobia
Ice	Cryophobia
Ideas	Ideophobia
Illness	Nosophobia
Imperfections	Atelophobia
Infection	Mysophobia
Infinity	Apeirophobia

TYPE OF FEAR	NAME OF PHOBIA
Injections	Trypanophobia
Inoculations	Trypanophobia
Insanity	Lyssophobia or dementophobia
Insects	Entomophobia
Itching	Acarophobia
Jealousy	Zelophobia
Justice	Dikephobia
Knees	Genuphobia
Lakes	Limnophobia
Learning	Sophophobia
Left side	Levophobia
Leprosy	Leprophobia
Light	Photophobia
Lightning	Astraphobia
Machinery	Mechanophobia
Making decisions	Decidophobia
Many things	Polyphobia
Marriage	Gamophobia
Meat	Carnophobia
Men	Androphobia
Metals	Metallophobia
Meteors	Meteorophobia
Mice	Musophobia
Microbes	Bacilliphobia
Mind	Psychophobia
Mirrors	Eisoptrophobia
Missiles	Ballistophobia
Moisture	Hygrophobia
Money	Chrometophobia
Monsters	Teratophobia

TYPE OF FEAR	NAME OF PHOBIA
Motion	Kinesophobia
Moving	Tropophobia
Nakedness	Gymnophobia
Names	Nomatophobia
Narrowness	Anginaphobia
Needles	Belonophobia or acusophobia
Neglect of duty	Paralipophobia
Newness	Neophobia
Night	Nyctophobia
Noise	Phonophobia
Novelty	Cenophobia
Numbers	Numerophobia
Odors	Osmophobia
One of something	Monophobia
Oneself	Autophobia
Open spaces	Agoraphobia
Pain	Algophobia
Parasites	Parasitophobia
People	Anthropophobia
Pins	Belonophobia
Places	Topophobia
Plants	Botanophobia
Pleasure	Hedonophobia
Points	Aichurophobia
Poison	Toxiphobia or iophobia
Poverty	Peniaphobia
Precipices	Cremnophobia
Pregnancy	Maieusiophobia
Public performance	Halophobia
Public places	Agoraphobia

TYPE OF FEAR	NAME OF PHOBIA
Public speaking	Halophobia
Punishment	Poinephobia
Rabies	Lyssophobia
Railways	Siderodromophobia
Rain	Ombrophobia
Rats	Rottephobia
Reptiles	Herpetophobia
Responsibility	Hypegiaphobia
Ridicule	Katagelophobia
Riding in a car	Amaxophobia
Right side	Dextrophobia
Rivers	Potamophobia
Robbers	Harpaxophobia
Ruin	Atephobia
Russia	Russophobia
Rust	Iophobia
Sacred things	Hierophobia
Satan	Satanophobia
School	Scholionophobia
Sea	Thalassophobia
Sea swell	Cymophobia
Sex	Genophobia
Sexual intercourse	Coitophobia
Shadows	Sciophobia
Sharp objects	Belonophobia
Shock	Hormephobia
Shouting	Phonophobia
Sinning	Peccatophobia
Sitting idle	Thaasophobia
Skin	Dermatophobia

TYPE OF FEAR	NAME OF PHOBIA
Skin of animals	Doraphobia
Sleep	Hypnophobia
Smell	Olfactophobia
Smothering	Pnigerophobia
Snakes	Ophidiophobia
Snow	Chionophobia
Society	Anthropophobia
Solitude	Eremophobia
Sound	Akousticophobia
Sourness	Acerophobia
Speaking	Halophobia
Speaking aloud	Phonophobia
Speech	Lalophobia
Speed	Tachophobia
Spiders	Arachnophobia
Spirits	Demonophobia
Standing upright	Stasiphobia
Stars	Siderophobia
Stealing	Kleptophobia
Stillness	Eremophobia
Stings	Cnidophobia
Stooping	Kyphophobia
Storms	Astraphobia
Strangers	Xenophobia
String	Linonophobia
Sun	Heliophobia
Surgery	Ergasiophobia
Swallowing	Phagophobia
Syphilis	Syphilophobia
Taste	Geumantophobia

TYPE OF FEAR	NAME OF PHOBIA
Teeth	Odontophobia
Telephone	Phonophobia
Thirteen	Triskaidekaphobia
Thunder	Brontophobia or keraunophobia
Touching	Haphephobia
Travel	Hodophobia
Trees	Dendrophobia
Trembling	Tremophobia
Tuberculosis	Phthisiophobia
Ugliness	Dysmorephobia
Vehicles	Amaxophobia
Venereal disease	Cypridophobia
Virgins	Parthenophobia
Void	Kenophobia
Vomiting	Emetophobia
Walking	Basiphobia
Wasps	Spheksophobia
Water	Hydrophobia
Weakness	Ashenophobia
Weight gain	Dysmorephobia
Weight loss	Dysmorephobia
Wind	Anemophobia
Women	Gynophobia
Words	Logophobia
Work	Ergasiophobia
Worms	Helminthophobia
Wounds	Traumatophobia
Writing	Graphophobia[9]

CONSCIOUS MEMORIES

Brain scan findings point to the hippocampus and nearby tissue as being instrumental in the recall of a previously studied word. Other areas at the front of the brain coordinate attempts to retrieve the memory of the word before its conscious return. The hippocampus is a sea horse–shaped structure located beneath the cerebral cortex. According to the head of the team making the discovery, Dr. Daniel Schacter,

> Our results suggest that hippocampal activation is more closely associated with the actual recollection of a past event than with the effort involved in attempting to remember the event.[10]

HEAD SHOTS

Most people think that children recover from injury and trauma much better than adults and even adolescents. But research suggests that this is not at all the case with gunshot wounds to the head. Dr. Linda Ewing-Cobbs and colleagues studied thirteen children with head wounds due to shots. It was found that kids between five and fourteen years of age show no difference in eventual degree of recovery. Nearly all were moderately disabled. And Ewing-Cobbs even suggests, "The consequences of brain injury might be more widespread in young children."[11]

Chapter 13
The **Gluttonous Brain**

Obesity may soon become a thing of the past.

In a world first, researchers have succeeded in shutting off the signaling system of the brain that triggers the desire to eat.

After years of work, it is now possible to develop drugs that will control hunger pangs in the same way that we already control headache pains. Thus, we will be able to stop the craving for food that causes so many dieters to fail.

For the first time in human history, we will be able to control when and whether we want to eat.

Medical and behavioral science research reveals that we eat for a variety of complex and interrelated physiological and psychological reasons. But research also reveals that many of us overeat because our brains predispose us to overeating. Through no fault of our own, some of us possess what has become known as "the gluttonous brain": a brain that oversignals

YOU USE UP TO
7 million brain
cells every day.

the desire to eat. Furthermore, this overeating tendency has a genetic basis and thus runs in families.

Latest evidence suggests that the difference between the gluttonous brain and the nongluttonous brain may simply be an overproduction of one or more of six neurotransmitters known to stimulate a desire for food. These neurotransmitters carry a "must eat" signal between various nerve cells in the brain.

In particular, one of these neurotransmitters, a simple molecule called neuropeptide Y (NPY), may be the one most responsible for this "must eat" message.

In the early 1980s, researchers discovered that NPY, when injected into the brains of normal rats, signals them to eat uncontrollably. According to one of these researchers, Dr. Glenn Stanley,

> High dose injections of NPY certainly do make rats eat as much as they are physically capable of eating. In our early experiments they continue to eat like this for a minimum of five hours! . . . [NPY injections] give rats a sort of starch craving. This tends to make them refuse all other food to gorge on carbohydrates. This is enough to convert normal rats into obese ones.[1]

As this research continues, what is most exciting is the discovery of an antiserum to NPY that has been tested successfully. The antiserum consists of "antibodies that recognize and latch onto NPY." This stops NPY from doing its job of binding to its receptor on the nerve cell.[1]

In a series of experiments, Stanley and colleagues injected

normal rats with high doses of NPY. The rats ate voraciously and became obese. But when they received the antiserum, they returned to normal.

Moreover, when the antiserum was injected into normal rats that had received no NPY, the animals ate about 60 percent less food than previously. More impressively still, they even ate less food when allowed to reach a state of semistarvation, deprived of food for up to six hours—a virtual eternity for a hungry rat!

From their experiments, Stanley and colleagues have concluded that "NPY regulates eating behavior on a normal basis, and not just when it is injected in high doses."[1]

According to the researchers, their results also suggest that interrupting the NPY pathway is a practical method for controlling overeating in humans. The next phase of their research is the development of a drug for humans that blocks the receptor so NPY cannot go to work. If all goes well, there are only the practical hurdles to overcome in developing the ideal, brain-based diet drug.

Such a drug would be head and shoulders above any previous diet pill.

Conventional diet pills sold around the world usually contain phenylpropanolamine (PPA), a mild stimulant chemically similar to amphetamines. PPA-based diet pills are very popular. Studies indicate that they are the fifth most common class of drugs sold throughout the Western world. Unfortunately, some research indicates that they can become habit forming and may produce side effects such as headaches, anxiety, car-

DO YOU EVER talk to yourself while you think? Research suggests that many people do and that it's a good indicator of intelligence. When you talk to yourself out loud, you actually teach yourself things.

A LARGER PER-
centage of left-
handers than
right-handers
smoke cigarettes.

diac irregularities, and even stroke. Caffeine may exacerbate the risk.[2] Moreover, they can be easily misused by those on crash diets or suffering from eating disorders such as bulimia. Sadly, this is all too often the case with emetics (vomiting-inducing sub-stances) and laxatives. However, other evidence indicates that the dangers of PPA-based drugs are exaggerated, and they pose no major problems when used properly under medical supervision.[3]

All of this aside, it seems likely that an NPY pathway–blocking drug will not cause such problems.

Taming the gluttonous brain, succeeding in dieting, and controlling one of our basic biological drives may finally be within our own hands—and within our own minds.[4]

YOU'VE HAD ENOUGH!

When does the brain know when the body should stop eat-ing? Psychologists at Johns Hopkins University have identi-fied a novel method by which the brain evaluates the contents of the stomach and intestinal tract. The vagus nerve, which carries signals between the brain and the stomach and intestinal tract, carries distinctly different pat-terns of electrical signals in response to carbohydrates compared with proteins. These signals largely influence stomach contractions, which help digest food. Furthermore, hormone-like peptides produced by the stomach and intes-tinal tract, in response to food, amplify the signals. When you've had enough, the signals tell your brain to stop.[5]

THE GOURMAND SYNDROME

Swiss researchers have discovered a new eating disorder in which certain types of brain lesions cause average eaters to become addicted to thinking about and eating gourmet food. The new disorder, the gourmand syndrome, was observed in thirty-six patients studied over three years. The syndrome was first seen in two men recovering from strokes in a Swiss hospital. They displayed unusual desires for gourmet dining as they were getting better. One of the men, a forty-eight-year-old journalist, is now his newspaper's restaurant critic. According to Dr. Theodor Landis, "Gourmand syndrome is a rare, benign eating disorder strongly linked to damage of the right hemisphere of the brain." And Dr. Marianne Regard adds, "This new syndrome shows the public that addiction and compulsive disorders, even ones that aren't debilitating, can be due to damage to a limited area of the brain."[6]

SUGAR ON THE BRAIN

Sugar may be a handy tool for boosting your short-term memory. A California researcher found that glucose, a simple form of sugar, "enhances a rat's ability to remember what it learned up to seven days earlier but doesn't improve recall for older memories."[7]

WHY IT TAKES MORE AND MORE SPEED

Speed, the potent drug methamphetamine, appears to deplete a chemical in the human brain responsible for pleasure. Research by psychiatrists at the University of Toronto indicates that the chemical effects on the brain may explain why methamphetamine users often need ever-increasing dosages of the drug in order to achieve the same high. It may also provide a clue to the violent and aggressive behavior that is often associated with "speed freaks." Repeated use of speed appears to deplete stores of dopamine in the brain. Dopamine is a hormone-like chemical linked to body movement and motor control as well as the sensation of pleasure. Dopamine levels are as much as 55 percent lower in speed users than in nonusers. Low levels of dopamine have also been associated with schizophrenia and Parkinson's disease.[8]

A KISS ON THE HAND CAN BE QUITE NEUROLOGICAL

Our brains come equipped with neurons that let you find your lover's lips, even in the dark. Whether you enjoy a kiss on the hand or the face, some neurons in the brain's premotor cortex seem to do two related tasks: They are important for tactile sensation and for visual awareness of the area immediately around the face. In experiments with monkeys exposed to light and dark, Princeton researchers found that certain bimodal neurons in a monkey remain active after they should switch off like other neurons. This allows the brain "to keep track of the position of the head relative to the stimulus" even in darkness, and that makes kissing in the dark a cinch.[9]

Chapter 14
The **Hallucinating Brain**

There's still so much about the brain we don't understand. Take hallucinations, for instance.

A hallucination is defined as any false perception occurring without an external stimulation. This simply means that one sees, hears, tastes, smells, or feels things that just are not there.

Hallucinations are extremely common. In fact, we all have them every night when we dream. These are called transient hallucinations, which also frequently occur during the hypnagogic state between sleeping and waking. Hallucinations happen in young and old alike. Children who lead a particularly active fantasy life may occasionally think they hear voices, see people or objects, or invent imaginary friends.

Both positive and negative hallucinations can be produced in normal people by hypnotic suggestion, sensory deprivation, solitary confinement, extreme exhaustion, or hallucinogenic drugs. In most of these cases, the hallucinations usually are poorly formed, lack a full sense of reality, and possess limited significance as indications of the true personality or as symptoms of mental illness.

Research at the University Hospital Nijmegen in the Netherlands indicates that Charles Bonnet's syndrome (CBS)—the presence of complex visual hallucinations in psychologically normal people—is far more common than was previously thought. In a study of 505 visually handicapped people, it was found that 60 met the criteria for CBS. Normally in CBS, the patient has hallucinations but does not have the delusions or loss of insightful cognition that is characteristic of, for instance, hallucinations of schizophrenics. The researchers state, "CBS should be considered as a diagnosis in patients who complain of hallucinations and who meet defined diagnostic criteria. There is no proven treatment, but many patients will benefit from reassurance that their hallucinations do not imply mental illness."[1]

YOUR CENTRAL nervous system tosses out 99 percent of what your senses register so as not to bother your brain with unimportant matters.

However, psychiatric hallucinations may be associated with physical or emotional disorders. In either case, the patient accepts and responds to these false perceptions as reality. Many authorities consider hallucinations of this type to be perceptual expressions of underlying wishes, feelings, and needs. For example, they may reflect a need to escape from reality, to enhance self-esteem, to relieve a sense of guilt, or to fulfill aspirations. Personality needs of this kind may influence the content not only of emotion-based hallucinations but also of hallucinations produced by physiological conditions such as brain damage or illnesses or through taking a drug, poison, or toxic substance.

Interestingly, the type of hallucination itself seems to be determined to some extent by psychological factors. A person who is ridden by guilt might hear condemnatory voices. One who is beset by fear may have visions of terror. And victims of sexual anxieties usually see themselves surrounded by sexual symbols.

YOUR MIND constantly distinguishes the true from the false. Memory tests show that people tend to recall what they believe to be true and tend to forget what they believe to be false.

Hallucinations fall into six categories. The auditory type is by far the most common.

Auditory Hallucinations

With auditory hallucinations, the person hears strange noises, muffled voices, disconnected words, or his or her own thoughts in speech (the French call this *écho des pensées*). But most often they clearly hear remarks addressed to them alone. The voices usually are attributed to a particular person, or to God, "friends," or even "enemies." The voices may appear to come from such sources as automobiles, animals, light fixtures, dolls, heaters or air conditioners, or imaginary telephones. Voices may also emanate from parts of the person's own body or from two or more directions at once. Such voices may be pleasant, accusatory, or commanding. Often obscene language is "heard." Sometimes the patient answers back. Occasionally, the voices may issue commands that lead to violence against

IN HUMANS, the left side of the brain controls speech. In birds, the left side of the brain controls song. In this similarity at least, we humans are "bird-brained." Recent evidence indicates we have greatly underestimated the intelligence of birds.

oneself or others. The infamous New York "Son of Sam" serial murders involved a man who believed that his dog and his gun commanded him to kill his victims.

One fascinating form of auditory hallucinations is musical hallucinations. According to psychiatrists from the Hospital Tenon in Paris, these hallucinations usually consist of hearing musical memories from one's past (e.g., childhood songs, favorite songs, past hits). When there is silence in a patient's room, he or she often starts uncontrollably hearing such songs, and the songs get louder and louder unless real noise occurs in the room. The researchers report that of their seven patients with musical hallucinations, "by concentrating, 3 patients could change the on-going tune for another." [2]

Musical hallucinations can be caused by many things, including brain cancer.[3] Interestingly, culture also can influence the type of music that makes up the hallucination.[4]

Auditory hallucinations often are seen in acute alcoholic hallucinosis, senile (paranoid) psychosis, and affective psychoses (for example, the depressive phase of manic–depression) and in a variety of other patients.

Visual Hallucinations

Although visual hallucinations sometimes are pleasant, more often than not they are disgusting or frightening. One vivid example of this is the Lilliputian hallucinations involving tiny, fast-moving animals that terrify alcoholics suffering delirium tremens.

Visual hallucinations also predominate in psychoses associated with acute infectious disease and in toxic poisonings.

> YOU HAD MORE brain cells at age two than at any other time in your life.

Tactile Hallucinations

In tactile hallucinations, sometimes called haptic hallucinations, the patient feels electric impulses in various parts of the body or feels sexual sensations. A variant of this is formication, or the sensation of insects crawling on or under the skin.

Kinesthetic Hallucinations

In this type, various parts of the body feel as if they are changing their shape, size, or movement. Interestingly, hallucinations of this kind involving nonexistent body parts sometimes occur in patients who have undergone amputation.

Olfactory Hallucinations

Most hallucinated odors are repulsive (such as decaying flesh or feces), seem to be associated with unconscious feelings of guilt, and may occur along with accusatory voices.

Gustatory Hallucinations

Hallucinations of taste often are associated with hallucinations of smell. Often, the patient complains of tasting poison in food or states that his or her mouth is full of horrible substances such as burning acids.

All types of hallucinations occur in paranoid schizophrenia, Alzheimer's disease, epileptic disorders, and psychoses associated with brain tumors, advanced syphilis, cerebral

WHAT ANIMAL has the largest brain in proportion to its size? It's the ant. Humans aren't even close.

THE WEIGHT OF one's body is about forty times greater than the weight of one's brain.

arteriosclerosis, cocaine addiction, and many other conditions.[5]

Research continually sheds more light on the matter. For example, psychiatrists at the University of Vienna reported on their intriguing discovery that auditory hallucinations in normal people are fundamentally different, neurologically, from auditory hallucinations of psychotic patients.[6] But why this is so is anyone's guess.

There is still so much about the brain that we do not understand.[7, 8]

HALLUCINATIONS AND SOLAR WIND

Here's a weird one. University of Iowa psychologists have found surprising data from the nineteenth century on the occurrence of visual hallucinations and the magnetic disturbances from solar winds. It seems that the two phenomena are statistically correlated and that the magnetic disturbances influence the production of the pineal hormone melatonin. Some research suggests that melatonin is associated with the ability of the brain to regulate sleep. In fact, melatonin has been advocated as an insomnia treatment, particularly in older adults. But other researchers scoff at such a notion and attribute melatonin's alleged sleep promotion to a placebo effect.[9]

A FISH BEATS US BRAINS DOWN

One of the things that sets humans above all other creatures is the large size of our brain as a percentage of overall body mass. And another is the high percentage of oxygen in the body devoted to the brain. The human brain is 2.3 percent of body mass and uses 20 percent of the oxygen in the body. This is far more than what occurs in other vertebrates, where the brain is 1 percent of body mass and uses 2 to 8 percent of the oxygen in the body. But scientists have discovered that a fish has knocked us off both of these brain pedestals. The brain of the tiny African elephant-nose fish is 3.1 percent of body mass. And it devotes a whopping 60 percent of its oxygen to the brain. Scientists theorize that such a great deal of oxygen is needed because the brain is so unusually large and the fish is so unusually cold-blooded.[10]

Chapter 15
The **Happy Brain**

It's the quest for the happy brain.

Would you take a pill to make you happy and keep you that way?

Science has developed the real potential for just such pills. And that leads us to the story of fluoxetine (commonly known by its brand name, Prozac). Some call it "the Alice in Wonderland drug," others the "liberation drug," still others "the feminist drug." But everyone agrees it is a drug that transforms.

When fluoxetine was introduced in 1987, the antidepressant enjoyed the fastest acceptance of any psychotherapeutic medicine in history. In the United States alone, 650,000 new prescriptions were written per month. Despite a backlash of claims that the drug causes side effects from suicide to homicide, its popularity continues to soar.

Listening to Prozac, by Dr. Peter Kramer, documents the

drug's dramatic rise.[1] The book was number one on the non-fiction best-seller lists all over the world.

Kramer, a professor of psychiatry at Brown University, believes that the drug has "transformative powers." Patients not only receive a cure for their depression but also undergo a change in personality. Indeed, they become "better than well. Not only does their depression lift, but also they become more gregarious, socially and mentally adept and assertive." He adds, "It is now sometimes possible to use medication to do what once only psychotherapy did—reach into a person and alter a particular element of personality."

In his book, Kramer presents several cases of his own patients who underwent a remarkable personality metamorphosis after only thirty days of taking the drug once a day.

One patient is Tess. After an abusive childhood with an alcoholic father and a depressed mother, Tess was suffering from deep depression when she first saw Kramer. She was suicidal because of the disaster of her latest self-destructive relationship. "Within weeks of going on Prozac, she is attracting men—good ones—and having fun. For the first time in her adult life she feels alive."

Kramer claims that fluoxetine lessens sensitivity to criticism or rejection, reduces obsessive–compulsive behaviors, soothes

ACCORDING TO experts, if you are typical, your mental health is at its best before the age of twenty-four and after the age of sixty-four. In your twenties, energy is high, as are hope and confidence to overcome setbacks. In your sixties, although energy and hope may be lower, you are more confident that not much can set you back that you haven't already encountered.

homesickness, and even diminishes interest in pornography. Furthermore, the drug is useful in treating eating disorders, premenstrual syndrome, attention deficit disorder, substance abuse, and sexual problems ranging from loss of libido to premature ejaculation.

For these reasons, fluoxetine has been dubbed "the Alice in Wonderland drug," after Lewis Carroll's Alice, who took one drug to make her larger and another to make her small. It is also called "the liberation drug" because patients are set free from their debilitating depression. And it has been dubbed "the feminist drug" because most of the people who are prescribed it are women. Often, after trying every other therapy, women taking fluoxetine gain the confidence they need to become more effective in their own lives. According to Kramer, they often gain the courage to boldly walk out of exploitive jobs, oppressive domestic conditions, and even brutal relationships.[1]

EVERYONE'S brain starts out as female. The brain of a male becomes masculinized by the male hormone testosterone. If the testosterone is not strong enough early enough, then masculinity does not occur. The experiments with laboratory rats continue.

Kramer argues that we are moving into the era of "cosmetic psychopharmacology." We can now change our mood or personality medically, just as we can bob a nose or remove wrinkles.

Kramer maintains that depression is a progressive disease and must be treated early. He theorizes that early trauma can change the anatomy of the brain and leave people with a heightened sensitivity to loss or rejection. This makes them vulnerable to serious depression later on. He also believes that some people may be born with a predisposition for a specific personality type that may lead to depression. He describes research on babies who exhibit extreme shyness at infancy in combination with physiological signs of stress. Kramer argues that, for these people, depression may come from a mismatch between their coping style (introverted, unassertive,

> IN 1900, IT COST the equivalent of $8.10 for an hour-long therapy session with Sigmund Freud.

inhibited) and the social style that society rewards (extroverted, assertive, uninhibited).[1]

Of course, this suggests a possible downside of fluoxetine. An effective "transformative" drug could be used as an agent of social engineering. "Transformative drugs" could be used to alter and control people's behavior toward a manner deemed to be more socially useful or desirable. In that sense, fluoxetine would be a drug reminiscent of the mind-numbing soma used to placate citizens in Aldous Huxley's *Brave New World*.

Thus, fluoxetine may be the realization not of Lewis Carroll's dream but of Aldous Huxley's nightmare.

That is precisely what is argued by the critics of happy drugs. Drs. Seymour Fisher and Roger Greenberg, psychologists at the New York Health Sciences Center in Syracuse, state that we must be very, very cautious in the use of such drugs. And we should also be aware that studies backing happy drugs often are methodologically flawed. Furthermore, they say, "administering a therapeutic drug is not simply a medical, biological act. It is a complex social act."[2] As such, it has implications for all of us.

If we attain the chemically altered happy brain and become a society of people continually drugged up with and dependent on happy pills, what manner of society will we possess, and what type of people will we have become?[2,3]

CONFIDENCE IS MORE IMPORTANT THAN BRAINS

It seems that brains may not matter as much as confidence in scholastic success. Research by Dr. Marianne Miserandino indicates that belief in one's ability matters more than natural ability or potential. In a study of seventy-seven eight- and nine-year-old children, it was found that "those children who were certain of their abilities reported feeling more curious and participated in, enjoyed and persisted more at school tasks." However, "those children that were uncertain of their ability and motivated by external reasons lost interest in school, did not partake in as many activities, felt angry, anxious and bored, and suffered a decline in their academic performance."[4]

CONSCIOUSNESS AND THE COMPREHENSIBLE BRAIN

What is consciousness? Why does it exist? What does it do? How does it emerge from the intricate cellular processes of the brain? These are big questions. A helpful insight is provided by Dr. David Chalmers:

> From an objective view, the brain is relatively comprehensible. When you look at this page, there is a whir of processing: photons strike your retina, electrical signals are passed up your optic nerve and between different areas of your brain, and eventually you might respond with a smile, a perplexed frown or a remark. But there is also a subjective aspect. When you look at the page, you

are conscious of it, directly experiencing the images and words as part of your private mental life. You have vivid impressions of colored flowers and vibrant sky. At the same time, you may be feeling some emotions and forming some thoughts. Together such experiences make up consciousness: the subjective, inner life of the mind.[5]

THE BRAIN'S THESAURUS

When we need an equivalent word and can't find one, we look it up in a thesaurus. Well, it seems the brain has one too. A team of scientists exploring the human brain's exotic terrain of soft furrows has discovered where the brain handles distinct categories of words and the concepts they describe. The brain appears to use a kind of interactive mental thesaurus dispersed in many separate parts of the left cerebral hemisphere. The finding may offer provocative new insight into how the brain retrieves words to describe the world around it.[6]

Chapter 16
The **Hypnotic Brain** 1:
Bigger Breasts Through Hypnosis, or How to Pull a Rabbit Out of a Hat

Is there such a thing as a hypnotic brain? Of course, we're not talking about the kind you see in a science fiction movie but the real thing. Why is it that some people are easily hypnotized but others can't be hypnotized at all? To what extent is the brain involved? Do some people have a hypnotic suggestion–prone brain whereas others do not?

Researchers, including psychiatrists, neurologists, and

medical hypnotists themselves, have never been able to describe precisely those who are more likely to be hypnotized. But there are some clues; just ask the theatrical hypnotists.

How Does the Theatrical Hypnotist Get Volunteers from the Audience to Make Fools of Themselves?

A theatrical hypnotist playing to a house of 500 usually will narrow down the entire audience to about 10 volunteers who will perform on stage:

> *The main secret of stage hypnotism is that the performer selects only the best subjects from a large group of volunteers . . . someone who is very cooperative, outgoing, and funny; natural hams who will play along, enjoy themselves, and not do anything to spoil the show.[1]*

But who are the best?

The theatrical hypnotist tests the entire audience before the show begins. The first to be eliminated are those who do not volunteer. Every theatrical hypnotist knows that only the people who volunteer would even consider being involved in the show. The second to be eliminated are those who were "volunteered" by someone else. Those put up to it by a partner or friend, volunteering on a dare, make poor stage subjects.

The theatrical hypnotist then asks all remaining volunteers to perform some very specific task while still seated in the audience. Most commonly, they are asked to hold up their right arm as straight as they can. Here is where the best volunteers distinguish themselves from the rest. Some people will not hold up their arm at all. They're eliminated. Others will hold it up but limply or at an angle. They're eliminated, too. The theatrical hypnotist wants people who hold their arms straight up, as stiffly as possible, and as long as possible, as instructed. People who follow orders best during the preshow test are the most likely to follow orders during the show.[1]

The people who act like fools on stage actually choose themselves.

As long as we're on the subject of tricks played on the mind, how does a magician fool our eyes and brain? For example, how does a magician fool us by pulling a rabbit out of a hat?

This classic magician's trick has been performed much the same way since biblical times.

The rabbit trick usually is the first trick in the magician's act. This is done to lower the animal's stress level and the magician's dry cleaning bill.

The top hat is indeed empty when first shown to the audience. The rabbit is hidden somewhere else. It is in a special pocket or dark cloth bag concealed in the magician's suit, somewhere on the set, or in an assistant's clothing. The rabbit does not move because of a long-known principle of rabbit behavior: A rabbit will not struggle in the dark.

In the classic version of the trick, when the magician demonstrates the hat to be empty, he or she manages to turn it so that the brim faces the rabbit bag. A bit of misdirection, such as the arrival of a scantily clad assistant, helps divert curious eyes from the magician as his or her fingers undo snaps in the bottom of the bag, causing the rabbit to

THE ODDS ARE that you can hypnotize yourself. Studies show that 70 to 90 percent of people who attempt it can do it. Athletes, actors, and political candidates are said to be accomplished at it.

plop neatly into the hat. The magician then may produce the rabbit whenever convenient.

If you keep a close eye on the performer you can often spot a bulge. Black hides the bulge best, which is one of the reasons stage magicians traditionally wear black. In a business suit or tuxedo jacket, rabbit pockets usually are toward the lower front at about breastbone level.

The rabbit bag may also be connected by a strong nylon string to the magician. A popular method is to tie the cord to one wrist, run it up that shirt arm, across the shoulders, and down the other shirt arm, where it terminates, just outside the sleeve, in a knot securing the bag. In a right-handed magician, the magician has the rabbit bag behind the right hand and must be careful to keep it out of sight. The hat is smartly snapped to scoop up the rabbit. The left hand takes the hat as the rabbit is released into the hat with the right hand. The magician then pulls the rabbit out with the left hand and holds it up. While all eyes are on the rabbit, the right hand holds up the hat. Raising both arms makes the suit ride up and causes the nylon string to retract the rabbit bag up the sleeve and safely out of sight.[1]

This trick has mystified audiences for hundreds of years, and we will love it for hundreds more.[2]

Bigger Breasts Through Hypnosis

Can hypnosis alter the size or shape of the body? As bizarre as the research findings might be, they seem to suggest that a person can alter his or her body size and shape—at least a little bit.

Studies have documented that women have achieved bigger breasts through hypnosis.

A chic Beverly Hills hypnosis clinic offers "breast enlargement

YOUR BRAIN waves have much to do with your sex appeal. If these waves somehow match those of a prospective partner, the attraction is immediate. Or so believe some specialists who work with the encephalograph. They're trying to see whether they can match up compatible lovers just by looking at their encephalographic readings.

through hypnosis" to "perfect-10-conscious" women living in Hollywood's most famous upmarket suburb. In fact, more than 50 percent of patients attend the clinic for breast enlargement.

Surprisingly, behavioral science research supports the view that breast size can be increased solely through hypnosis. In fact, some argue that hypnosis ought to be tried before any medical intervention takes place. If some women feel that they absolutely must have bigger breasts and will stop at nothing to get them, even risking their own health in doing so, hypnosis may be the best option. It is safer than surgery, injections, implants, or other possibly hazardous medical interventions.

In 1974, Dr. James Williams published an article in the *Journal of Sex Research* in which he described the first "successful use of hypnosis to stimulate breast growth."[3] A few years later, the most famous study in this line of research was published by Dr. Richard Willard, a medical doctor, in the *American Journal of Clinical Hypnosis*.[4]

Willard conducted a controlled study of twenty-two women between the ages of nineteen and fifty-four. Before beginning the experiment, he had another physician "who was not involved in the design of the experiment"[4] take careful measurements of five aspects of each breast to denote height, diameter, and circumference. Measurements were taken six and twelve weeks after the experiment began.

The twenty-two women were treated once a week for twelve weeks. In each session, they were given hypnotic suggestions for deep relaxation. They were told to imagine warm water flowing over their breasts, to imagine a heat lamp warming their breasts, and to imagine the feeling of their breasts pulsating. Tape recordings were made of these suggestions so that the women could think of these "visual images" at home when they were no longer under hypnosis. At the end of the twelve weeks, Willard reported,

> LEGENDARY psychiatrist Carl Gustav Jung said, "Beautiful bodies and beautiful personalities rarely go together."

28 percent had reached the goal they had set at the beginning of the program and desired no further enlargement. There were 85 percent who could tell a significant enlargement in their breasts had been accomplished, and 46 percent found it necessary to buy a larger brassiere. Forty-two percent had a loss in weight of more than 1 kg and still had enlargement of their breasts. The average increase in circumference was 3.3 cm; the average increase in the vertical measurement was 1.7 cm and the average increase in horizontal measurement was 2.5 cm. . . .

It was gratifying to note that 78 percent of the subjects noticed other positive changes in their lives while participating in the experiment, such as better bowling scores and improved golf games. At the end of 12 weeks, 85 percent of the patients could obtain a spontaneous feeling of warmth or pulsation in their breasts while doing other things, such as driving a vehicle, working or watching television. . . . [I]n this study, 63 percent of the subjects had children and complained of pendulous breasts. These subjects expressed a desire to regain the fullness and contour of the breasts which they had before the pregnancies. All of these subjects reported they were very pleased with the increase of fullness and firmness of their breasts at the end of the study.[4]

The mechanism of breast enlargement by hypnotic suggestion is not known. It may involve selective dilation of blood vessels in the breast, leading to engorgement or hormonally triggered proliferation of breast tissue.

Few studies have tested the findings of Williams or Willard. But so far, the ability of hypnosis to enlarge breasts has not been disproved by behavioral or medical science. Thus, until evidence to the contrary emerges, the findings of Williams and Willard will have to stand.

Needless to say, present evidence alone is more than enough for the Beverly Hills clinic to proceed full speed ahead. It advertises "75% improvement rates" for breast size. Indeed, the clinic supposedly is seeing male patients, too, but not for breast enlargement. These men must think that hypnosis can increase what they need most to be built up—perhaps their egos.[5]

WHEN YOU CAN'T STOP MOVING

Akathisia is a condition in which you cannot stop moving. One of the behaviors brought on by this condition is compulsive marching; the body simply will not sit down. Akathisia is fairly common in epileptics and sometimes temporarily arises as they adjust to new medications to treat their seizures.[6]

THE BRAIN'S HEAD START

Unlike other organs that constantly replace cells, the brain does not. Instead, the brain starts out with more cells than it ordinarily needs in a lifetime. According to Dr. Samuel Weiss, "Nature gives you too many brain cells to start with and assumes that you won't do anything silly like get into a boxing ring or ride a motorcycle without a helmet. And in most cases nature has done well, because most of us don't need replacement."[7]

Chapter 17
The **Hypnotic Brain** 2: Memory, Regression, and the Svengali Effect

As to the relationship of hypnosis, the mind, and the brain, there are three common questions: Can hypnosis help memory? Can a person under hypnosis regress to childhood? Can a hypnotized person be forced to act against his or her will?

Can Hypnosis Help Memory?

It is not widely known, but behavioral science research largely discredits the notion that hypnosis results in improved memory (hypermnesia). It seems that hypnosis does not assist in the calling-up of previously "hidden" facts with more accuracy and detail. This runs counter to the popular view sustained by the occasional media account wherein a witness under hypnosis helps police reconstruct a crime.

Instead, research tells us that hypnosis creates and boosts feelings of confidence for already accessible but uncertain information. Thus, hypnosis increases the probability that such remembered information will be reported with a greater degree of conviction.

One of the most important studies supporting this conclusion came from researchers at the University of Pennsylvania.[1] They conducted a simple experiment. They had seventy-eight volunteer subjects view a fifteen-minute video. During two test sessions several days apart, the subjects were asked a standard set of questions about what they had seen. After each answer, subjects were asked to rate their "confidence in its accuracy using a 4-point scale."[1]

During the first session, no subjects were hypnotized. But during the second, half the subjects were hypnotized and half were not. At this second session, those hypnotized were given the hypnotic suggestion that their answers "would come more easily than before."[1]

Both hypnotized and nonhypnotized subjects were equally able to recall additional correct details on the second test. But although hypnosis did not improve a

IS IT TRUE THAT if you sleep on a problem you'll be better able to solve it in the morning? There is some evidence that this is indeed true, although perhaps not with all problems in all situations. Research shows that your short-term memory is about 15 percent more efficient in the morning than in the evening. So if you put something down during the day and can't recall by evening where you put it, wait overnight and rethink it in the morning.

BRAIN WAVES come in four lengths: alpha, when we let go of anxiety; beta, when we puzzle over problems; theta, when we come up with bright ideas; and delta, when we sleep.

subject's memory, it did have "a slight effect" of instilling more confidence in the subject's responses that were earlier designated as only guesses.[1]

The researchers add that their experiment confirms conventional wisdom in psychology "that hypnosis engenders a shift in the subjective criterion for what constitutes a 'memory.'"[1]

At first it might appear that the confidence-boosting effect of hypnosis may make it useful in the case of a witness to a crime who has an incomplete memory of what happened. Unfortunately, the researchers point out that "our data indicate that hypnosis differentially increased confidence only for erroneous uncertain responses, and not for uncertain information that happened to be correct."[1]

Furthermore, they argue,

> *[Although] hypnosis or any other procedure that liberalizes report criterion may yield additional leads, . . . there is a considerable risk that the inherent unreliability of information confidently provided by a hypnotized witness may actually be detrimental to the truth-seeking process.*

Thus, they stress, "if hypnosis is permitted to form the basis of testimony in court, the confident 'recollections' of a previously hypnotized witness could very well create a serious miscarriage of justice."[1]

Finally, the researchers claim that many studies suggest several other ways of bringing about hypermnesia that are often more effective than using hypnosis. They assert that "a lack of advantage to hypnosis may be particularly evident when contrasted with the effects of motivating instructions . . . or the use of other cognitive retrieval strategies."[2]

Can a Person Under Hypnosis Regress to Childhood?

Behavioral science research largely discredits the notion that hypnosis helps a person regress to childhood.

There are between 60 and 100 studies on this question in the behavioral science literature. Psychologist Michael Nash has provided an important review of this research.[3]

Nash says that if adults are hypnotized and are then told to be and feel like a child, their behavior is still "essentially adult." That is, their mental and moral functioning is still more like that of adults than of children. Furthermore, nearly all studies show that if you take a group of hypnotized and nonhypnotized adults and ask both groups to act like children, the nonhypnotized adults succeed in acting more like children.

Nash concludes, "There is no evidence for a literal reinstatement of childhood

WE USUALLY think of the brain as the master control organ of the human body. But at least one commentator thinks the brain's role is greatly overstated. Dr. R. Bergland from the Harvard Medical School argues that the brain is merely a gland and depends on changes of hormones and molecules for its functioning. Furthermore, he maintains that although there is no denying that electrical impulses occur in the brain, they are only superficial signals and not as important as hormones in conveying messages to the brain, within it, and throughout the body.

YOU NEEDN'T
expect to under-
stand more than
70 percent of
what you hear. The
brain automatically
fills in the gaps.

functioning during hypnotic-age-regression procedures."

When a stage show hypnotist suppos-edly regresses a person to some alleged pre-vious life many centuries ago (say, to ancient Egypt), the regressed person never speaks in the language of that time. Cer-tainly, if such entertainers can regress some-

one to a former existence, regressing them to their own childhood should be no problem at all. However, research says that even this feat cannot be done. Apologies to Shirley MacLaine.[2]

Can a Hypnotized Person Be Forced to Act Against His or Her Will?

Behavioral science research gives us no clear answer to one of the most controversial and common questions about hypnosis.

During theatrical hypnotism acts, we have all seen people make fools of themselves. The stage hypnotist has a volunteer from the audience bark like a dog, strut like a rooster, or dance a striptease. Popular belief holds that if someone submits to being hypnotized and is successfully put under by some Svengali-like figure, he or she is invariably open to all sorts of suggestions, will lose all inhibitions, and could do just about anything.

But is a hypnotized person really acting involuntarily or voluntarily? Can a hypnotized person resist a hypnotic sugges-tion? How strong is the so-called Svengali effect?

The bulk of behavioral science research suggests that the majority of people, if not all of us, can resist a hypnotic sugges-tion, that a hypnotized person probably acts voluntarily, and that the Svengali effect does not really exist. But there is conflicting evidence.

Many studies over the years have tested the ability of subjects to resist hypnotic suggestions. In the late 1920s, it was reported that if first given the autosuggestion that they could resist a later hypnotic suggestion if they chose to do so, subjects successfully resisted when they wanted to.[4,5] But another study, in 1940, was unable to replicate those results.[6]

In a 1963 study twelve subjects were tested to see whether they could resist two hypnotic suggestions. Six subjects resisted both. Five resisted only one. One could resist neither.[7]

In the 1980s, experiments were undertaken to see whether subjects could resist hypnotic suggestions if they were bribed to do so. In a series of experiments, subjects were offered money ranging from $5 to $100. About 60 percent of subjects were able to resist. However, nearly 40 percent of subjects were unable to resist even if they were offered the maximum $100. The researchers concluded that "hypnotic influence is truly coercive for a small number of subjects and that their hypnotic performance is in fact truly involuntary."[8]

Thus, it seems that some are able to resist whereas others cannot or at least do not. But why this difference?

Psychologists at Ohio University propose a theory: "Hypnotizable subjects can resist suggestions when resistance is defined as consistent with the role of a good hypnotized subject."[9]

The Ohio team argues that being hypnotized has social as well as psychological dimensions. When people volunteer to be hypnotized, they voluntarily take on a social role: being a hypnotized subject. In this role, they behave according to the norms of behavior that they think are appropriate for this role.

If a person believes that it is socially correct for a hypnotized subject to resist a suggestion, then he or she is able to resist when hypnotized. However, if a person believes that resistance is not socially correct, then he or she is unable to resist.

Thus, hypnotized people may make fools of themselves in front of an audience because they believe that looking foolish is appropriate social behavior under those circumstances. Alternatively, they may refuse to make fools of themselves if this is outside their definition of appropriate social behavior.

In this way, performing the role of being a hypnotized subject is no different from performing the role of being a spouse, a parent, an employee, a voter, or any other social role. The governing principle is that people tend to act in ways they think appropriate.

Committing a crime via hypnotic suggestion exists only in theory. This is because too many existing social norms would have to be violated.

The Ohio team suggests that behavior under hypnosis is voluntary rather than involuntary for at least two reasons. First, a person chooses whether to undergo hypnosis in the first place. Second, based on the team's own laboratory research, people usually believe that resistance to any hypnotic suggestion is acceptable social behavior, and they choose to resist accordingly. Indeed, the team concludes,

Hypnotic responses have all of the properties of behavior that is typically defined as voluntary. That is, they are purposeful, directed toward goals, regulated in terms of subjects' intentions, and can be progressively changed to better achieve subjects' goals.[9]

In a strange way, then, it is we who ultimately control our own actions, even while under hypnosis.

The power of Svengali is in each of us.[10]

ACHROMATOPSIA: THE CURSE OF THE COLORLESS

The brain sees color, but the eye must send the right color message. Ordinary color blindness is almost always partial. It results from a genetic defect in the retinal cells of the eye and is much more common in men than in women. In fact, perhaps one in twenty men suffer from red–green color blindness, the most common form. Total color blindness is another matter. It is called achromatopsia. Again, the cause is genetic. Achromatopsia is very rare, affecting as few as one in 30,000 to 40,000 people. However, the native inhabitants of Pingelap, a tiny atoll among the Pacific Islands, are an exception. They suffer congenital achromatopsia in exceedingly high numbers because of intermarriage arising from the atoll's isolation. What has emerged on Pingelap is a color blind community.[11]

FORGET IT!

Cells throughout the body are constantly being replaced, but that's not so in the brain. Why? One simple explanation is that if brain cells were replaced, we would lose our memories. You can lose skin cells, liver cells, or bone marrow cells, but when you lose brain cells, forget it![12]

Chapter 18
Kleptomania:
The Taking Brain, or When You've Just Gotta Have It

We tend to snicker when we hear of some faded Hollywood film star or politician's wife arrested for petty shoplifting. But there's no cause for chuckles because these people and many like them could be suffering from kleptomania.

The internationally accepted definition of kleptomania is the recurrent failure to resist impulses to steal objects not needed for personal use or their monetary value.

What goes wrong in a kleptomaniac's brain is as perplexing as it is interesting. Yet what could be even more interesting is that research has found that kleptomaniacs may lose most or all of their urge to steal if treated with antidepressant drugs. At least this is the startling finding of research by a team of six Harvard University psychiatrists.[1,2]

These Harvard kleptomania studies are fascinating in several respects, not the least of which is the fact that they shatter several myths about kleptomania. For example, the Harvard team found that kleptomaniacs, rather than being obsessive–compulsive people with irresistible urges to steal, often suffer major mood disorders and alcoholism, anorexia, or bulimia. Furthermore, it was discovered that many kleptomaniacs have been victims of a major traumatic event in their life such as physical or sexual abuse, the violent death of a loved one, the loss of a home in a fire, or involvement in a fatal car accident. The researchers speculate that such events probably trigger the kleptomania.

It was also found that kleptomaniacs may suffer from a lack of serotonin in the brain. Serotonin is a brain chemical long known to be associated with moods. Theoretically and in practice, the researchers argue that restoring normal brain serotonin levels through antidepressant drugs could alleviate kleptomaniac symptoms.

Other studies tend to confirm this view. For example, psychiatrists from the Institute of Mental Health in Singapore reported that a previously very difficult to treat patient "who failed to respond to psychotherapy, behavioral therapy and pharmacotherapy . . . was successfully treated with the serotonergic agent fluvoxamine."[3]

When the Harvard team set out to understand more about kleptomania, they were surprised to discover that very little was actually known about it. Although behavioral and medical science, as well as the public, had some knowledge of what kleptomania was, only scant attention was paid to the subject in the in the psychiatric literature. The Harvard team decided to learn more about kleptomania by studying the life and treatment histories of several kleptomaniacs and comparing them.

They eventually settled on the cases of twenty kleptomaniacs at Boston's McLean Hospital, and they investigated these twenty cases in depth. They discovered that kleptomaniacs are more often women: Fifteen of the twenty patients were female. Contrary to the view that kleptomaniacs are either young adults or older people, the study found that most kleptomaniacs were in their mid-thirties. Furthermore, although it was common for the stolen items to be used, often the items were hoarded. And, interestingly, it was found that kleptomaniacs, as often as not, gave away whatever they stole.[1]

It was found that all twenty kleptomaniacs experienced major mood disorders. Of the twenty kleptomaniacs in the study, sixteen were diagnosed with anxiety and twelve with eating disorders.

Major mood disorders are psychological disturbances that often are characterized by dependence on alcohol or other addictive drugs, by panic attacks, by antisocial behavior, or by eating disorders such as anorexia nervosa or bulimia.

Anorexia nervosa is sometimes called Karen Carpenter's disease because it claimed the life of the American pop singer in 1983. It involves severe emaciation and wasting resulting from long-term refusal to eat, based on an intense fear of becoming fat. Anorexia nervosa also causes physical problems such as disruption of the menstrual cycle in women and a variety of psychological problems associated with bizarre notions of body image.

A WOMAN over age forty is 28 percent more likely to bear a left-handed child.

Bulimia is distinguished from anorexia

nervosa chiefly by its characteristic episodes of starvation followed by episodes of binge eating. Strict dieting, excessive exercise, forced vomiting, and laxative and diuretic abuse are associated with bulimia. Indeed, syrup of ipecac, a poison when taken to excess but a common household item kept for inducing vomiting in an emergency, was found at near toxic levels in Karen Carpenter's bloodstream at the time of her death.

The Harvard team believes that kleptomania should be classified along with obsessive–compulsive disorder, major mood disorders, and eating disorders. And they argue that all may be triggered by a psychological event in the sufferer's life or by a chemical imbalance in the body.

Under no circumstances should the kleptomaniac be blamed or treated as a criminal. The tortured mind or the brain itself is more likely to be at fault. The victim steals but is not really a thief.[4]

KLEPTOMANIA FROM A BLEEDING BRAIN

It doesn't happen often, but sometimes trauma to the head can cause kleptomania. In 1994, two German doctors reported the case of a forty-seven-year-old woman from Hannover who developed dramatically worsening kleptomania after suffering a brain hemorrhage. Before the trauma, she was able to control her urges and not steal. However, after the trauma, even though the bleeding was stopped, brain damage left by the trauma to the basal forebrain resulted in her becoming a kleptomaniac with uncontrollable urges regardless of drug use and therapy.[5]

WHEN AGING IS IN THE AIR

Research suggests that, within the brain, the vulnerability of proteins to attacks by highly reactive, oxygen-based free radicals appears to determine where and how quickly the brain ages. The irony is that the same oxygen that suffuses the body with life can quickly assume a destructive role, altering or destroying cells. Researchers at the University of North Texas found that the brains of old mice contain many more oxygen-damaged proteins than do those of young mice.[6]

THE BRAIN'S SHORT STROKES

A transient ischemic attack (TIA) is a condition in which the blood supply to the brain is interrupted temporarily. This results in strokelike symptoms usually lasting from two to not more than thirty minutes. In other words, the brain has a short stroke. The most common cause of TIA is a tiny blood clot or lipid fragment (embolus) from elsewhere in the body. Unfortunately, about one third of TIA sufferers fall victim to a genuine stroke within five years of their first TIA. That's the long and the short of it.[7,8]

Chapter 19
The **Mercurial Brain**:
The Mad Hatter and Isaac Newton's Madness

The great scientist Sir Isaac Newton, the Mad Hatter in *Alice's Adventures in Wonderland*, and Japanese children born with birth defects in the 1950s are all strangely related.

Sir Isaac Newton (1642–1727), the legendary mathematician, physicist, and natural philosopher, is considered to be one of the greatest scientists of all time. He was celebrated in his own day, as he is in ours, as one of the most original and influential theorists in the history of science. From Newton we get the three laws of mechanics (Newton's laws), the law of gravity

("What goes up must come down"), the theory of planetary motion, calculus (co-invented with philosopher Gottfried Wilhelm Leibniz), and numerous other ideas and discoveries.

But what is not widely known about Newton is that twice during his lifetime he went "mad." He suffered prolonged periods of abnormal, even bizarre behavior. He experienced severe insomnia, extreme sensitivity in personal relationships, loss of appetite, delusions of persecution, memory difficulties, and some overall decrease in mental acuity. Today we might have classified Newton as a borderline psychotic.

Although he was not left permanently deranged, these two bouts of "madness" left their mark on him. And most strangely of all, historical evidence reveals that Newton caused his own "madness." In fact, it was a direct product of his own work.

Newton's first such episode lasted through most of 1677 and 1678. The second began in 1693 and was more widely reported because Newton was by then a public figure.

What really happened to Newton's brain?

Over the years, biographers of Newton have proposed many theories to account for his two "mad" periods. Among these are psychological trauma caused by the shock of his mother's death, depression caused by a fire that destroyed some important papers, exhaustion after the writing of his *Principia Mathematica* (1687), depression caused by failure to obtain a desired post in London, extreme religious fervor, and anxiety caused by local problems at Cambridge University—all interesting but all incorrect.

Instead, the best evidence indicates that the true reason for Newton's "madness" was something far simpler: mercury poisoning.

In the 1970s, an examination of Newton's records of his experiments revealed that he undertook many chemical experiments shortly before the first signs of each of his "madness" episodes.[1] Newton experimented with sulfur, ammonium chloride, sulfuric and nitric acids, arsenic, copper, lead, and several other substances. Mercury was chief among these.

Newton heated the metals, their ores, or their salts in order to convert them into a volatile form suitable for experimentation. During this time, he was continually breathing in the fumes, which we now know to be highly toxic. In some experiments, Newton even tasted the heavy metals. Furthermore, devoted scientist that he was, Newton regularly slept in his laboratory, not leaving for weeks on end.

Thus, Newton probably was poisoned by his own experiments.

Neurologist Dr. Harold Klawans claims that Newton showed many symptoms commonly seen in mercury poisoning victims, as described in modern toxicology textbooks, and concludes, "1. Newton had sufficient exposure. 2. Newton had a clinical picture that is consistent with mercury poisoning, including neurologic findings."[2]

Mercury poisoning has a curious history. In Europe and America, until the end of the nineteenth century, mercury was used as a stiffening agent in the making of felt hats. Felt hats were extremely popular. Workers in the hat industry often suffered symptoms of mercury poisoning such as frequent tremors,

THE GREAT composer Mozart left letters that contained gross obscenities. Some psychiatrists claim that this is evidence that Mozart suffered from Tourette's syndrome. Those suffering from the neurological disease sometimes uncontrollably blurt out obscenities. However, Mozart wrote them down. This is not the usual blurting form of Tourette's.

mental aberrations, loss of memory, and odd behaviors. The tremors themselves were called hatters in the United Kingdom and the Danbury shakes in the United States (after a major hat-making plant in Danbury, Connecticut). In *Alice's Adventures in Wonderland* (1865), Lewis Carroll based his character the Mad Hatter on a real-life hatter he knew whose mental illness was almost certainly caused by mercury poisoning.

Mercury also causes birth defects. Such birth defects usually occur on a small scale, but not always.

In the 1950s, a Japanese chemical plant using inorganic mercury dumped effluent into Minamata Bay. Some of the mercury had been converted to methylmercury before discharge. The compound rapidly entered plankton, accumulated in fish, was eaten by humans, and eventually poisoned more than 2,900 people, 46 of whom died. When pregnant women ate the fish, often they spontaneously aborted, or their children were born with abnormalities such as horribly contorted bodies, brain damage, inability to coordinate muscles, and sensory loss or impairment.

According to Dr. Minoru Inouye, head of the National Institute for Minamata Disease in Minamata City and the leading authority on the mercury poisoning disaster,

> *More than 2,900 persons were poisoned by consuming much contaminated fish. They developed symptoms of constriction of visual field, sensory disturbance, ataxia [failure of muscular coordination], etc. with a very wide variation among individuals. More than 60 children have been affected during either or both the prenatal and neonatal periods after their mothers had eaten these contaminated fish. In addition, many cases of spontaneous abortion were*

recorded. The clinical features of the children were motor dis-
orders resembling cerebral palsy and mental retardation. A
pathological study of two autopsy cases revealed that the
brains were hypoplastic [incompletely developed] and also
involved in the neuronal damage which was more diffuse
than in adult cases. Experimental studies have confirmed
that the fetal brain is susceptible to developmental distur-
bance in early pregnancy and to neuronal degeneration in
later pregnancy. And fetal neurons are more vulnerable to
methylmercury than maternal ones." [3]

Other major environmental disasters involving mercury poisoning occur from time to time. In 1971 in Iraq, 459 people died and 6,530 were hospitalized after eating mercury-contaminated grain. In 1980 in Argentina, 7,000 to 10,000 infants were exposed to phenylmercury after that chemical was used as a fungicide in their cloth diapers. In 1990, during environmental spot checks, the Health Department of the city of Columbus, Ohio found mercury vapor levels in one typical apartment at 800 times the acceptable level.[4] A child living in the apartment was diagnosed as having acrodynia (from the Greek word meaning "pain in the extremities"). In acrodynia caused by mercury poisoning, an infant or child's body is racked by pain, swelling, skin rashes, irritability, failure to thrive, and other symptoms. Teeth often drop out, and fingers and toes turn pink.

According to Dr. Thomas W. Clarkson of the University of Rochester, cerebral palsy is a common mercury poisoning symptom in a newborn infant, and doctors should consider mercury poisoning as a possible cause in any case of cerebral palsy.[5]

Mercury poisoning can come from many sources. Reports

A PREMATURE infant is five times more likely to be left-handed.

have documented poisoning sources ranging from Chinese patent medicines to beauty creams.[6,7]

Much has been made of mercury (amalgam) dental fillings as a possible source of mercury poisoning. Some people have had their fillings removed after complaining of headaches, behavioral changes, and other symptoms supposedly caused by the fillings. If mercury is leaking in people with amalgam fillings, there is no evidence that any damage is being done. In a 1995 study of nuns between the ages of 75 and 102, University of Kentucky researchers concluded that "existing amalgams are not associated with lower performance on eight different tests of cognitive function."[8]

Nevertheless, airborne mercury poisoning is an international public health problem. In 1990, scientists meeting in Sweden declared airborne mercury contamination to be the largest source of mercury environmental pollution throughout the world. Furthermore, they warned that concentrations of mercury up in the atmosphere caused by humans down on Earth are now reaching "dangerous levels world-wide" and constitute a public health risk.[4]

This seems to be yet another reason why we humans should work even harder to clean up the environment, cleanse the air in which we breathe, and keep contaminants out of the sky. As Newton would say, "What goes up must come down."

GHOSTS AND THE BRAIN

Why do some people think they see ghosts? How does the brain become fooled? It has been seriously suggested that people see ghosts in haunted houses because they ingest spores broadcast by psychoactive fungi growing on the old walls. This is not a new idea. It first appeared in *The Gentleman's Magazine* in 1883.[9]

PREGNANCY SHRINKS THE BRAIN

Women sometimes complain that their brains do not seem to function as well during pregnancy. For example, their concentration skills may be less. A team of British researchers has uncovered an explanation for this: Women's brains shrink during pregnancy and take up to six months to regain their full size. This unexpected happening may help explain phenomena such as postpartum depression.[10]

Chapter 20
The **Murderous Brain** I: What Makes a Murderer?

As research shows, the brain of a criminal may contain a mechanism known as the criminal high. But what about the most vicious criminal: the murderer? Do murderers unconsciously seek to boost their level of arousal through murderous acts? Does this mechanism explain thrill-killing, for example?

Behavioral and medical scientific evidence is equivocal. So far we haven't been able to specifically define a "murderous brain" other than by extrapolation from those who seek the criminal high. Nevertheless, research continues, and the picture could change.

However, since the 1960s research has defined the early behavioral warning signs in children of later homicidal behavior. Although this research area is enormously controversial, with no two experts fully agreeing, the same factors reappear in the childhoods of murderers.

In a 1966 study, Drs. Daniel Hellman and Nathan Blackman described three types of childhood behavior that they believe best predict later adult homicidal acts: bed-wetting late into childhood, fire-setting, and cruelty to animals.[1]

According to Hellman and Blackman, bed-wetting indicates deep emotional disturbance, fire-setting indicates little or no regard for society or its rules, and cruelty to animals shows both a lack of respect for a life and a tendency toward violence—essential elements in the murder equation. These factors have since become known as the early warning triad and remain classic factors still frequently cited in the research literature.[1]

In a 1974 study, Dr. Blair Justice and two colleagues argued that four additional factors ought to be added to the triad: fighting with older children, temper tantrums, school problems and truancy, and the inability to get along with others. These behaviors, although quite normal to small degrees in children, become a problem when exaggerated or persistent.[2]

The Justice team based their conclusions on an exhaustive analysis of fifteen hundred studies of individual violence gleaned from 237 academic journals. Of these, 188 references mentioned symptoms or behavior patterns. In addition, they conducted 779 tape-recorded interviews with pathologically violent people and with those who worked closely with them. The researchers also examined another 1,055 case histories.

At the end of this process, the Justice team concluded that "fighting was the most commonly cited early predictor of potential violence." They then presented a number of illustrative case studies of violent prison inmates who clearly showed in childhood many of the warning signs.[2] One typical example is the following:

> *Donald, age 19, was serving a life sentence for murder with malice and theft. When interviewed by the visiting teacher at age 10 he was inattentive in school, lied, was involved in fights two or three times a week, was a bully, and was having moderate to severe difficulty in reading, spelling, and arithmetic. He had few friends and spent most of his time watching television or wandering around alone. At age 10 he began skipping school and dropped out in the seventh grade. He began stealing (taking candy bars) at age six.[2]*

In a 1983 study, Dr. Dorothy Lewis and colleagues presented compelling evidence for additional factors: the father factor, the mother factor, and the childhood health factor.[3]

First, the Lewis team discovered that, during childhood, murderers often have fathers who behave violently, indeed often homicidally, toward them or toward others. Furthermore, the mother often is on the receiving end of the father's pernicious attentions, although such violence may also involve siblings. And related to this, murderers often experience in childhood the absence of the biological father. The father may leave the home for extended periods or may be permanently absent.

In addition, they discovered that a murderer's father was more likely to suffer from alcoholism or drug addiction. This is not surprising because many studies before and since point to strong links between alcohol and drug abuse and murder.

Second, the researchers found that mothers of murderers are far more likely to have been hospitalized for a psychiatric disorder and tend to be more prone to child abuse than other mothers. They point out that research clearly shows that future murderers are more likely to both witness and experience child abuse and other forms of domestic violence.

CHANCES ARE slight that anything will go wrong with your mind if something hasn't already gone wrong by the time you're age seventy.

Third, the Lewis team discovered that murderers, much more than other people, suffer from a variety of physical and mental health problems beside bed-wetting. Chief among these is brain seizures in childhood. This could indicate many things, including the possible existence of organic brain damage as contributory in any murder case. If so, then this raises a number of legal issues involving diminished capacity.

The researchers found that, compared with nonmurderers, in murderers persistent psychotic and sociopathic symptoms and various neurological impairments appear in early childhood. Indeed, much more often than usual, murderers entertain and express suicidal thoughts in childhood. Many eventual murderers attempt suicide during childhood, and many seek help or therapy, sometimes long before they kill.[3]

In fact, the same early warning signs come to the fore in related behavioral studies that do not involve murderers as such but that do involve other violent pathologies.

In a 1985 study, Drs. Stephen Kellert and Alan Felthous examined childhood cruelty toward animals, one of the factors of the early warning triad. They looked at this behavior in three groups: aggressive criminals (only some of whom were murderers), nonaggressive criminals, and noncriminals. The researchers discovered that cruelty to animals

*occurred to a significantly greater degree among aggressive
criminals than among non-aggressive criminals or noncriminals. . . . Family violence, particularly paternal abuse and
alcoholism, were significantly more common among aggressive criminals with a history of childhood cruelty towards
animals.*[4]

In a 1986 article, Drs. Jane Kelso and Mark Stewart examined
characteristics predicting what they call "aggressive conduct
disorder."[5] Again they found the familiar constellation of factors emerging: "Among the predictors of persisting conduct
disorder were a variety of antisocial or aggressive symptoms,
fire-setting, early age of onset, and family deviance."[5] They
suggested an additional factor: Violence-prone adults tend to
have been accident-prone children.

In 1991, a disturbing study by Dr. Alain Labelle and colleagues attempted to explain why the murder rate by adolescents is climbing at an alarming rate in many nations
throughout the world. The researchers suggest that to understand why young people commit murder, we should look first
to the murderer's family. Despite the rising tide of youth violence throughout the world, "it is surprising to observe that
our understanding of murder committed by adolescents is still
fairly limited."[6]

They add that although the motivation to commit murder
is reported to be present in all murderers, "the factors which
lead a person to actually commit the act are still unclear, particularly for adolescent murderers."

The Labelle team notes that the typical murderer is between
twenty and thirty years of age. Adolescent murderers are those
under age twenty. They are the third most likely age group to

commit murder. Moreover, the incidence of homicide increases through the adolescent years. Thus, sixteen-year-olds commit more murders than fifteen-year-olds, seventeen-year-olds more than sixteen-year-olds, and so on. Murder before adolescence, in childhood, is extremely rare. And as with adult murderers, adolescent murderers usually are male, at a ratio of ten to one.

The Labelle team observes that many professionals in the field are of the opinion that those who commit murder, adults or adolescents, usually do not have a history of mental illness. However, the researchers suggest that what may really be happening is that mental illness exists but is undiagnosed or untreated before the murder. In fact, in one study 89 percent of adult murderers had not undergone previous psychiatric treatment or evaluation. But 70 percent of these people were subsequently found to be not only suffering from mental illness but suffering from one particular type of mental illness: dissociative state. In other studies, the majority of adolescent murderers were found to be schizophrenic, psychotic, or suicidal.

Many professionals also believe that murderers have a long criminal history before the murder. Again, the Labelle team suggests that this may not be true. They cite a study of 200 murderers that showed that only 38 percent had criminal records of any kind.

And many think that murderers are below average in intelligence. However, the Labelle team notes that, here too, research conclusions are unclear. They cite a study showing that adolescent murderers are actually above average in intelligence. However, they also cite a study showing that only one in seven has an IQ above 90—that is, 10 points below average.

The Labelle team confirms that adult murderers usually are acquainted with their victims. In fact, one study shows that murderer and victim are strangers in only 15 percent of cases. Furthermore, 70 percent of adult murders occur after a domestic quarrel. In addition, the researchers argue that "the availability of firearms or lethal weapons in the house of the perpetrator are important environmental factors in cases of both adolescent and adult murderers."

The Labelle team maintains that it is also widely believed that alcohol and drugs often are linked with adult violence and assaults. But surprisingly, they claim that this relationship "has not been clearly defined" by research. For example, one study of 621 murderers, looking at drug use by both the murderers and their victims, was "inconclusive." They add, "Others identified alcohol as occasionally contributing to crime, but found no differences in alcohol use between violent and non-violent offenders."[6]

Nevertheless, the Labelle team confirms the previous research indicating the three childhood behaviors frequently mentioned as being associated with murderous behavior later on: cruelty to animals, bed-wetting well into later childhood, and juvenile fire-setting. Furthermore, they hint at other possible factors that could be added to the list, including hyperactivity (attention deficit disorder hyperactive), head injuries, and central nervous system damage. The Labelle team argues that these should be considered factors because all have been shown to be associated with other antisocial behaviors. However, the researchers admit that contrary evidence exists that disputes these associations.

But most importantly of all, the Labelle team found family breakdown to be the single most important factor associated with adolescent murderers:

Chronic maladjustment in the family affecting one or both parents has been reported in cases of adult and juvenile murder . . . acts of violence . . . and delinquency. Studies on adult, adolescent and child murderers also unanimously report the presence of serious family disorganization. Persistent physical brutality either inflicted or witnessed in childhood or adolescence is also frequently reported. . . . The actual incidents range from emotional deprivation, fighting between parents, physical punishment, intense parental brutality, deliberate cruelty and sexual abuse by relatives.[6]

Behavioral and medical scientists continue to debate the relative roles and weightings of childhood predictors of homicide. But regardless of their eventual precise order of importance, it seems that most if not all early warning signs probably have been identified already. Yet in such an inexact science, new discoveries could occur at any time. For example, biochemical factors affecting the central nervous system have only begun to be explored. Exciting findings could evolve from this line of research. We've seen what has started to emerge from research on thrill seeking and the criminal high.

Nevertheless, murder is a complex, baffling behavior that confounds experts. And this has always been so. Commenting on the 1920s trial of German mass murderer Fritz Haarmann, Professor Theodor Lessing remarked at the time,

We do not even know if, when animals tear each other to pieces, they do not experience a certain sensual pleasure, so that when the wolf strangles the lamb, one can say equally well, "he loves lambs" as that "he hates lambs."[7]

So until the research picture changes, we are left with the oldest finding in behavioral science: To understand why kids go wrong, look to the family.[8]

DO BRAIN SEIZURES CAUSE MURDERERS TO ACT?

A Harvard University psychiatrist argues that a small percentage of people who commit brutal and inexplicable murders may have suffered brain seizures immediately before the violent acts. Such seizures may temporarily suppress their inhibitions against killing. Dr. Anneliese Pontius adds that, later, when they recover from the seizure, they are horrified at what they've done. "They suddenly find themselves with a dead body. They have no idea what happened or why." Based on her work with hundreds of murderers, Pontius theorizes that the seizure occurs in the brain's limbic system, causing "the limbic psychotic trigger reaction."[9]

THE DECEIVING BRAIN

Why are eyewitness stories so often contradictory? Why is it that two witnesses who observe the same crime from the same vantage point often give different accounts, sometimes even wildly different? Israeli researchers think they know why: What we see may literally depend on our state of mind. Using voltage-sensitive dyes that light up brain cells when stimulated, Israeli researchers measured brain reactions when subjects were given different visual stimuli. It has been established that the brain reacts differently when the eye sees something familiar compared with something novel. The Israeli team discovered that a person's present thought and mood also influence the brain. If the mood is not right, then a person's brain may not be ready to see in the same way in which the person standing next to him or her may be ready.[10]

Chapter 21
The **Murderous Brain** 2:
The Serial Killer

What makes a serial killer?

Research tells us that the typical serial killer is a sexually dysfunctional man who lives alone or with a parent. He is not capable of a healthy sexual relationship with another person. Indeed, his immediate motive is hardly grand: He wants sexual gratification. Killing is merely a characteristic of the way he rapes. Torture and murder arouse him.[1]

"I have yet to see a serial killing that did not have some sexual motivation," claims Robert K. Ressler. And "I have never seen a serial killer who is a happily married family man, or who had a long-term relationship with a woman."

Ressler is a former U.S. Federal Bureau of Investigation (FBI) agent and perhaps the world's top expert on the psychology of the serial killer. In the 1970s, Ressler coined the term *serial killer* and was a pioneer in the development of psychological profiles of serial killers at the FBI's training academy in Quantico, Virginia.

In *Whoever Fights Monsters: My Twenty Years Hunting Serial Killers for the FBI*, Ressler argues that, above all else, serial killers are made and not born.[2]

"All serial killers share a common childhood history. They start life with an unloving mother and an absent or abusive father. Largely because of this, they never learn right from wrong." Quite often the father has left the family home after the child has been the victim of psychological, physical, or sexual abuse. The mother may continue the abuse. According to Ressler, "if such children do not get help from siblings, school, or social services, they enter adolescence lonely and without interpersonal skills. Eventually, they become obsessed with abnormal sexual fantasies."

Studies also show that fantasy usually is an important part of the motive for serial killings. Furthermore, a serial killer's behavior from childhood onward often includes chronic excessive daydreaming, compulsive masturbation, extreme self-isolation, habitual lying, truancy and rebelliousness, compulsive stealing, and cruelty to other children and animals.

According to New York forensic pathologist Dr. John Hayes Jr., many serial killers use a confidence trick or a ruse to lure their victims to their deaths. This may be money, a promise of a good time, or even a job offer. And as they go on with their killings, they gradually evolve more sophisticated methods to lure victims and to avoid detection.

Hayes adds that serial killers have definite patterns that eventually surface in the course of police investigations. For example, all the murdered women may have a common background or a particular physical resemblance. Sometimes such women are similar to those in failed relationships with the murderer.

Serial killers often perform highly ritualized acts before and after the murder as well as during the murder itself. Such preparation may take hours or even days.

Nevertheless, according to Ressler, "the key to these murderers, if there is one, lies in the unremittingly sexual nature of their deeds." Ressler has interviewed more than 100 violent criminals. He claims that "to a man, they were dysfunctional sexually; that is, they were unable to have and maintain mature, consensual sexual experiences with other adults, and they translate that inability into sexual murders."

Indeed, Hayes notes, the serial murder itself may be a twisted method to achieve what the rest of us achieve through more normal means. For example, serial killers who like to strangle their victims do so because it creates a bizarre intimacy in that they are face-to-face at the point of death.

In his book, Ressler recounts his twenty-year FBI career and provides an inside look at cases in which he used psychological profiles to help direct police to murderers. He also details his face-to-face meetings with dozens of imprisoned killers, including Jeffrey Dahmer, Charles Manson, Ted Bundy, and David ("Son of Sam") Berkowitz.

Ressler argues that "even outrageous, unspeakable criminal behavior is not unique and not incomprehensible. These sort of murders have occurred before and, when properly analyzed, can be understood well enough so that we can even break them down into somewhat predictable patterns." In fact, Ressler has divided serial killers into two basic types: disorganized and organized.

Disorganized killers kill in spontaneous outbursts, often choosing a victim who is close at hand. They kill quickly, often do not complete the sex act, and make little or no effort to cover up evidence of the crime.

However, organized killers plan their crimes in detail, hunting for a particular kind of victim, and often use the same confidence trick to lure their victims to their doom. Organized killers often use restraints such as handcuffs or ropes. They usually kill slowly, dispose of the body carefully, and often take items from the victims as trophies.

In Ressler's book, the interviews with serial killers provide extremely revealing personal glimpses into savagely contorted minds. For instance, David Berkowitz told Ressler that he liked the idea of being notorious and that he started trying to kill someone in each of New York City's boroughs in the 1970s only after the media speculated on whether he would.

Richard Trenton Chase, the blood-drinking "vampire" killer who murdered six people in Sacramento, California in the 1970s, said that he chose victims simply by going down a street and trying to find an unlocked door. Ressler asked Chase why, if he found a door locked, he did not break it down. Chase answered, "Oh, if the door is locked, that means you're not welcome."

Edmund Kemper, who killed and beheaded eight women in the Santa Cruz area of California in the early 1970s, said that he delighted in visiting his mother, whom he hated, while a dead body was in the trunk of his car. He even buried the head of one victim beneath his mother's bedroom window.

Surprisingly, perhaps, Ressler does not support the death penalty for serial killers. Instead, he believes that they should be sentenced to life in prison in order to be studied. But he doubts that any of them can be rehabilitated:

*These are men who have never known how to relate to
other human beings; it is not likely that such a fundamental interpersonal skill can be taught in prison. To turn
angry, resentful, aggressive men into sensitive people who
can fit into society is almost an impossible task.[2]*

Nevertheless, despite the heinous nature of these acts, psychologists and psychiatrists are divided as to whether serial killers
are insane. For example, Dr. Joan Ullman, a clinical psychologist from the University of Chicago, who attended the trial of
Jeffrey Dahmer, cites one such instance of this division: A psychiatrist testifying against Dahmer's insanity plea observed that

*Dahmer had proved his sanity by "remembering to reach for
a condom" before copulating with his "dead corpses" or their
dissected parts. The psychiatrist testified that Dahmer's capacity to delay gratification and his capacity for impulse control
showed he could conform his conduct to social norms.[3]*

But for most of us, so horrific are the acts of serial killers that we
could well be excused for wondering whether such people are
really members of our own species or some cruel mutation.

In the book *The Silence of the Lambs*, Hannibal ("The Can-
nibal") Lecter (played by Anthony Hopkins in the movie) says
to Officer Clarice Starling (played by Jodie Foster),

*Nothing happened to me, Officer Starling. I happened. You
can't reduce me to a set of influences. You've given up good
and evil for behaviorism, Officer Starling. You've got every-
body in moral dignity pants—nothing is ever anybody's*

fault. Look at me, Officer Starling. Can you stand to say I'm evil? Am I evil, Officer Starling?[4]

MENTAL MOVIES

Most people think that the things we see are somehow projected onto a single mental movie. But research suggests that vision is more like a multiplex theater where each screen shows a slightly different version of the same film. Different brain areas take up different jobs in the vision process.[5]

SPEAR PIERCES MAN'S BRAIN—BUT HE LIVES!

The *Weekly World News* tabloid featured a story about a Melbourne skin diver who accidentally shot himself through the forehead with a spear gun and lived. The barbed and pointed weapon just missed the man's right eye but pierced two thirds of the way through his brain. Doctors took almost three hours to remove the spear from Van Hoa Pham, aged thirty-three, of Mill Park, Victoria. According to neurosurgeon Dr. Graeme Brazenor, miraculously Mr. Pham should suffer no long-term damage from his injuries.[6]

Chapter 22
Obsessive–Compulsive Disorder: Trapped by Your Own Rituals

What happens in the human brain when the mind is compelled to take refuge in rituals—the rituals of obsessive–compulsive disorder?

Obsessive–compulsive disorder (OCD) is a condition in which a person finds security by repeating a particular behavior over and over and over again. OCD is silent and invisible. It can take any form imaginable. It can ceaselessly plague people who may otherwise lead entirely normal lives. But it can also debilitate many more, robbing them of their power to perform simple, everyday tasks.

OCD can emerge in anyone at any age. You, or the person

next to you, may harbor one or several forms, perhaps without even knowing it. Yet despite extensive studies over generations, science is still largely baffled by OCD. And people go right on suffering from it, sometimes for life.

The world's leading authority on OCD is Dr. Judith Rapoport, chief of the child psychiatry branch of the U.S. National Institute of Mental Health in Washington. According to Rapoport, there are three basic forms of OCD rituals: "checkers," "exacters," and "washers." "Checkers" check lights, doors, windows, and locks perhaps 10, 20, even 100 times. They repeat actions, often very peculiar ones, oblivious to other concerns. "Exacters" often spend hours producing symmetry in a ritualized manner. For example, shoelaces must be exactly even, eyebrows must be identical, and so on. However, most people with OCD are "washers." "Washers" believe that they must repetitively cleanse the articles in their environment, despite the fact that no dirt can be seen on an article and with the sufferer's full knowledge that the article was washed perhaps just a few minutes before.

In her classic study *The Boy Who Couldn't Stop Washing*, Rapoport says,

> *All of these problems have common themes: you can't trust your ordinary good judgment, can't trust your eyes that see no dirt, or really believe that the door is locked. You know you have done nothing harmful, but in spite of this good sense, you must go on checking and counting. You can't dismiss the idea. The compulsion keeps coming back, and you ask yourself "Do I really know? I still feel something is wrong." The compelling need to repeat small and private, or elaborate and conspicuous rituals which are irrational and*

*bizarre is dramatic and remarkable. This is the nature of
compulsions.*[1]

The term *obsessive–compulsive disorder* comes from the fact that
most experts maintain that obsessions and compulsions are
linked and inseparable. An obsession is a persistent idea,
impulse, or image that intrudes on a person by causing distress,
consuming time, upsetting routine, disturbing occupational or
social activities, or interfering with normal personal relationships. The person knows the obsession exists only in his or her
mind, and this is disturbing. He or she attempts to ignore, suppress, or neutralize the obsession by overly relying on less disturbing thoughts, feelings, or actions. A compulsion or
compulsive behavior is a repetitive, purposeful, and intentional
act performed in response to an obsession.

Obsessions differ from delusions because with delusions
the person believes that something is being imposed on his or
her own mind by some outside force. And with OCD, often
the obsessed person wants to resist the compulsion. In fact, he
or she tries very hard to resist performing the compulsive
behavior. However, the tension builds and builds until the person invariably yields.

Literary titan Samuel Johnson (1709–1784) exhibited
step-counting and stair-counting compulsive behavior. In *The
Life of Samuel Johnson* (first published in 1791), James Boswell
reports that he observed Johnson "upon innumerable occasions" suddenly stop while walking

*and then seem to count his steps with a deep earnestness;
and when he had neglected or gone wrong in this sort of
magical movement, I have seen him go back again, put*

himself in a proper posture to begin the ceremony, and, having gone through it, break from his abstraction, walk briskly on, and join his companion.[1]

According to Rapoport, "Boswell felt that the mannerisms were 'of the convulsive kind'" and that this notion "anticipated our new biological interest in obsessions and compulsions."[1]

The most famous obsessive–compulsive of this century was arguably industrialist, aviator, and film producer Howard Hughes. After having affairs with some of the world's most glamorous women of the 1930s, 1940s, and 1950s, Hughes became a complete recluse in the last years of his life. He walled himself off from the outside world because he was preoccupied with being contaminated by dirt. He almost certainly suffered from fears of personal contamination and spermaphobia (a morbid fear of germs). He had all papers and food brought to him by employees who wore surgical masks and special gloves. This was so that no one could possibly touch what he would touch. Obsessive–compulsive cleaning rituals eventually took up his entire day. Rapoport writes,

Toward the end of his life, paradoxically, Hughes became a filthy, unkempt figure with unwashed, matted hair, a scraggly beard, and fingernails and toe-nails of such length that they curled in upon themselves. He either went nude or dressed only in a pair of undershorts. Most probably the rituals of bathing and grooming became so overwhelming in Hughes's case that he was ultimately incapable of even the simplest self-care.[1]

Singer Michael Jackson's reputed obsessions are fairly well known. Like Hughes, he is supposedly afraid of germs and lives as a recluse except while on tour. He sleeps in a pressurized oxygen tent, although this could damage his heart and lungs. It is quite possible that this may have contributed to his 1990 heart attack scare. He eats a rigidly restrictive diet of food prepared to his precise instructions. Obsessively desiring a perfect body, Jackson fasts and exercises to the point at which he probably injures his health. He is also reputedly "addicted" to plastic surgery and the skin-bleaching process used to treat vitiligo. Vitiligo is a skin disorder resulting in blotchy patches on the body, caused by lack of uniformity in skin pigmentation.[2]

If this last notion is indeed true, Jackson may suffer from a variant of Munchausen syndrome. This is a factitious disorder nicknamed by psychiatrists ironically, if not facetiously, as doctor addiction.[3]

But although Jackson may be obsessed with obtaining the perfect body, he is also reputedly fascinated by misshapen ones. In the 1980s, Jackson tried to purchase the deformed skeleton of Joseph Merrick, "the Elephant Man," once the toast of Victorian London society. He is morbidly fascinated with dangerous pets, such as tarantulas and snakes, and is obsessed with animals generally. His well-known preoccupation with children, his building of a private Disneyland-type park where childhood can be preserved, and his religious-like interest in Peter Pan (hence his sometime nickname of "the Peter Pan of Pop") all indicate a man walking a tightrope of many obsessions.[4]

Much was made of the tragic and pathetic obsession of Hollywood director Peter Bogdanovich with his former lover, Playboy model and movie starlet Dorothy Stratten. After Stratten was murdered by her jealous husband, Bogdanovich married Stratten's teenage sister, paid for her acting and dancing lessons, and induced her to have plastic surgery so that she would be the mirror image of her slain sister.[5]

Another Hollywood director, Alfred Hitchcock, was famous for his classic thriller and suspense movies. And he was also known for his obsession for blond leading ladies. Among them were Ingrid Bergman, Grace Kelly, Kim Novak, Eva Marie Saint, and Tippi Hedren. Hitchcock is believed to have suffered from the psychiatric disorder known as scopophilia (gaining sexual gratification by watching others). Film historians think that this is why he was constantly suggesting that his leading ladies be seduced or raped while he was behind the camera. Actress Vera Miles walked out on Hitchcock for this very reason, and so did Audrey Hepburn (a rare Hitchcock brunette).

Hitchcock's films often depict psychiatric problems of various kinds: *Marnie* (1964) (kleptomania, or compulsive stealing), *Frenzy* (1972) (serial killings), *Vertigo* (1958) (acrophobia, or fear of heights, and erotomania, or obsessive pursuit of another person), *The Birds* (1963) (zoophobia, or fear of animals), and *Psycho* (1960) (homicidal transvestic fetishism), to name a few. And Hitchcock's own disorder, scopophilia, figures prominently in *Rear Window* (1954).

Much of the psychological literature on obsessions concerns sexual obsessions. In 1886, German psychiatrist Richard von Krafft-Ebing shocked his Victorian audience with his book *Psychopathia Sexualis*. Perhaps better than anyone before or since, Krafft-Ebing chronicled the sexual obsessions of his nineteenth-century European contemporaries. According to British author Colin Wilson,

The most striking thing about it [Psychopathia Sexualis]
is the sheer range of sexual perversions it describes. After
reading a dozen or so cases, the reader begins to feel that
the streets of 19th century Berlin or Vienna must have been
packed with sadists, masochists, voyeurs, fetishists and trans-
vestites. [6]

Naturally, it was a huge best-seller, but it nearly resulted in Krafft-Ebing being thrown out of the British Medico-Psychological Association.

The obsessions of most people remain their private affair and usually do not warrant the attention of anyone beyond their family, close friends, and physician—unless laws are broken. But as in the cases of celebrities, the obsessions of some can be anything but private. Indeed, the public has an insatiable appetite for the behavioral oddities of the rich and famous. In other words, the public is obsessed by the obsessions of the beautiful people.

Very little is known about the causes of OCD. Although OCD usually emerges in adolescence, it can show itself much earlier. Rapoport says,

I have seen a two-year-old start to walk in circles around
manhole covers; ten years later he couldn't go to school
because of this bizarre compulsion to draw Os! How these
complex behaviors spring up in childhood is mysterious but
suggests that some innate program of behavior is running
wild in this disease. [1]

Moreover, OCD affects males and females equally. OCD can last for months, years, decades, or an entire lifetime. The symptoms in children or adults are very similar. Most people with OCD exhibit more than one symptom, and they usually try to hide their problem for as long as possible. The prevalence of symptoms can wax and wane over time. Major depression and drug abuse can be complications of OCD.

> LEFT-HANDERS tend to use their right hands more frequently than right-handers use their left hands.

Researchers are exploring the physiology and brain functioning of people with OCD. For instance, it has already been discovered that those with OCD have an abnormally fast metabolism in certain brain structures. Specific small portions of the brain burn energy at excessive rates. Such findings have located the point of the fastest burn. This is the brain's basal ganglia and the caudate nuclei deep in both hemispheres and upper brain stem.[7, 8]

Researchers using magnetic resonance imaging suggest that other parts of the brain could be involved as well. Indeed, they claim that OCD sufferers may also have smaller brains overall compared with control subjects.[9]

The good news is that OCD is treatable. In fact, treatments are continually improving with each passing year. According to Dr. Frederick Toates, treatment leads to a good prognosis for nearly every patient.[10]

Formerly, psychosurgery was used in extreme cases. But as we now know, such surgery has dire repercussions. In fact, Rapoport's first obsessive–compulsive patient eventually underwent a lobotomy. She writes, "Sal had the operation and was cured, in a sense."[1]

Most current treatment strategies consist of either behavior modification or drug therapy. Behavior modification may involve exposing the patient to the very obsession that stimulates

FROM THE EARLY
1900s until the 1950s,
the prefrontal lobotomy
was being perfected and
used in mental hospitals
throughout the world.
Portuguese neurologist
António Egas Moniz
received the 1949
Nobel Prize in Medicine
for much of this work.
The hope was great
that this form of therapy
would prove to be as
popular in neurology as
aspirin is for the family
doctor. But by 1960,
most of the medical
community had rejected
lobotomy as a medical
monstrosity. By the way,
doctors did not rou-
tinely prescribe aspirin
for a headache (or for
anything else, for that
matter) until about half
a century after it was
invented by Karl Ger-
hardt in Germany in
1853.

the compulsion. For example, after teaching a spermaphobic how to relax, the therapist might shake hands with the patient several times without gloves and then might prevent the patient from washing his or her hands.

Drug therapy usually involves anti-depressants such as fluvoxamine, fluoxetine, and especially clomipramine.

In January 1990, clomipramine was approved by the U.S. Food and Drug Administration for use in OCD. Clomipramine enhances the brain's ability to use serotonin. This is one of the brain's neurotransmitters, chemical messengers allowing vital communication between brain cells to take place.

But according to Dr. Alan Ringold, a Stanford University psychiatrist specializing in treatment of OCD whose research helped clomipramine gain approval, "one day pretty soon, I am sure, this medication will be replaced by something much better."[1]

Unfortunately, patients with severe OCD can expect to be in therapy for a long time, perhaps the rest of their lives.[11, 12, 13]

Therefore, until therapies improve, a person's own thoughts—

although perhaps perfectly normal in every other way—will still be able to make that person feel "crazy," "psychotic," or "out of control." Such is the power of OCD.

Sadly, this disorder is utterly dispiriting to the patient. The frustration is enormous as OCD produces an inability to accomplish that which others seem to achieve effortlessly. Moreover, it is particularly demoralizing when an embarrassing OCD is publicly exposed for all to see and devastating whenever social disapproval, ridicule, or discrimination follows.

An often cruel and unsympathetic society would do well to cultivate understanding, tolerance, compassion, and forgiveness toward those with OCDs. Indeed, we should do this immediately and with resolve.

In fact, it should be our obsession.

OCD: WHEN THE ORBITAL CORTEX IS HYPERACTIVE

In OCD, the brain's orbital cortex, which lies just above the eye sockets, is hyperactive. Researchers hypothesize that the orbital cortex alerts the brain to a problem and that in OCD it sends out repeated false alarms. With the help of the thalamus, a part of the brain that helps process signals from the cortex and other brain areas, those signals go to the caudate nucleus. The caudate nucleus, deep within the brain, is instrumental in controlling movement of the arms and legs. At the same time, the alarm signal moves from the caudate nucleus to the cingulate gyrus, also deep inside the brain. This makes the heart pound and the stomach churn.[14]

GLUG, GLUG

A rare but not unheard-of compulsion is compulsive water drinking. One case reaching the tabloid media was that of Donna Cassaria. The nineteen-year-old Detroit woman drank seven gallons of water per day. This caused her to vomit, strained her kidneys and heart, and required her to remain close to a toilet.

Compulsive water drinking is not uncommon among psychiatric patients, who sometimes drink so much water that their brain swells up in a condition called brain edema. Patients have been known to suffer permanent brain damage and even die from this.

Cassaria spent years suffering from this addiction. As a girl she excused herself from classes to drink water. When her parents locked the bathroom or kitchen doors, she sneaked water in bottles up to her room. If her parents cut off her water supply, she drank water from vases or drainage pipes. She eventually checked herself into a rehabilitation center. After one month of therapy, her water drinking was greatly reduced. She said, "Now I only really have the urge to drink water if I'm feeling blue or am under stress. And the doctors are teaching me how to handle my emotions without turning to water as a crutch."[15]

Chapter 23
The **Phobic Brain**

Ever since the fear of AIDS gripped the world, doctors have been reporting increases in related fears: blood and blood products (hematophobia), needles (belonophobia), and injections (trypanophobia). Dental phobics are hardly soothed when they see the dentist dressed up in AIDS-protective gear, looking more like an astronaut than a health care professional.

Dr. William Sherwood of the American Red Cross contends that the increased prevalence of AIDS-related phobias may be affecting the willingness of people to donate blood and to receive blood in an emergency transfusion.[1]

A hematophobic fears blood so much that he or she will avoid blood and any situation involving direct or indirect contact with blood—his or her own blood or anyone else's. Hematophobics often go to extreme lengths to avoid even the slightest risk of injury. For example, they will not use knives, rarely shave, and avoid everyday household tasks such as cooking, sewing, gardening, and minor carpentry. One male psychiatric patient could not remove pins from a new shirt. One female patient would avoid contact with paper so as to avoid paper cuts. Some people will not drive a car for fear of being involved in an accident wherein they or someone else is injured and bleeds.

A trypanophobic fears injections and may refuse life-saving medical efforts. Drawing a routine blood sample can cause such intense psychological trauma that trypanophobics have been known to deny themselves medical treatment (even to save their own life), avoid physical examinations, fail to get dental checkups, miss employment opportunities (where a physical examination is required), and even run away from police during investigations of drunk driving, which definitely makes matters worse. Such people cannot stand even to have their finger pricked.

A person with belonophobia (also known as acusophobia) is needled by intense fears of all long things with sharp points.

Previous estimates of the prevalence of hematophobia place it as affecting about one in every 25 adults, trypanophobia about one in every 10 adults, and belonophobia about one in every 100 adults. In most cases, these phobias seem to have been acquired sometime during childhood or adolescence, usually before age ten.

Obviously, these phobias can make life miserable for the sufferer. In fact, they can be as restricting and debilitating as many physical illnesses.

According to Dr. Lars-Goran Ost, "at least some blood-phobic persons report that they have had to decide on a vocation other than what they wanted or had to switch to another career during training because of their phobia."[2] Occupations in medicine, construction, and agriculture are rendered impossible. All contact sports and many leisure activities are out as well.

Ost adds that "some report being constantly worried at work about the possible occurrence of a situation involving blood or injury and in which they were responsible for taking action (e.g., as a nursery school teacher or at home as the parent of young children who may have an accident)."[2]

Some of these phobics remain childless, not daring to give birth because blood, needles, and injections are involved. Furthermore, the life of a trypanophobic or belonophobic can be painful. Some will refuse an anesthetic rather than receive one by way of a needle. Others remain unvaccinated, resulting in vulnerability to disease and restrictions on travel abroad. An injection-fearing diabetic may forgo life-saving insulin injections, and a patient with kidney disease may refuse critically needed dialysis.

For these phobics, if escape from a phobic situation is impossible, there is a high probability of fainting. In fact, according to Ost, people with such phobias have a marked history of fainting (syncope). Of 140 phobics studied by Ost, 70 percent of hematophobics and 56 percent of trypanophobics experienced at least one occurrence of fainting in their lifetimes. "These proportions are extraordinarily high in comparison with those of patients with other simple phobias or with anxiety disorders overall."[2]

The possibility of uncontrolled fainting poses the additional health risk of sustaining an injury in a fall. And the anxiety about fainting during an inescapable phobic situation creates an additional source of mental torment.

Ironically, Ost reports that during an inescapable phobic situation, such phobics often suffer a dangerously low drop in heart rate, pulse, respiration, and, of all things, blood pressure.

Again, it should be stressed that any phobia may be treated, often very successfully. Take, for example, arachnophobia.

Arachnophobia is the extreme fear of spiders. This is a very common phobia. A hugely successful 1990 film, *Arachnophobia*, played on the public's dual dread of and fascination with these eight-legged creepy-crawlies. Film critic Leonard Maltin said of this film: "Not recommended for anyone who's ever covered their eyes during a movie." [3] But interestingly, arachnophobia is one of the most easily treated phobias. In one study of thirty-eight arachnophobics, almost all of patients responded favorably to a treatment program involving seventy-two slides of pictures of increasingly fearsome spiders. [4] Interestingly, too, Australian research shows that one need not ever have been exposed to a spider to be deathly afraid of them. [5]

Dental phobia is the irrational fear of the dentist. For most, dental phobia results in broken appointments and sweaty palms in the waiting room. For others, their anxiety is so great that they avoid the dentist and thereby risk their oral health. But for a few, it is even worse. There are recorded instances of dental phobics attempting their own tooth extractions with pliers.

Modern technical advances have virtually eliminated pain suffered in the dentist's chair. But this has not stopped millions of people throughout the world suffering from dental phobia. It is estimated that perhaps 10 to 14 percent of Australians suffer from dental phobia to varying degrees. [6]

Dental phobia can develop at any time and has many causes. It is believed that a bad childhood experience may be at the heart of the fears of most dental phobics. But this need not always be so. Having a bad experience in the dentist's chair as an adult or merely hearing of the bad experiences of others can be implicated.

Dr. J. Gordon Rubin, a world authority on dental phobia, says that "many of these pre-adolescent experiences occurred 20 to 30 years ago when dentistry was much less sophisticated, but the phobic's fears persist, fuelled by vague memories."[7]

He adds that for many dental phobics, "the cost of their phobia can be very high, in terms of pain, humiliation, dangerous infections, marital problems and even career restrictions. Fear is the number one patient problem."[7]

Interestingly, it has been found that when there is a history of trauma in one's life, the chance of dental phobia being present goes through the roof. In a study of 462 women who had a history of childhood and adult traumas, it was found that, when compared with other women who had no dental phobia, "a history of trauma appears to be significantly associated with elevated dental fear."[8]

A South Australian study has also shown that dental phobics are significantly more sensitive to physical pain than are others.[9]

More than twenty major dental phobia clinics now operate in the United States. In Australia, dental phobics usually are helped at more generalist facilities. One of the oldest anti–dental phobia programs has been operating for nearly twenty years at the Oral Facial Pain Clinic at the Royal Dental Hospital in Melbourne. The head of the clinic, Jack Gerschman, points out that for almost two decades, all Australian dental students have been made aware of dental phobia.

Gerschman observes that in the mid-1970s, only 5 or 6 percent of the population admitted to having a dental phobia, but twenty years later this figure was 16 percent. He theorizes that there are two possible explanations for this. First, people are more honest now because there is less of a stigma about admitting to dental phobia. Second, anxieties generally are more widespread today, and dental phobia is no exception.

Treatment for dental phobia is a two-way affair. Both the patient and the dentist may have to change. For the patient, treatment usually consists of behavior modification and is similar to that used for treating fear of flying (aviophobia). Occasionally, drug therapy is used. Programs focus on making the patient feel more relaxed, comfortable, and in control during increasingly long periods in the dentist's chair. The patient learns to use imagining techniques not unlike those that mothers-to-be learn in prenatal classes to deal with labor pains. The patient practices fear reduction techniques until they become automatic. Slowly, in a process called desensitization the patient's confidence becomes so strong that he or she directly confronts the drill, the needle, and other objects of dental phobia. Finally, the last stage of therapy may involve a dress rehearsal in the dentist's chair.

Some studies show that just a single session of desensitization works wonders. One study from the Netherlands found that all fifty-two patients with dental phobia improved with one talk therapy session: "It is concluded that it is possible to obtain substantial reductions of dental trait anxiety through a single session of cognitive restructuring."[10]

The dentist may also have to modify procedures to cope with the dental phobic. For example, before work actually begins, the dentist might agree to respond to the patient's hand signals if pain is felt and allow more frequent rest breaks.

Research shows that dental phobics express anxiety about a shared list of things associated with the dentist. Pain is implied in some but not in all. The top ten fears in order of importance are (1) the drill, (2) the needle, (3) extractions, (4) choking or gagging, (5) losing control, (6) post-treatment swelling, (7) getting teeth cleaned, (8) the dentist ignoring the patient's requests, (9) the dentist being insulting or critical about personal oral health, and (10) making an appointment.[8, 11]

There is no rational reason for dental phobia, but this is true of all phobias.

Dental phobics can be comforted by the thought that perhaps the dentist also has a phobia. Perhaps it is claustrophobia (fear of enclosed spaces, such as the mouth), spermaphobia (fear of germs), hemophobia, belonophobia—or gephyrophobia (fear of bridges), while doing bridge work, of course.[12]

WHO IS A PHOBIC?

The following general characteristics are symptoms of a phobia, including dental phobia:

- The victim suddenly feels persistent and irrational panic, dread, horror, or terror when in a situation that is harmless.
- The person recognizes that the fear goes beyond the normal boundaries and the actual threat of danger.
- The phobic reaction is automatic, uncontrollable, and pervasive, practically taking over the person's thoughts in a barrage of imaginary threats and danger.
- The person suffers from all the physical reactions that extreme fears cause (rapidly beating heart, shortness of breath, trembling, and an overwhelming desire to flee the situation).
- The person flees the feared object or situation and goes out of his or her way to avoid it.[13]

FREUD'S PHOBIAS

The father of psychiatry, Sigmund Freud, suffered from agoraphobia (fear of outside spaces). This was not his only problem. Freud was a self-confessed neurotic who had frequent blackouts, was a compulsive smoker (refusing to quit even after thirty operations to correct extensive jaw damage due to cancer), abused cocaine for much of his life, and was fearful of his own telephone number. At age forty-three, Freud received the phone number 14362. He believed that this number predicted he would die at age sixty-one. Freud's dread of his "prophetic" phone number lasted for many years. Freud died by assisted suicide in 1939 at age eighty-three.[14]

RUBBER GLOVES AND DENTAL PHOBIA

A patient at King's College Hospital Dental School in London was so frightened by the thought of rubber gloves entering his mouth that his swallowing reflex was interrupted, retching occurred, and dental phobia persisted. After two therapy sessions aimed at achieving better relaxation, the reflex came back, the retching stopped, and the dental phobia disappeared.[15]

THE BRAIN'S LOGICAL MEMORY SWITCH

Researchers have found a protein that serves as a kind of logical switch that signals to a nerve cell whether a memory is to be stored for a brief moment or permanently shelved in the mental library. The protein is called CREB. Neurological investigations have revealed that CREB is a transcription factor that binds to DNA and causes nearby genes to spin into protein. And researchers have discovered how the nerve cell flips the CREB switch on and then switches memory on and off. It was found that when fruit flies were fortified with extra CREB, they learned more quickly how to distinguish certain smells.[16]

WHEN MEMORY TAKES A HOLIDAY

Nearly half a century ago, neurologists C. Miller Fisher and Raymond Adams, two neurologists from Boston, coined the term *transient global amnesia* (TGA) to describe temporary episodes in a person's life "in which the only major alteration in behavior is a marked disruption of memory." Memory takes a holiday.

Such episodes probably take place later in life. Often, they begin after emotional or physical stress. An odd symptom of TGA is that the patient continually asks the same question. For example, the patient will ask, "What day is it?" "Thursday," you reply. "I must mow the lawn today," he says. "You mowed the lawn yesterday," you say. "What day is it?" he asks again. Aside from memory, the patient is normal. In TGA cases, memory may return spontaneously—and just as mysteriously as it left.[17]

AT OUR WITS' END?

The information-processing capacity of the human brain is just about at its limit. Researchers claim that if we are not now at our intellectual limit, we are no more than 20 percent away from it. They also argue that any radical improvement in information-processing capability is impossible because of the careful balance between the size of our brain and the blood vessels that nourish it. Given the structure of our body and our brain, we humans may now be as smart as we're ever going to get.[18]

EMBALMER'S CURSE

In 1988, doctors at the Massachusetts General Hospital in Boston succeeded in explaining the cause of a previously baffling affliction suffered only by those involved in the funeral industry, known as embalmer's curse. The sufferer, always a man, experiences headaches, mood shifts, depression, loss of libido, and impotence. Sometimes they experience physical symptoms such as loss of body hair, growth of breasts, and shrinking of the testes. It was discovered that these symptoms were caused by the brain being assaulted by an overproduction of the female hormone estrogen. And this occurred in the male embalmers because they came into direct physical contact with chemicals used in embalming creams, which trigger estrogen production. The key to preventing embalmer's curse was thus very simple: Embalmers should wear rubber gloves.[19]

Chapter 24
Prosopagnosia: When You Can't Recognize Your Own Face in the Mirror

If you think you are poor at remembering faces, consider those suffering from prosopagnosia.

Prosopagnosia is the complete inability to recognize a familiar face after seeing it. If you suffer from this brain disorder, upon seeing the picture of someone's face, you would not know whether you have known the person all of your life, have just been introduced to the person a moment before, or were viewing the face of a complete stranger for the first time.

The memories of people with prosopagnosia may be perfectly normal in other respects. Their inability is in recognizing faces only. People with prosopagnosia may still be able to determine whether someone is familiar to them but not by merely seeing the person's face. They need other sensory cues. For example, they may recognize a person from the sound of his or her voice or even by smell. Moreover, seeing a part of the body other than the face may provoke recognition. Perhaps even the way a person walks could trigger the "this-person-is-familiar-to-me" response.

Prosopagnosia is one of several forms of agnosia. These are sometimes called processing disorders or category disorders. All agnosias are characterized by the brain's inability to recognize the importance of a domain of sensory stimulation. Acoustic agnosia is the inability to recognize the significance of sounds. Finger agnosia is the inability to indicate one's own fingers or those of another. Body image agnosia is the inability to recognize the shape of one's own body or that of someone else. Time agnosia is the loss of comprehension of the sequence or duration of events. And there are many others.

Prosopagnosia is caused by a loss of nerve cells in the part of the brain responsible for processing shapes and textures. One is not born with prosopagnosia. Nor is it merely a neurosis, as was once thought. Nor does it come from disease. Instead, prosopagnosia almost always results from an injury to the right rear of the brain. Technically, the region involved is the brain's inferomesial areas of the temporal and occipital lobes.[1] A head injury from a traffic accident or a bullet wound may bring it on. And according to experts in the field, prosopagnosia remains for life.

WHILE THEY ARE thinking, the blood flow to the brain is greater in women than in men. The significance of this, if any, is unknown.

As unusual and fascinating as prosopagnosia is, much about it is unknown, and much remains controversial. For example, even the manner in which it is diagnosed stirs debate among experts. Diagnosis depends solely, or at least primarily, on the patient's verbal self-report. The patient says that he or she simply does not recognize a face as familiar, and the doctor notes it down (taking it at face value, so to speak). But some experts express concern that any diagnosis derived from a patient's self-report is unscientific, unreliable, subjective, and impossible to verify and may hide the true dimensions of the disorder or mask some other problem.

> YOUR BRAIN puts about 25 million nerve cells into play when you do nothing more than notice that some geometric shape is a circle, a square, or a triangle.

Other experts have observed that, even though patients with prosopagnosia may not feel familiar with a face when they see it, they may still show indications that they recognize the face on some deeper, unconscious level. Perhaps it is a level that science has yet to uncover, appreciate, or fully understand.

What causes the brain's sight recognition to shut down—and then only for faces?

Over the last decade or so, a few experts have theorized that patients with prosopagnosia may have unusual "recognition resources." Alternatively, we all have these resources, but only certain people are forced to draw on them by a damaged brain.

One theory is that there are "islands of spared recognition ability" in people with prosopagnosia, based on the observation that the level of electricity generated by the skin measurably changes when prosopagnosia sufferers view a face that seems familiar but is unrecognized.[2]

Furthermore, the precise cortices involved in prosopagnosia have been identified through computed tomography.[3]

Another theory concerns unusual brain potentials, which are event related in patients with prosopagnosia. Such patients have covert processing abilities that are prolonged more than is normal.[4]

Nevertheless, there is much to be learned about this disorder. According to Dr. Antonio Damasio, when we understand

> the strategies the brain uses to process categories, we have a chance to develop improved re-education strategies in brain-injured patients. Such strategies would use sensory or cognitive pathways left undamaged by the initial injury. . . . Almost everything that gets done one way can be done another way.[5]

Of course, what is most fascinating about prosopagnosia is the many peculiar forms it takes in patients.

An early case was described in 1956. A thirty-two-year-old man was rendered unconscious for three weeks after a car accident. He "complained, exclusively, of an inability to recognize faces, even those of his wife and children." However, he could recognize the faces of three coworkers: one with a eye-blinking tic, another with a large mole on his cheek, and the last with an extremely long face. Each was "recognized solely by the single prominent feature mentioned." Everyone else, including members of his own family, could be recognized only by their voices.[6]

A more recent case was described in 1993. W.J. had very severe prosopagnosia:

> After a stroke he became a farmer and acquired a flock of sheep. He learned to recognize and name many of his

sheep, and his performance on tests of recognition memory and paired-associate learning for sheep was significantly better than on comparable tests using human face stimuli. It is concluded that in some instances prosopagnosia can be a face-specific disorder.[7]

In 1995, the intriguing case was reported of a sixty-eight-year-old woman who could recognize familiar people not by their faces but only by their names.[8]

Prosopagnosia is forcing us to reexamine our basic notions of familiarity, recognition, awareness, and knowledge and question what these concepts really mean in the human brain.[9]

Case Study: The Man Who Mistook His Wife for a Hat

Perhaps the most famous prosopagnosia case is that of Dr. P., the brain-injured musician who became the basis for *The Man Who Mistook His Wife for a Hat*, by clinical neurologist Oliver Sacks. Sacks writes, "A face, to us, is a person looking out—we see, as it were, the person through his persona, his face. But for Dr. P., there was no persona in this sense—no outward *persona*, and no person within."[10]

THE BRAIN SEES US DIFFERENTLY

The brain allocates cerebral space to the parts of the body most in need of coordination. Indeed, in terms of space allocation in the brain, the human brain perceives the body differently from the way we see ourselves. In terms of their share of brain space, the hands (especially the thumbs), shoulders, lips, tongue, and feet loom large. The rest of the body shrinks proportionately. If the human body physically reflected the brain's view, we would be a deformed assemblage of enlarged or stunted parts, looking rather like a frog.[11]

THE BOY WITH TWO BRAINS

A Chinese baby with two brains is doing well but hardly sleeps because his brains work in rotation, according to the Xinhua News Agency. The little boy, born in Chaoyang City in northeastern Liaoning Province in July 1995, is growing well and does not need surgery, the official agency quoted doctors as saying. However, the baby sleeps only for about one hour a night—and sometimes for as little as twenty minutes—and seldom sleeps during the day, Xinhua says. "Doctors have found that the youngster has two brains, which work on a rotating basis, which means the baby sleeps less."[12]

Chapter 25
The **Remembering Brain**: Déjà Vu, or Haven't We Met Before?

What is memory? How do we remember? And how do we forget? How is the brain involved?

A fascinating book challenges our traditional assumptions about memory.

We usually think that our brain functions as a huge computer that stores data and that our memory is the mechanism used to retrieve it. But according to a New York psychiatrist, this view of memory is pure myth: Memory is largely invented.

In his book *The Invention of Memory*,[1] Dr. Israel Rosenfield claims that we have no "permanent memories stored in our brains." Instead, we have fragmentary ones that are continually

ACCORDING TO Johns Hopkins University researchers, as men and women grow older, women can remember better.

being reconstructed by emotions. He contends that because "emotions structure recollections and perceptions," we should never think of memories without also thinking of how we act on our memories with our feelings.

It seems that our brain, our so-called computer, has a heart.

Rosenfield traces the development of this controversial theory back through the writings of early psychologists, even citing Freud as supporting his view. He contends that research into the brain's physiology, the role of the limbic system in particular, lends weight to his argument.

Although memory may be invented, no one doubts it can be improved.

Mnemonics is the art of memory improvement. The key to perfecting this art involves learning how to do four things: focus attention better, improve concentration skills, organize and mentally cross-index information better, and construct meaningful associations based on strong visual images that themselves are unforgettable.

Most memory improvement books use one or more of the following mnemonic techniques:

Make up a "memory jog" sentence or acronym. For example, to remember the order of Sydney streets from Hyde Park (standing on Park Street) and looking west (Elizabeth, Castlereagh, Pitt, George, York, Clarence, Kent, and Sussex), think of "Elizabeth Castlereagh fell in the Pitt as George York and Clarence Kent Sussed-out sex." The funnier and more outrageous the thought, the better.

Make up rhymes and even put the rhymes to music. Nobody ever forgets the useful "I before E, except after C" to spell *receive* or "a rat in the hat might eat the ice cream" to spell "arithmetic." Also, putting to music a list of household chores that must be remembered makes them unforgettable. For example, to the tune of "Mary Had a Little Lamb," you could sing, "Put out the garbage bin tonight, bin tonight, bin tonight."

Compose mental pictures. This is especially recommended when you are trying to remember a person's name. "Marie Loftus" might become "Marie Antoinette sitting in a hay loft."

Repeat or rehearse new facts. "G'Day, Marie" is what you say when you are first introduced. A few minutes later you say to yourself, "That's Marie Loftus." A few minutes after that, imagine yourself sitting in the hay loft with Marie, perhaps eating cake.

Use a loci system. *Loci* is Latin for "places." This involves taking a series of facts to be remembered and matching each one with a specific site you can easily visualize—your kitchen, for instance. For example, if you are to chair a meeting and must make eight introductory points about a subject, imagine placing one point in the refrigerator, the next in the oven, the third in the sink, and so on. When you give your talk, make another mental tour of the kitchen and pick up your points as you think about your kitchen.

Write things down. Writing notes and making lists will often fix things in your mind and provide a record. Also, seeing words as you write them down involves another sensory experience with which to hang on to the information.

Organize and structure your life. Make sure that everything
in your house has a place. The hook in the garage for
the spare set of house keys is a mnemonic device.
Thus, you will always know where to look first.

Search for opportunities to exercise your memory and
improve your mind. For example, play games such as
crossword puzzles, Trivial Pursuit, and Scrabble. Make
up lists of miscellaneous information just to test your
recall. For example, make a list of "All the films I've
ever seen starring Tom Cruise" or "All the world
heavyweight boxing champions since John L. Sullivan." Test yourself periodically.

Relax your body when trying to remember, be patient, be
persistent, but do not expect superhuman memory
miracles. Something may not surface when you first
concentrate on it ("It's right on the tip of my tongue"),
but later it just pops up with no trouble.

Improve your mind in all ways you can. Reading, attending talks, enrolling in courses, and joining discussion
groups will introduce new stimuli and sharpen your
mind.

There are other mnemonic techniques, but it's hard to
remember them all.[2]

What of memory itself? What do we really know?

Research suggests that although we still know little for sure
about the precise relationship between memory and the brain,
we know a little about how memories move within the brain.

Studies using brain imaging suggest that "cellular information" speeds through disparate parts of the brain to coordinate
memories for personally experienced events. These are known

as episodic memories. Using positron emission tomography (PET) images, researchers in Toronto are offering the first data suggesting that "this memory thoroughfare turns left at the front of the brain to store recollections and veers right to retrieve them."[3] Blood flow jumps sharply on the left side of the prefrontal cortex (which lies just behind the forehead) as new information enters episodic memory. Furthermore, blood surges in the right prefrontal cortex as episodic memories resurface. Thus, this movement constitutes a memory highway in the brain.

IF YOU ARE TYPIcal, your short-term memory is more efficient in the morning, whereas your long-term memory is more efficient in the afternoon. Forget the evening.

The existence of such a memory highway is supported by findings from London. Also using PET scans, the researchers found a distinct module of interconnected structures in the brain's outer, cortical layer, and in other areas of the cerebrum that could orchestrate mental encores of past experiences. A clump of tissue in the right temporal cortex, near the ear, appears to serve as a hub in this module. The London team's work backs up the Toronto team's research showing that part of the right frontal cortex aids in the retrieval of personal memories.[4]

What about the most fascinating memory phenomenon, déjà vu?

Although most of us have experienced déjà vu at least once ("Haven't we met before?"), this peculiar phenomenon continues to puzzle behavioral and medical science. Researchers and clinicians are unable to agree as to what it is, how common it is, what causes it, or what it really means. What happens in the brain that brings about déjà vu?

Déjà vu comes from French and means "already seen." Basically, the déjà vu experience occurs whenever we know that something is unknown, but we perceive it as somehow familiar. For example, it happens when we meet someone for the first time, yet his or her face seems oddly familiar. Or it happens when we travel to a new city for the first time, yet it seems like a place we have been to before. As such, déjà vu can be very confusing, a little disconcerting, and, when we admit to it out loud, occasionally embarrassing.

Sir Walter Scott writes of it in his journal (1828). Charles Dickens describes it in *David Copperfield* (1849). Leo Tolstoy mentions it several times in his autobiographical trilogy, *Childhood* (1852), *Boyhood* (1854), and *Youth* (1856) and in *War and Peace* (1869). Marcel Proust refers to it in *Remembrance of Things Past* (1913–1927). Alfred Tennyson explores it in two poems, "To— (As When with Downcast Eyes)" (1832) and "The Two Voices" (1833). The songs "Where or When" by Rodgers and Hart (1937) and "Déjà Vu" by David Crosby (1970) capture its romantic aspects. The 1985 Madonna film *Desperately Seeking Susan*, directed by Susan Seidelman, portrays the heroine having an amnesiac déjà vu experience after a head injury. Déjà vu, it would seem, is part of our culture.

It is also quite common. Between 30 and 96 percent of humans have experienced déjà vu at one or more times in their lives. Opinion differs on this rate because researchers cannot agree on a definition of déjà vu. However, researchers do agree that déjà vu apparently occurs just as often in men as in women. Yet they do not agree as to whether déjà vu is related to factors such as ethnicity, social class, or level of education.[5]

Several studies point out that age is a factor in déjà vu.

Déjà vu occurs somewhat more often in younger people than in older people. But no one knows why this is so.

Although déjà vu is sometimes seen in patients with various medical and psychiatric maladies, it also occurs in healthy, perfectly normal people (as many of us can attest). Déjà vu has been found by some researchers to be observed in people with anxiety and dissociative neuroses, mood and personality disorders, schizophrenia, and organic brain disorders and syndromes. It is also thought to be occasionally the result of psychological trauma, emotional exhaustion, or drug use, especially where fatigue, stress, and physical illness are involved. In particular, a few studies point to déjà vu being associated with epilepsy. Nevertheless, Dutch researchers claim, there is no absolute connection between déjà vu and any single psychiatric or neurological disorder.[5]

Déjà vu is sometimes confused with flashbacks, actualized precognition, or cryptomnesia. But the four are quite distinct. In flashbacks, a person may conceive of himself or herself as actually being back in time and space; his or her past unfolds, almost as if it were on videotape. In actualized precognition, a person has the impression that the present situation he or she is in has been foretold; he or she knows what is going to happen before it does. In cryptomnesia, a person has the sense that his or her own past, which should be familiar, is strangely unfamiliar. Thus, cryptomnesia can be thought of as the opposite of déjà vu—and just as baffling to explain.

EXPERTS CLAIM that when they walk into a room, left-handers tend to turn left, right-handers turn right.

RESEARCHERS claim that although many right-handers are completely right-handed, no left-hander is completely left-handed.

LEFT-HANDERS have an advantage as musicians because in their brains, the parts that deal with sound are larger and better developed.

ON AVERAGE, right-handed people live nine years longer than left-handed people do.

IN AUSTRALIA each year, more than 170 left-handed people a year are killed by using products made for right-handed people.

There have been numerous attempts to explain déjà vu. Sigmund Freud described déjà vu as "uncanny" and "miraculous." In *The Psychopathology of Everyday Life* (1901), he then went on to explain it as involving the recollection of an unconscious fantasy or wish. Since Freud, others have tried to explain déjà vu as a form of amnesia, a disturbance of attention, or a problem of visualization and imagery. Still others have suggested that it results from a confusion of dreams or a complex memory mix-up.[6, 7]

One theory is that déjà vu may involve either the right or the left temporal lobe. Neurologists have succeeded in stimulating déjà vu experiences by electrically stimulating the temporal lobes. But they also stimulated hallucinations in the same patients, with the same electrodes, applied to the same spot.[8]

In 1990, in a vigorous attempt at a theory for déjà vu, Drs. Herman Sno and Don Linszen proposed what they call a hologram model to explain déjà vu. Briefly put, in photography, a hologram is a three-dimensional picture composed of tiny squares of information assembled in such a way as to resemble a mosaic. Sno and Linszen claim that perceptions and memories are like holograms. Déjà vu is produced when enough of the pieces of one hologram (the present perception) resemble enough of the pieces of another (the past memory), causing either to be confused with the other.

It is a interesting theory. Oddly enough, it seems very similar to a déjà vu explanation proposed by a psychiatrist named Dr. Harold Levitan way back in 1969.[9] In any case, it looks awfully familiar.

Perhaps it's déjà vu?[10]

ICTAL DÉJÀ VU

Ictal refers to that which pertains to a stroke. Strokes can trigger the phenomenon of ictal déjà vu, according to one study. And it seems that handedness is a factor as well. Researchers at the University of Arizona report that in eight patients with ictal déjà vu, all right-handed patients had damage to their right temporal lobe, and all left-handed patients had damage to their left temporal lobe. Right-handers are left-hemisphere dominant, and left-handers are right-hemisphere dominant. The researchers speculate that déjà vu may be located in the nondominant brain hemisphere.[11]

WHEN IS A VEGETABLE NOT A VEGETABLE?

When someone has massive brain damage and permanent unconsciousness, some people cruelly call this person a "vegetable." Frightening research claims that people very often are misdiagnosed as "vegetables"—nearly half in one study! Researchers closely examined forty patients. They gave a much more thorough check for signs of alertness and awareness than was previously given by the hospital staff that rendered the initial vegetative state diagnosis. Seventeen of the forty patients believed to be in "a persistent vegetative state" were later found to be alert, aware of what was happening to them, and often able to express themselves in simple forms of communication (for example, a head nod, an eye blink, or a finger movement).

As head of the study, Dr. Keith Andrews, says, "It is disturbing to think that some patients who were aware had for several years been treated as being vegetative. It must be extremely distressing to be aware but unable to make contact."[12]

According to the American Neurological Association, people in a vegetative state show no awareness of themselves or their surroundings, do not respond to questions or physical stimuli except reflexively, but open their eyes and appear to go through waking and sleeping periods. The state is defined as persistent if it lasts longer than a month.[13]

COMA COMMUNICATING

British researchers are experimenting with a possible way to help doctors communicate with people in comas. Scientists in London will use a "hairnet" of electrodes, connected to a computer, to "read" a comatose person's thoughts. The comatose patient will be asked to think about moving a part of the body. If he or she could hear, he or she could think, and the computer could detect this thought and translate it into either a "yes" or "no." This would constitute a simple form of communication—not a great deal, but it's better than nothing. According to the head of the research team, Dr. Steve Roberts:

> There are a lot of people who have had severe injury, come out of coma and tell of a nightmare situation of being conscious of their surroundings but utterly unable to communicate in any way. It is hoped in a lot of these cases patients will be able to respond to this analysis and we would be able to assist their rehabilitation out of coma. There's even a glimmer of hope that we might be able to say "there's someone in there," which will be of some comfort to the patient.

Such communication is possible because earlier studies have established that the brain "rehearses" movement, and the same part of the brain is activated whether a person actually moves or just thinks about it.[14]

Chapter 26
Savant Syndrome: The Ultimate Specialist, a "Genius" in One Thing but an "Idiot" in Everything Else

When it comes to parceling out brain abilities, nature usually is pretty even-handed. Most of us have roughly normal abilities—but not always.

Take, for example, savant syndrome.

Do you remember the character played by Dustin Hoffman in the 1988 film *Rain Man*? He was an autistic savant. Although classified as mentally retarded, he had an extraordinary memory, which came in very handy while he gambled in Las Vegas with his brother, played by Tom Cruise.

A savant is the ultimate specialist. He or she can do one thing very, very well but most other things incredibly badly. We classify such people as retarded, and we often institutionalize them as incompetent. But in reality savants are extraordinary people.

Today, behavioral scientists continue to be baffled by savants. All that we really know for sure is that savantism is a rare and spectacular condition that still defies full explanation.[1]

Savantism is an extraordinary ability, knowledge, skill, or talent in an otherwise intellectually handicapped person.

Let us look at some of these extraordinary people.

A "mentally subnormal" patient could repeat verbatim a newspaper's entire contents after it was read to him. Still another could repeat verbatim the newspaper's contents—but this time backwards.

A so-called "imbecile boy" of twelve years who could not read or write nevertheless could correctly multiply any three figures with lightning speed.[2]

A twenty-two-year-old woman with "a mental age of five" was able to recall the dates of every visit that had ever been made to her home and the names of each of the visitors.

A "retarded" patient could remember the day every person had been buried in the local parish, going back some thirty-five years, complete with the age of the deceased and the names of the mourners attending the funeral.

An "idiot savant" can achieve fame. For instance, "the genius of Earlswood Asylum" was a deaf "imbecilic" patient possessing remarkable skills in drawing, invention, and mechanical dexterity. He was widely known and respected for these talents.[2]

Thomas Fuller, an eighteenth-century Virginia slave, was judged by all to be a hopeless "imbecile." But he could rapidly calculate in his head the exact number of seconds in seventy years, seventeen days, and twelve hours, taking into account the seventeen leap years involved. By the way, the answer is 2,210,500,800.[3]

Gottfried Mind, regarded as a "dull-witted cretin," had a marvelous faculty for drawing cats. His cats were so lifelike that he was known throughout Europe as "the cat's Raphael." One of his cats graced the collection of King George IV.

"Blind Tom" Bethune was a well-known autistic savant with an extremely limited IQ who played Mozart works on the piano at the age of four and could play back flawlessly any musical piece, no matter the complexity. He could also repeat a discourse of any length, in any language, without the loss of a single syllable. Once tested with two compositions of thirteen and twenty pages, he repeated them without error.[4]

Ellen Boudreaux, described as a "profoundly retarded" blind girl, although affected with rickets and crippled, had great musical talents. She could repeat perfectly any song sung or played to her, no matter the complexity, after hearing it only once.

Kiyoshi Yamashita, although of "seriously subnormal intelligence," was a genius in graphic art. Indeed, he was known as "the van Gogh of Japan."[5]

Alonzo Clemons, with a measured IQ of 40 and living in a home for the developmentally disabled in Boulder, Colorado, has nonetheless produced hundreds of pieces of sculpture. One such artwork sold in 1992 for $45,000.[3]

E.C., an intellectually subnormal man living in Canada, has better drafting skills than professional draftsmen who were compared with him. According to his doctors, E.C. has an incredible ability to see a three-dimensional perspective "without the use of explicit or implicit perspective rules."[6]

Stephen Wiltshire, a man with a measured IQ of 30 who lives in London, has produced several books of extraordinarily beautiful drawings. One of these, *Floating Cities*, was a number-one best-seller in the United Kingdom.[3]

George and Charles, the so-called calculator twins, are identical, intellectually handicapped twins with an uncanny ability to remember certain aspects of every day going back 80,000 years. For example, they can tell you what day of the week was April 24, 929 B.C. They can also recall, in detail, the weather conditions for every day of their adult lives.[3,7]

Leslie Lemke, born prematurely and blind, possesses an extraordinary memory. He sings, plays, and has appeared on numerous television shows. He has also been the subject of two films, *The Woman Who Willed a Miracle* (1983), which won four Emmy awards, and *An Island of Genius* (1987).[8]

Kim, a mathematical savant who lives in Salt Lake City, Utah, was the inspiration for the character played by Dustin Hoffman in *Rain Man*.[3]

Dr. Darold Treffert has been working for many years with autistic savants. In fact, he served as a consultant for *Rain Man*. Treffert has written what is probably the most famous book on savants, *Extraordinary People: Understanding "Idiot Savants."*[8] He sums up best what little we know about this mysterious condition.

"The savant syndrome," the term Treffert prefers to the more widely known

LEFT-HANDERS tend to be better at algebra. It is theorized that left-handers' brains are better suited to dealing with the abstract.

"idiot savant," is a comparatively rare condition. Strangely, about 10 percent of autistic children may be autistic savants,
according to some authorities. One survey
of 90,000 residents in mental health facilities "turned up 54 savants, or about one in
every 2,000 residents."[1] Males outnumber
females by a ratio of six to one.

Treffert contends that "no single theory, as yet, can explain
this mystifying phenomenon." Indeed, he writes, "the theories
are nearly as individual and as numerous as the case reports."[8]

Nevertheless, six types of theories have emerged. However, all of them are somewhat wanting.

First, some believe that savants have eidetic imagery powers
far beyond normal. This is the ability to visually scan quickly,
store, and recall vast amounts of information. But this theory
certainly cannot explain all autistic savants. Not all savants have
this ability. In fact, some are blind and cannot scan at all.

Second, some contend that savants inherit skills from parents. But perfectly normal and ordinary parents produce
savants, and savants produce perfectly normal and ordinary
children in nearly all cases.

Third, some assert that savants suffer sensory deprivation
and social isolation. This may be true for some. But it may be
the result rather than the symptom of the condition. Also,
many savants experience completely normal upbringings.

Fourth, some argue that savants possess an impaired ability
to think abstractly. However, Treffert argues that this view is a
description rather than an explanation.[8]

Fifth, some maintain that savants develop compensatory
skills such as deliberate memorization as a means of coping

with an impairment. But here, too, Treffert maintains that "they cannot by themselves account for the condition."[8]

Finally, some hold that savants are the victims of organic brain damage or have problems with brain localization (right brain versus left brain hemisphere lateralization, and so on). But many savants have normal electroencephalographic and computed tomography scan readings and show no organic brain damage whatsoever.

Therefore, Treffert concludes that savant behavior "is complex and difficult to comprehend, and despite the fact that it clearly does exist, this behavior remains unexplained in individuals and in the aggregate. The search for an explanation continues. No model of brain function, particularly memory, will be complete until it can include and account for the syndrome. This astonishing condition remains a challenge to our capabilities."[8]

What is the lesson for us?

The phenomenon of the savant illustrates the extremes of human capability—the ironic interconnection between "genius" and "idiot"—all in one human body. It underscores that we must strive to understand and appreciate the extremes of humankind and never ridicule or condemn. Most of us are similar. Some of us are different, and a few of us are very, very different.

As the brain exhibits yet another oddity, the savant is the ultimate specialist.[7, 9]

Case Study: Memories of T.M.

Psychologists at the University of London have presented evidence that people with extraordinary memories are really not that extraordinary after all. They describe the mental workings of T.M., a twenty-five-year-old man who is an accomplished user of mnemonics. He astounds audiences with his seemingly impossible memory feats. But these feats are no mystery to T.M., and he carefully explains how it is all mnemonics and nothing paranormal. For example,

> *T.M. asks audiences for birthdates and very quickly gives the day of birth. . . . The day of birth calculations were originally carried out through use of a system of numerical codes for years and months which were combined and subjected to certain calculations. However, with practice many shortcuts and mnemonics have been developed and now T.M. often knows instantly that certain dates imply certain days, like learning the multiplication tables. Every year and month had a code from 0 to 6 and T.M. has learned the codes (by the method explained below) for all years from 1900 to 2000. For any given date the method is to add the codes for the month and the year and divide the total by 7; the remainder gives the day of the week. For example, 27 October 1964 gives 27 + 1 (the code for October) + 3 (the code for 1964) = 31. Dividing by 7 gives a remainder of 3 which is the third day of the week, Tuesday.* [10]

THE BUSY BRAIN: USE IT OR LOSE IT

A cliché among brain experts is that the more you use your brain, the better it performs. It's the old idea, "Use it or lose it." But does research really support this belief?

A team of psychologists at the University of California put a group of their fellow academics through a five-part series of mental experiments and compared their performance with that of nonacademics of the same age. The experiments targeted memory in particular. The assumption was that academics are more likely to be in the "use it" category than in the "lose it" one. In any case, consistent with the belief, it was found that academics did indeed fare better in the mental tests. But mental powers do eventually erode with time. According to Dr. Arthur Shimamura, head of the research team, "No matter how mentally active you are, you're going to slow down." Yet a brain that's kept busy lasts longer.[11]

Chapter 27
The **Schizophrenic Brain**: When You Think You're Split in Two

There are many, many unanswered questions about schizophrenia.

But first, here are some of the basics.

Schizophrenia is a very common mental health problem. About one person in every hundred Australians will suffer from schizophrenia at some point. Thus, almost everyone in Australia will know someone with schizophrenia or someone who has a schizophrenic in his or her family.

Schizophrenia is a complex entity and difficult to define, but at least some of the following symptoms must be present: There are disorders in both form and content of thought, disturbances in perception (such as hallucinations), and disorders of attention, volition, motor functioning, emotion, interpersonal relations, incoherent trains of thought, inappropriate or blunted emotions, and a deep-seated sense of apathy and hopelessness.

Schizophrenia unhinges mental life with an array of symptoms.

There are two broad types of schizophrenia (acute and chronic) and at least six subtypes (paranoid, hebephrenic, catatonic, simple, defect state, and affective). Fortunately, schizophrenia is treatable with cognitive therapy but more often with drug therapy.

Hearing voices, as if you were split in two, is the hallmark symptom of schizophrenia.

Many myths surround schizophrenia. One is the conventional view that schizophrenia occurs in higher proportions in rural areas than in urban areas. Moreover, it is widely believed that schizophrenics in rural areas often drift to cities as part of their disease in order to create a self-imposed isolation. However, studies challenge this myth.

A study of schizophrenic Swedish men that found that instead of moving to cities after developing schizophrenia, men raised in cities were more prone to develop it. The researchers further suggested that urban areas are more schizophrenia-prone than rural areas. Indeed, the researchers argue that there may be an environmental cause common to cities that puts people at risk of becoming schizophrenic.[1]

But myths aside, what causes schizophrenia is still a mystery. It was once believed that schizophrenia was caused by poor parenting; usually a cold and distant mother was involved. But this view is now rejected by almost all authorities, and parental guilt has been lessened.

In 1990, Johns Hopkins University researchers discovered a link between the shrinkage of the brain's superior temporal gyrus and severe schizophrenic auditory hallucinations. The theory put forward was that schizophrenia results from damage to a specific portion of the left side of the brain.[2] Thus, when the "voices" occur that the schizophrenic "hears," there is actually heightened activity in the same part of the brain that people use when they speak or think words.[3]

In 1992, this theory was strengthened by a major Harvard study that found a link between schizophrenia and shrinkage of the brain's left temporal lobe, especially the part essential for hearing and speech.[4]

The study found a strong relationship between the degree of thought disorder and size of the superior temporal gyrus. This is a particularly elevated portion of the brain formed by the way in which the cerebral cortex is folded. The study was based on magnetic resonance imaging scans of fifteen people with schizophrenia and fifteen people without it. The Harvard team found that the schizophrenia sufferers had nearly a 20 percent smaller superior temporal gyrus.

Although this work to finger the cause of schizophrenia does not provide new types of treatment, the researchers believe their discovery is "a hopeful sign for research into this severely disabling disorder."[4]

Hopeful research signs occur frequently these days. For example, evidence from a 1995 University of Iowa study suggests that schizophrenia may spring from abnormalities in the thalamus and areas throughout the brain with anatomical links to that structure. Prior evidence, it was argued, indicated that the thalamus, located deep in the brain, helps to focus attention, filter sensations, and process other types of information.

Indeed, such "troubles in the thalamus and its related structures, which extend from above the spinal cord to behind the forehead, can create the full range of symptoms observed in schizophrenics."[5]

It could be that the whole brain is involved in schizophrenia and that psychological notions such as existing self-concept may be involved. As Dr. Philip McGuire says, "A predisposition to [hearing voices] might depend on abnormal activity in brain areas implicated in perceiving inner speech and determining whether it is of self or alien origin."[6]

When is such brain damage likely to occur? Although the symptoms of schizophrenia emerge during young adulthood, the brain damage that causes it may occur in infancy. "The exact nature of this neural damage remains poorly understood, but [it reflects] disruptions of brain development that originate before or shortly after birth."[7]

But a few researchers argue that schizophrenia is caused by a virus, and a familiar one at that. A controversial but very intriguing finding as to the cause of schizophrenia comes from Dr. John Eagles of the Royal Cornhill Hospital in Aberdeen.[8] Eagles argues that the virus that causes polio may also cause schizophrenia. Moreover, he claims that schizophrenia may be part of the post-polio syndrome.

Eagles bases his contention on the fact that in England, Wales, Scotland, and New Zealand, schizophrenia rates have fallen by around 50 percent since the mid-1960s. This parallels the introduction of antipolio vaccines in those countries. The oral vaccine was introduced in the United Kingdom in 1962. Thus, when polio was stopped, so too was a lot of schizophrenia, without anyone knowing that this would happen.

Eagles adds that in Connecticut, it has been found that

those admitted to hospital for schizophrenia "were significantly more likely to have been born during those years when high rates of poliomyelitis infections were reported."[8]

Furthermore, Eagles points out, unvaccinated Jamaicans who immigrated to the United Kingdom "have markedly increased rates of schizophrenia compared with the indigenous [U.K.] population."[8]

Eagles observes that over the last few years, post-polio syndrome has been identified by medical science. In this syndrome, about thirty years after being struck down with paralysis from polio, survivors suffer from severe fatigue, neurological problems, joint and muscle pain, and increased sensitivity (especially to cold temperature). About 50 percent of polio sufferers get post-polio syndrome. According to Eagles,

since the mean age of onset of schizophrenia is close to 30 years of age, these data and similar models would accord with the concept of schizophrenia as a "post-polio syndrome" which follows perinatal poliovirus infection."[8]

Drs. David Silbersweig and Emily Stern of Cornell University argue that there may be little wrong with the brains of schizophrenics, but nevertheless they've found something very intriguing. Using positron emission tomography (PET), they've devised a clever means of exposing the brain's blood flow during the act of schizophrenic hallucinating. They examined six schizophrenic men, all of whom heard voices and were unresponsive or unexposed to treatment. One had visual hallucinations as well. While connected to the PET scanner, each subject was asked to press a button with his right thumb when he hallucinated. It was found that when each hallucinated, parts of the brain located near the surface and needed for hearing were activated. Furthermore, all had increased blood flow in several deep regions of the brain: the hippocampus, the parahippocampal gyrus, the cingulate gyrus, the thalamus, and the striatum. Do schizophrenics really hear voices? Their brains say they do.[9]

> THE LEFT SIDE of your brain is responsible for your choice of words, the right side for your tone of voice.

Schizophrenics often speak in an illogical, incoherent, rambling manner. In earlier times, this was believed to be evidence of demonic possession. But researchers have been investigating a far less supernatural explanation. According to neuroscientist Dr. Patricia Goldman-Rakic, the speaking problem of schizophrenics may merely reflect a deficit in short-term memory. It has been found that the prefrontal cortex is significantly less active in schizophrenics. This is the area of the brain believed to be where short-term memories reside. As Dr. Goldman-Rakic says, "If they cannot keep the subject of a sentence in mind by the time they get to the verb or object, it's going to be fragmented and incoherent."[10]

This is all very interesting. There are many unanswered questions about schizophrenia.[11]

IS SCHIZOPHRENIA THE RESULT OF MATERNAL IMMUNE RESPONSE OR MALNUTRITION?

Some researchers argue that disruptions in fetal brain development promote schizophrenia. A University of Pennsylvania study of the medical records for the entire population of Denmark concluded that severe malnutrition in the early months of fetal development may contribute to schizophrenia, as may a mother's immune reaction to her unborn child.[12]

THANKS FOR THE MEMORIES

As people get older, an enzyme called prolyl endopeptidase (PEP) increasingly degrades the neuropeptides involved in learning and memory. In Alzheimer's disease, the process is speeded up. This causes memory loss and a shortened attention span. Scientists from Suresnes, France have discovered compounds that prevent PEP from breaking neuropeptides apart. In laboratory tests with amnesic rats, these compounds almost completely restored memories.[13]

Chapter 28
The **Self-Mutilating Brain**

Most of us protect our bodies from pain and disfigurement—but not all.

Gary David, the controversial inmate and founding member of the self-amputation Van Gogh Club at Pentridge Prison in Melbourne, inflicted injuries to his own body on seventy-seven separate occasions.

David has cut, slashed, burned, pierced, poisoned, or amputated numerous parts of his body. He has eaten pieces of glass and drunk brass cleaner, sulfuric acid, and the contents of a nine-volt battery. He has sliced off both ears (eating one) and amputated his nipples, parts of his penis (twice), his scrotum, and one of his heels. He has shoved fish bones in his eyes and wire up his urethra. He has severed his Achilles tendons, nailed both feet to the floor, injected urine, extracted a quart of blood from his arm using part of a fountain pen, and inserted razor blades up his anus.[1]

But as extreme and bizarre as his behavior may seem at first, research suggests that self-mutilation among institutionalized people is extremely common.

According to the world's foremost expert on body mutilation, Dr. Armando Favazza, self-mutilation in some form is practiced by the majority of the world's incarcerated people. Furthermore, he argues that such self-mutilation is done for reasons that make perfect sense given the conditions in institutions. Moreover, far from being regarded as a deviant act, self-mutilation can be viewed as a form of "symptom-reducing self-therapy." It is the person's way of reasserting the self in a hostile, dehumanizing, and destructive environment.[2]

Ironically, self-mutilation becomes a form of self-protection.

In his classic book on the subject, *Bodies Under Siege: Self-Mutilation in Culture and Psychiatry* (1987), Favazza says that "forced institutionalization . . . often creates feelings of desperation, and boredom among inmates, who may resort to self-mutilation to deal with these feelings." Self-mutilation ranges from tattooing to trephination (cutting and removing skull bone).

Favazza adds that an inmate's self-mutilation actually maintains or restores the mutilator's sense of the integrity of his or her own physical body. By slicing flesh or otherwise damaging himself or herself, the mutilator is able to experience a temporary respite from intolerable inner tensions, from overwhelming feelings of depression, depersonalization, anxiety, guilt, helplessness, and rage.

IF YOU COULD harness the power used by your brain, you could power a ten-watt lightbulb.

To illustrate his theory, Favazza cites the case of one Canadian prison for juvenile girls where 86 percent of the inmates "carved-up" their bodies in "an epidemic of self-cutting." He argues that the girls' self-mutilation represented "the epitome of personal freedom by which they could reassure themselves that they had some mastery over their fate."[2]

ACCORDING TO the California Medical Association, 87 percent of professional boxers suffer some sort of brain damage.

He recounts that the staff of the prison found that traditional measures to stop the epidemic failed. These included lectures, medications, psychotherapy, threats, and punishments such as removal of privileges and solitary confinement. In fact, such measures increased the rate of "carving" tenfold. Finally, the prison staff tried something novel. They first fooled the girls into thinking that their carving actually played into the staff's hands. More importantly, they then conceded more autonomy to the girls within the institution. The epidemic then came to an immediate end.

Sadly, Favazza notes that after a time, the staff could not tolerate their own loss of control. They reversed their concession, halted the unique autonomy program, and thereby encouraged a return to inmate self-mutilation.

In her review of Favazza's book,[3] Dr. Nancy Scheper-Hughes recalls the writings of Italian psychiatrist Franco Basaglia.[4] Scheper-Hughes says,

> *From the perspective of the psychiatric patient, what message is conveyed by locked doors, padded cells, barred windows, cold packs, and other physical restraints, if not the taunting dare to lash out, to resist, to escape? Within a life-defying*

total institution, only the forbidden act remains as a token of one's former autonomous existence. "I cut myself, I cut myself," Loretta told me during her 16th involuntary admission to the locked wards of Boston State Hospital in 1980, "to prove that I am, to prove that I can."[3, 5]

GENITAL MUTILATION AND BODY PIERCING

Doctors in London argue that "genital mutilation may be partially understood as a consequence of delusionally motivated action against a background of low self-esteem, premorbid body-image preoccupation, forced early sexual activity and hence profound ambivalence towards adult sexuality."[6] If so, this era of body piercing and tattooing is understandable. Many young people have low self-esteem and body image preoccupation. How far is their fashionable body piercing from psychiatric genital mutilation? Probably not very far at all.

MENTAL ILLNESS AND THE SUN

Here's another weird one. A team of Israeli psychologists have found startling evidence of surprisingly high correlations between solar activity and psychiatric illness. The team examined the admission records of one psychiatric unit over ten years in order to determine whether there was any correlation between ten psychiatric behaviors and geophysical activity. Four of the ten behaviors (unspecified in the study) were significantly correlated:

—0.274 with sudden magnetic activity

—0.216 with the index of geomagnetic activity

—0.262 with the number of hours of positive ionization of the ionosphere in the corresponding month. Percentages of variance accounted for were very small.

Thus, the sun may have an effect on mental illness, but science has not been able to determine what these statistical associations mean.[7]

ET EPILEPSY

Dianne Neale, a forty-nine-year-old woman without a history of epilepsy, apparently suffered epileptic seizures upon hearing the voice of Mary Hart, co-host of the TV show *Entertainment Tonight* (*ET*). The patient experienced an upset stomach, a sense of pressure in her head, and confusion. Laboratory tests confirmed the abnormal electrical discharges in her brain. The patient held a press conference to deny she was crazy, to express resentment about being the object of jokes, and to attribute no blame to Mary Hart. Hart apologized on air for the problem. The case was written up in *The New England Journal of Medicine*.[8]

THE HYPOTHALAMUS: A VITAL BRAIN REGULATOR

The hypothalamus of the brain is the lower part of the diencephalon located above the inner regions of the nose. A hanging stalk from this area supports the pituitary gland

and connects it to the hypothalamus. The hypothalamus functions as a vital brain regulator that controls several important body processes:

> Regulation of the heartbeat
> Regulation of the rate of breathing
> Regulation of body temperature
> Regulation of the sleep–wake cycle
> Regulation of the biological timing of the beginning of sexual maturity.[9]

Chapter 29
The **Shrinking Brain**

The forms of human mental illness are as many as the stars. Cultural psychiatry is a branch of psychiatry that emerged in the 1970s from both anthropology and psychiatry. Practitioners from both disciplines attack the prevailing notion in mainstream psychiatry that mental illnesses are universal phenomena stemming from identical underlying biological mechanisms, even though symptoms may vary from culture to culture. Although some diseases such as schizophrenia appear in all cultures, other mental diseases do not. Moreover, the features of an illness, such as the course that it takes, vary so "dramatically [from culture to culture] that a physician may as well be treating separate diseases."[1]

Moth Madness

Moth madness is a disease among the Navajos of the American Southwest. It is regarded by the Navajos as AIDS is regarded by Europeans: with great dread. Moth madness consists of epileptic-type seizure symptoms, leading to uncontrollable frenzy and hysterical, self-destructive behaviors. Often the sufferer believes that a part of his or her body, such as the head, the torso, or the sexual organs, is shrinking. However, the sufferer shows no physical signs of any disease whatsoever when examined by a doctor. It is purely psychosomatic. It is called moth madness because of the flickering nature of a moth's movements, its tiny size, and its short lifetime.

Anthropologists at the University of Arizona argue that among the Navajo, moth madness is believed to occur whenever the taboo against incest has been violated: "Even if the onset [of moth madness] is in the first few years of life, it is believed that one of the parents has transgressed a taboo and the disease has been transmitted to the child by prenatal contact."[2]

Koro

Another shrinking disease is called koro. This little-known disease strikes mostly South and Southeast Asians and consists of intense and often debilitating anxiety attacks accompanied by an overwhelming fear that the sexual organs are shrinking, dropping off, or being sucked into the abdomen. The patient usually is convinced that, should the genitals do this, death will quickly follow. This psychiatric disorder is believed to be far more common among men (involving the penis and testes) than among women (involving the breasts, vulva, or labia). Medical and behavioral scientists do not know why koro takes the form that it does or why it occurs mainly in Asian countries.

Koro is the Malaysian name for the disease and the accepted medical and behavioral science term. However, in China it is known as *saoyang*, and it is known by a variety of folk names elsewhere. Although anthropologists have written of koro epidemics affecting entire villages, the clinical literature is scant, especially regarding causation. Men suffering from this disease have been described as "immature and dependent, lacking confidence in their own virility and in conflict over the expression of genital impulses."[3] Koro cases have also been described as being "often coincident with fears of the dangers of masturbation or sexual excesses or drug induced."[4]

Koro attacks can last for hours, days, or much longer. Modern treatment consists of drugs and psychotherapy. However, traditional folk treatments can certainly be more colorful, such as efforts made "by family and friends to hold the penis for fear it would slip into the abdomen."[4]

In 1987, the first koro case in an adult, native-born U.S. national was reported by Dr. Maryonda Scher. She describes a koro patient, admitted to a Seattle hospital, as

> *a Caucasian, unmarried man in his mid-twenties with no previous psychiatric history. . . . He came to the hospital complaining that he had been unable to get an erection for the past 4–5 days. He stated, "something is wrong down there. It's shrinking, so I play with it a lot to make sure it's still out." He feared that both testes and penis would disappear into his abdomen. [Furthermore,] since the onset of his difficulty, he had become extremely anxious. He had slept poorly and his thoughts were "delayed and confused." He had told his parents about his trouble 1–2 days before admission, and they responded with confusion and anger*

which increased his terror. . . . [Finally,] the night before
admission, he loaded a shot gun in front of his mother and
mentioned suicide. His sister brought him to hospital the
following morning.[5]

A clinical session with Scher uncovered a troubled and pitiful figure. The patient's eldest brother developed schizophrenia in Vietnam. He and his mother were "especially close." He and his entire family, of which he was the fifth of eight children, all lived in the same house or very nearby. They all practiced the same fundamentalist religion. Scher adds that this patient had always been shy and nervous, had always done poorly in school, had held only occasional jobs, and had been unemployed for three months before hospital admission.[5]

In addition, Scher points out that he was obese, suffered from high blood pressure, consumed large amounts of alcohol daily, and masturbated five or six times a day, although "he was conflicted about his masturbation because his religion prohibited it." Scher notes that her patient "felt that he 'added stripes to Christ's back every time' he did so." Furthermore, the patient was not attracted to men and had always failed in relationships with women. He had given up all hopes of marriage or of ever leaving home. He was hospitalized for thirteen days and given low dosages of psychotherapeutic drugs, along with much reassurance that his symptoms were only imagined. He was an outpatient at the time of Scher's report. And there is one last irony, small but sad. At age twelve, Scher's patient experienced a brief incestuous relationship with his sister—the same one who drove him to the hospital.[5, 6]

The Windigo Psychosis

Among the Algonquian-speaking Native Americans of north-eastern Canada is the belief in the terrible, fearsome monster known as the Windigo. The Windigo is a giant, stonelike creature five yards tall that craves human flesh. The Windigo has a frightening and menacing mouth with tremendous, jagged, razor-sharp teeth. It continually hisses and makes other loud and eerie noises. Its eyes drip blood and are protuberant, rather like those of an owl. Its feet are three feet long, with one great clawed toe. It lives in dark forests and is completely impervious to cold. Killing it is virtually impossible. Once it stalks its victim, the victim has no escape. When a hunter fails to return from a hunting expedition, it is assumed that he has been taken by a Windigo.

Among these people, the Windigo psychosis is the belief that one has been possessed by the spirit of a Windigo. The failure to provide food for one's family—the greatest personal failing and social transgression in this society—is believed to be the cause. Like the Windigo monster itself, Windigo psychotics experience an intense, compulsive desire to eat human flesh. They usually direct their cannibalistic urges toward members of their own family. They will kill and eat their loved ones unless stopped first. They believe that they have lost permanent control over their own actions and that the only solution is death. According to Morton Teicher, in one of the classic works of psychological anthropology, *Windigo Psychosis*, Windigo psychotics often plead for their own destruction and raise no objection to their own execution.[7]

Such cannibalism violates the greatest taboo among the Algonquian-speaking Indians, whose traditional food supply is uncertain, especially during the long winters. Historically, starvation is a constant threat in this part of the world. It is understandable that cannibalistic impulses, conscious or unconscious, are resisted only with discipline.

Susto

Throughout Central America, *susto* is the name given to a mental illness in which a person believes that he or she has lost the vital life force. Sufferers become restless during sleep, listless, and depressed, lose their appetite, neglect dress and personal hygiene, and fail to undertake the normal duties of everyday life. A person can die of susto, and many do. Although they waste away, there is no physical sign of any disease or injury. Sufferers say that susto is caused by a sudden fright or other trauma. Susto is also called *espanto*, *perdida del alma*, or *chibih*.

Anthropologists at the University of California analyzed this intriguing disorder as it is commonly seen in the Mexican state of Oaxaca.[8] Of the forty-eight susto sufferers of varying ages they studied, eight were dead within seven years. This compared with no deaths among the forty-eight non–susto sufferers they studied as a control group. The researchers discovered that the basis for this disease is social, not biological. They theorize that people experience susto when they are unable for some reason to meet the important social expectations placed on them. If they cannot fulfill the role into which they have been socialized, they find escape in illness and eventually in death.[8, 9]

Amok

This psychiatric illness consists of intense brooding followed by aggressive, violent, or even homicidal outbursts. It is often prompted by a perceived insult and apparently afflicts only

Navajo men and men from Laos, the Philippines, Malaysia, Polynesia, Papua New Guinea, and Puerto Rico.

Brain Fag

Brain fag is a psychiatric syndrome reported to be exclusive to West Africa. The sufferer experiences a general sense of "brain fatigue" that makes concentrating and remembering difficult. Interestingly, it is common in university and high school students undergoing extreme mental stress.

Ghost Sickness

Among various Native American tribes, this malady includes bad dreams, physical weakness, confusion, a sense of futility, a sense of danger, loss of appetite, fainting, dizziness, and hallucinations. Ghost sickness is linked to the preoccupation with death and the dead, which is very characteristic of many Native American cultures.

Taijin Kyofusho

Limited to Japan, this psychiatric illness involves an intense fear that a person's body is offensive in appearance, movement, or odor. The sufferer sometimes believes that his or her body can be shrunk by the power of other people looking at it.

Hwa-Byung

In Korea, the suppression of intense anger can bring on an illness that involves insomnia, acute panic, a morbid fear of impending death, indigestion, heart palpitation, and intense aches and pains throughout the body.

Sleeping Blood

Among the Portuguese of the Cape Verde Islands, this malady is known as *sangue dormido*—literally "sleeping blood." When a person has transgressed important social laws, his or her blood can "sleep" in the body. The illness is marked by pain, numbness, paralysis, convulsions, stroke, infection, blindness, heart attack, and miscarriage. Sometimes the brain is believed to be shriveling within the skull.[10]

A lesson for us in all of these illnesses is that we must always look for the social and cultural components in mental disease. Mental disease sometimes is an escape from intense social pressure. For example, anorexia nervosa in Western women may be caused at least in part by their perceived failure to live up to the impossible image of body shape imposed on them.

As is seen from some of these illnesses, death is sometimes preferred to failure.

WHAT CAUSES ALZHEIMER'S DISEASE?

Many researchers believe that dwindling levels of the neurotransmitter acetylcholine may be responsible for the mental deterioration of Alzheimer's disease. Some think that a pill made of nicotinamide adenine dinucleotide (NADH), a substance cells use to produce energy, may help stimulate the production of acetylcholine, halt neuron loss, and stall Alzheimer's disease symptoms. In an Austrian study, patients with Alzheimer's who began taking daily doses of NADH showed improvements in memory after only two weeks.[11]

A NERVE GROWTH FACTOR TO FIGHT ALZHEIMER'S

CytoTherapeutics, a biotechnology company in San Diego, is conducting a large study investigating the efficacy of implanting a natural body chemical called nerve growth factor (NGF) into the brains of Alzheimer's disease sufferers in order to prevent neurons from dying. If NGF works, then the devastating symptoms of Alzheimer's disease could be delayed indefinitely.[12]

ALZHEIMER'S AND THE IMMUNE SYSTEM

No one knows precisely what causes Alzheimer's disease. But a surprising hypothesis is gaining support concerning the progression of Alzheimer's: The brain's immune system may be worsening the course of the disease. Within the brain, bits of a protein (beta-amyloid) build up alongside of brain cells instead of being eliminated by the body as they're supposed to be. They form sheetlike plaques. The immune cells in the brain try to destroy these plaques. As a by-product of the process, toxins are released that destroy healthy brain cells. Thus, Alzheimer's disease may be akin to other autoimmune diseases such as arthritis and lupus.[13]

Chapter 30
The **Shy Brain**

Behavioral scientists call extreme shyness social phobia. Probably 40 percent of people suffer from shyness to varying degrees, with an unknown percentage of these people being social phobics. A 1995 survey in *Psychology Today* found that 48 percent of Americans report they're shy.[1] A 1996 paper at the first Australian conference on social phobia gave a rough estimate that perhaps one in six Australians suffer from full-blown social phobia. If so, then social phobia would be the third most common psychiatric disorder, behind alcoholism and depression.[2] For shy people, life can be excruciatingly painful, yet they may be too shy to admit it.

Social phobia is a persistent fear of one or more situations in which the person is exposed to possible scrutiny by others and fears that he or she may do something or act in a way that will be humiliating or embarrassing. First described in the *British Journal of Psychiatry* in 1970, *social phobia* has been a standard clinical term since 1980.[3]

A situation producing social phobia is called a socially phobic situation (SPS). Researchers tell us that an SPS can be almost any place or forum in which two or more people meet and interact: at work, at school, at meetings, at parties, at sporting or entertainment events, even in the bedroom. That is, an SPS can be any place where one could be seen, judged, and possibly belittled by another. But unless a social phobic reveals his or her fears, we will probably never know their extent. What is completely unthreatening to us may be a torture chamber for someone else.

Nevertheless, the three most common SPSs are writing in front of others, eating in public, and, most importantly of all, public speaking. Public speaking is by far the single most fear-producing social situation. Ironically, humans are the only animals capable of sophisticated speech, yet all too often, public speaking makes us cringe.

Researchers also tell us that when confronted with an SPS, there are three common responses. The first is to avoid the situation, which is almost certainly done whenever possible. The second response is to act in an inhibited fashion with controlled behavior during the SPS until it is finally over. The third response is to show various physical symptoms indicating stress before, during, or after the SPS. These symptoms include blushing, sweating, muscle twitching, trembling, heart palpitations, and urinary urgency. Thus, it seems that possible exposure to the judgment of others and to the risk of mortification that this could bring is enough to cause some of us to literally shake with fright from head to toe.

Interestingly, these physical symptoms can be measured in the laboratory. In one series of experiments at the University of Pittsburgh, when subjects were asked to give an impromptu speech, their systolic blood pressure shot up alarmingly.[4]

Evidence also suggests that social phobia has its roots in early childhood. In fact, the physical symptoms of social phobia can start appearing as early as twenty-one months of age. This was revealed in a Harvard University study of shyness in children. In their six-year study of the heart rates of behaviorally inhibited and non–behaviorally inhibited young children, the Harvard team found that the heart rates of the behaviorally inhibited children (shys and social phobics) were far higher than those of the noninhibited kids. Furthermore, these rates stayed higher in the behaviorally inhibited children at all periods of measurement over the six years.[5]

Studies of how social phobics think confirm that social phobics are terrified of negative evaluations of themselves by others. But this is not the only thing happening in their minds. When surveyed, social phobics also have fewer positive and more negative thoughts than do others. This was the finding of several studies by Dr. Richard G. Heimberg and colleagues.[6]

It is a continuing debate among behavioral scientists as to where shyness ends and social phobia begins. Dr. Samuel Turner and colleagues have attempted to clarify this boundary. But they admit that this is difficult, especially because the same symptoms occur in people classified as either shy or social phobics.[7]

ACCORDING TO Stanford University researchers, shy people have less than normal amounts of the brain chemical dopamine.

Fortunately, counseling and other forms of therapy are useful in treating social phobia. Indeed, "in every case . . .

patients have improved after treatment," according to Dr. Harlan R. Juster and Heimberg.[8] Sometimes psychoactive drugs are necessary, too. For example, a Harvard University Medical School review of the pros and cons of using one such drug, clonazepam (an anticonvulsant), found that this drug is a pretty good treatment.[9]

> THE PART OF your brain just above your left ear governs reading, writing, and speaking.

What may be going wrong in the brain of a social phobic? Dr. James W. Jefferson argues that "several findings suggest that serotonin dysfunction [in the brain] may play at least a partial role in the etiology of social phobia."[10]

But regardless of how many people are shy and what percentage of these are social phobics, one need never be ashamed if one is either or both. Nor should one ever be reluctant to seek help. Never be too shy to ask.[11]

ELECTIVE MUTISM

Halophobia, the fear of public speaking, is the most common phobia seen in adults. But this refers to acts such as delivering a speech on a stage or speaking to a group, not normal conversation. *Elective mutism* is the term that some authorities have given to the reluctance to speak in unfamiliar social situations. This is the person who is always the quietest one in the group. Some experts believe that elective mutism is a separate diagnostic entity in itself, whereas others say it is a symptom of social phobia. Psychiatrists at the U.S. National Institute of Mental Health presented the case of a twelve-year-old girl with elective mutism, reviewed the literature on the subject, and concluded that elective mutism "may be a manifestation of social phobia rather than a separate diagnostic syndrome."[12]

STUTTERING MASKS SOCIAL PHOBIA

Stuttering is a widespread problem in children and adults. But according to a team of Canadian psychiatrists, many adults who stutter really have a problem with social phobia instead. And if a therapist follows the recommendations of the *American Psychiatric Association's Diagnostic and Statistical Manual of Mental Disorders* (DSM-IV, the Bible of psychiatry), the patient is being treated for the wrong thing: "Many adults seeking treatment for stuttering have salient difficulties with social anxiety that prove amenable to cognitive–behavioral interventions. By precluding a diagnosis of social phobia in these patients, DSM-IV may hinder the identification of social anxiety as a source of disability and may limit access to treatment."[13]

THE BRAIN'S STORE AND RECALL HELPERS

Research suggests that separate brain systems store and recall incidents in one's life. And each of these systems relies on its own helper areas that specialize in what happened, where it happened, and when it happened. According to Swedish research on positron emission tomography that measured blood flow to various areas of the brain when stimulated, each prefrontal area of the brain belongs to a general memory network that receives "dispatches" from neural "correspondents" specialized in either contents, location, or time of an event. [14]

EPIDEMIC HYSTERIA

There have been many cases of the phenomenon known as epidemic hysteria. For no apparent reason, a group of people will experience symptoms of illness. This may involve children of an entire school, travelers on a bus, or the whole audience at a rock concert. Besides fainting and hallucinating, symptoms include vomiting, diarrhea, fever, and dehydration. Such epidemics may last several hours or even days. After obvious factors causing the hysteria are ruled out (such as heat stroke or food poisoning), a diagnosis of epidemic hysteria is the diagnosis of last resort. According to Dr. François Sirois:

> The main task [of diagnosis] is an accurate evaluation. The main differential diagnoses are (1) heat stroke, (2) food poisoning, (3) gas intoxication, (4) allergens, (5) infections, usually with a longer incubation period and secondary attack rates in [a] household.

When one person experiences the symptoms, other people, seeing that person, experience the symptoms too. When stress and perhaps moral conflicts are concerned, they identify with the ill person and follow his or her behavior. Sirois adds that an epidemic of hysteria (as opposed to other forms of disturbance) is based on three factors: the group regression, identification with the index cases, and the unconscious nature of the underlying conflicts or fantasies. [15]

Chapter 31
The **Suicidal Brain**

Is there such a thing as the suicidal brain?

Many brain scientists are now convinced that some of us are indeed more likely to commit suicide. That is, we are more inclined toward depression—the leading precursor to suicide—because of our brain's biochemistry. Thus, more and more scientists are coming to believe that the suicidal brain is real.

Research first reported in 1989 showed that the brains of clinically depressed or suicidal people harbor abnormal levels of the brain chemicals serotonin and norepinephrine. Two teams of researchers, one in Philadelphia and the other in Maryland, published articles in the same issue of the *Archives of General Psychiatry* showing that flaws in the brain's serotonin levels are linked to violent suicide attempts and aggression.[1,2]

In 1991, additional findings supported the theory that suicidal behavior is associated with specific biochemical abnormalities in the brain. Researchers showed that the brain cells that regulate the perception of pleasure and pain in suicide victims differ markedly from the same cells in people who die of natural causes.[3]

The U.S.–Israeli research team was the first to look at opioid receptors in the brains of suicide victims. Opioid receptors are located on the surface of certain brain cells. They absorb tiny amounts of an opium-like chemical produced by the brain and play a critical role in pleasure and pain sensations.

The researchers measured opioid receptor concentrations in twelve drug-free and disease-free suicide victims presumed to have been depressed before they died. They discovered an 100 to 800 percent higher concentration of mu receptors (an opioid receptor) and a 50 percent lower concentration of delta receptors (another opioid receptor) compared with those in twelve people who died of other causes.[3]

Scientists admit that they know little about opioid receptor types or the specific brain opioids to which each type responds. However, the findings are all "very interesting," according to Dr. David Baron of the U.S. National Institute of Mental Health in Washington, D.C.[4] He adds that "it makes good sense that there would be or should be an abnormality in the opioid system. You often hear from suicide patients that 'I couldn't take the pain any more,' referring to physical or emotional pain."[4]

A member of the U.S.–Israeli team, Dr. Anat Biegon, says that

We know people suffering from depression have a very high incidence of chronic pain. This may indicate a defect in the opioid system. . . . The essence of depression is anhedonia— an inability to experience pleasure. And opioid receptors are the primary targets of the brain's reward system.[5]

Furthermore, Biegon admits that science cannot yet answer the all-important question of what causes the altered receptor concentrations in a suicide victim's brain. However, clues from animal experiments indicate that opioid receptor concentrations often increase in response to a lack of opioids. Also, environmental and genetic factors may directly affect receptor levels. But so far, this is only informed speculation. Nevertheless, Biegon thinks that, for now at least, "I would say that changes in the opioid system cause depression. . . . It's very possible that they contribute to the syndrome."[5]

The researchers are pressing on with other experiments using traceable antibodies directed against opioid proteins to directly measure opioid concentrations in brains of live people with and without depression.

After these experiments are completed, we may be closer to knowing whether some of us do indeed have a suicidal brain.

If there is a suicidal brain, is it possible to test to see whether you're prone to suicide? Such a test was once thought to be impossible because brain tissue would be needed. However, Illinois researchers have developed a simple blood test that measures blood platelet receptor levels that closely mirror those in the brain's tissues.[6]

In the twenty-first century, such tests will be routine.

Suicide Is Seasonal

Suicide is seasonal. In both the southern and northern hemispheres, the overall suicide rate peaks in spring and summer and drops off in autumn and winter. But it is slightly different in the two hemispheres because the Christmas holiday season—a period of abnormally high suicide rates—is in the summer in the south but in the winter in the north.

Several studies have shown that the level of chemical messengers in the brain that are involved in psychological reactions to various types of stress rise and fall throughout the year according to seasons. The types of stress include those from depression, unemployment, loneliness, and alcoholism.[7]

And It's Also Related to Weather

Research going back to the 1930s has shown that suicide is correlated with stormy weather. According to a classic study by C. A. Mills,

> *1. A strong suggestion of storm effect is seen in the distribution of suicides and homicides in North American cities. The rates are not highest where industrialization is most advanced, but rather where barometric pressure and temperature changes are most frequent and severe. 2. Suicides show a definite time relationship to weather changes as high- and low-pressure centers approach and pass by. With falling pressure and rising temperature, suicides rapidly rise. Most peaks in frequency occur at the time of a low-pressure crisis. With rising pressure and falling temperature few suicides occur.* [8]

WHEN DEPRESSION IS GREATEST, SUICIDE IS LESS

Of course, depression is a red flag warning of possible suicide. However, an ironic oddity of suicide research is the fact that those who are most depressed actually are less likely to commit suicide. In essence, they are so "down" that they cannot even raise a hand against themselves. For example, the most serious schizophrenic patients are most likely to suffer from what is called deficit syndrome. This syndrome involves lack of emotion, lethargy, absence of interest in anything, and a complete disengagement from all human interaction. In one 1994 study, it was reported that among forty-six schizophrenic patients, none with deficit syndrome committed suicide, compared to ten without it who did kill themselves. According to the researchers, ironically, deficit syndrome "shields its bearers from suicide."[9]

THE BRAIN'S ATTENTIONAL BLINK

Does the brain ever take a holiday? In a sense, it does. In fact, the brain takes many thousands of tiny vacations every day, every time we see something. After the brain absorbs visual data—such as a written word or a number on a page—it suffers an "attentional blink" lasting a few hundred milliseconds. During this time, the brain is unable to absorb anything else. Experiments show that during such "blinks," subjects cannot remember information presented to them. To what extent is the brain sleeping on the job? Is information not remembered, or is it not even perceived? In a series of recall tests, researchers have shown that the information is indeed perceived by the brain, but the brain fails to encode it into its short-term memory. At least the brain isn't falling down on the job entirely.[10, 11]

ERGOTISM

Ergotism is a medical condition in which people believe they will soon burst into flames. Sufferers experience excruciating convulsions, severe abdominal pain, and a sensation of being burned alive. Many victims go blind or insane, or they die. Patients have been known to inflict wounds on themselves to "keep the burning sensations away." They are convinced that they will soon be consumed by flames. There is no cure. Ergotism is caused by the poisonous ergot fungus. The fungus infests wheat and rye. When contaminated grain is made into bread, the fungus infects the brain and brings about the ergotism hallucinations. Epidemics of ergotism have involved entire towns, the last documented ergotism epidemic occurring in Pont-Saint-Esprit, France in 1951. As the epidemic spread, several people attempted suicide. One sixty-eight-year-old woman threw herself from a third-floor hospital window in order to escape the flames that she thought were engulfing her.[12]

Chapter 32
The **Thrill-Seeking Brain**

Why do so many of us love thrill-seeking? Why do we so often crave the brain rush of danger? Why do we bungee jump, skydive, mountain climb, skin dive near sharks, drive at high speed, and so on?

Research suggests that we, along with other primates, sometimes crave the arousal of danger.

In the 1970s, I. S. Bernstein reported the results of an experiment on monkeys. Several were placed in a compound with a set of vertical poles for them to climb. One of the poles was electrified at the top. Thus, when a monkey climbed that pole, it suffered a slight shock. It was found that the electrified pole was the most popular. All groups of monkeys observed showed an increase in climbing behavior for that particular pole. But when the power was turned off, that pole became no more or less popular than the other poles. Bernstein concluded that monkeys pursue excitement even if the price is pain. They seek the arousal of danger.[1]

Arousal in humans has been studied since the pioneering work in the 1920s by physiologist Dr. Walter Cannon. When the body is under threat, Cannon discovered the famous fight-or-flight reactions well known today.[2]

Subsequent research showed that arousal could be brought about without a physical threat—indeed, by emotions alone. Sexual arousal is an example. Emotions bring about sexual arousal, which in turn prepares the body for sexual activity.

Symptoms of arousal are intense alertness, pounding of the heart, deepening of breathing, increasing perspiration, drying in the mouth, and so on. Arousal symptoms are controlled by the autonomic nervous system (ANS) working with the reticular activating system (RAS) of the body. The ANS is spread throughout the body and controls "housekeeping" functions of the body such as heart rate. The RAS exists in the brain stem, a small structure at the base of the brain where the spine and brain meet. The RAS operates like a gate and "judges" environmental stimuli. If a stimulus is important enough, the RAS activates the brain's cortex so that closer attention is paid to that particular stimulus. But if a stimulus is unimportant, the RAS allows the cortex to ignore that stimulus.

But why do we crave the arousal of danger?

According to psychologist Dr. Michael Apter, we are danger-seeking animals because it is natural for us to be so. Unlike what Freud believed, we do not crave tranquility. Instead, we lust for excitement in all forms, including dangerous ones.

In *The Dangerous Edge: The Psychology of Excitement*, Apter asserts that our danger seeking is not only pleasurable for us as individuals but also necessary for our evolution. In earlier times, if at least some of the members of our species had not sought to obtain gains, even at the expense of the dangers associated with obtaining such gains, humans would still be living in caves. For example, an early human might have had to choose between attempting to steal food guarded by a lion or starvation. Although individuals undoubtedly perished, there were enough successful risk takers so that the species prospered. Apter believes that the risk-taking brain buzz is nature's extra little stimulus to push us over the edge to take the plunge. Over hundreds of generations, the pleasure from successful gain has evolved such that danger seeking has become an end in itself.

But what puts the brakes on danger lust?

Apter argues that humans have a built-in mechanism that controls their danger seeking. We have what he calls a "protective frame" that involves a balancing act of three behavioral zones of activity. At any given time, we live in one of the three zones:

> **The safety zone,** when we are at no physical risk and experiencing no arousal. An example of this is sitting in a living room lounge chair.
>
> **The danger zone,** when we are at physical risk and experiencing the arousal of flirting with catastrophe. An example of this is driving at high speed.
>
> **The trauma zone,** when we experience the catastrophe that comes from "falling from the danger zone." Driving at high speed causes accidents, resulting in injury or death.[3]

According to Apter, most of us live for most of the time in the safety zone. But we also enjoy living in the danger zone even if we occasionally fall into the trauma zone, just as the monkeys enjoyed climbing the electric pole even after being shocked.

Dr. Apter theorizes that we choose the amount of time we wish to remain in the danger zone by means of our protective frame dividing the danger zone from the trauma zone. Without the protective frame we would have only anxiety: the fear of the trauma awaiting in the trauma zone. We would avoid this. Furthermore, mentally disturbed people often have poorly functioning protective frames. However, Apter maintains that the protective frame allows us to pursue the arousal to the brink of trauma. He calls this "the dangerous edge."[3]

Apter says that

> *this protective frame may come from one's own confidence, the availability of others to help one, the presence of physical aids, and the like. The effect of it is that a person can get very close to trauma without actually being traumatized.*[3]

So when it comes to danger—and our desire for it—the protective frame is like a condom from the psyche.[4]

CAN ALL OUR BRAINS TRAVEL ALONG THE INVISIBLE INFORMATION SUPERHIGHWAY?

Philosopher Carl Jung believed that all humans share a collective unconscious. That idea may not be too far from the truth. Fascinating research reveals that, theoretically at least, all human brains could communicate with each other. Because of the electromagnetic nature of the human brain, the communication would work rather like radio. This is because human brains may operate within a fairly narrow frequency range, perhaps varying by only 0.1 hertz. According to neurologist Dr. Michael A. Persinger,

> Within the last two decades, a potential has emerged which was improbable but which is now marginally feasible. This potential is the technical capability to influence directly the major portion of the approximately six billion brains of the human species.[5]

DOES THE BRAIN MAKE A GREAT ATHLETE?

Perhaps it's brains over brawn after all? Evidence suggests that the reason that some great athletes are superior to others is that their brains are able to produce faster reflexes. Chicago neurologist Dr. Harold Klawans gives the example of Canadian ice hockey star Wayne Gretzky, who has the fastest reflexes that professional neurologists have ever registered. Gretzky has superb "long loop" reflexes (muscle movements triggered by lengthy loops of brain cells). This may be why Gretzky, with lightning speed, can intercept a puck from an opposing player and shoot it past the goalie better than any professional player who ever lived.[6]

Chapter 33
The **Time-Twisted Brain**

Can simply altering our perception of time help diagnose and treat mental illness?

Some behavioral scientists think it can. And this theory is guiding the research of several teams of investigators around the world. Some researchers are building temporal isolation chambers (TICs), placing patients or other subjects inside them, and then studying what happens to behavior and health when time is artificially manipulated. One of the more notable research centers using TICs is at the University of Pennsylvania Hospital in Philadelphia.

As one enters a TIC, at first glance it appears similar to a freshly painted, moderately priced hotel room, complete with a modern bath. But closer study reveals major differences.

There are no windows, the ceiling is covered with panels of lights, and two very thick doors separate it from other rooms.

Inside a TIC, behavioral scientists can create the illusion of fifty-minute hours, thirty-six-hour days, or nights during which the sun shines. They can seemingly twist time in ways found nowhere in nature. By manipulating lights, clocks, temperatures, and other factors in the TIC, scientists hope to alter a subject's perception of time and use the results to diagnose and treat mental illnesses.

Using video cameras, computers, and medical equipment, researchers hope to learn more about anxiety disorders, schizophrenia, depression, sleep disorders and the effects on the human mind and body of shift work, jet lag, and sleep denial.

"The range of things we can study here [at the University of Pennsylvania Hospital's TIC] is staggering," according to Dr. David Dinges. "Living in here is like living in a room sealed off from the outside world—there are no windows, no radios, no telephones, or anything else that allows you to realize the time of day."[1]

Each TIC is carefully shielded from radio waves, changes in temperature, the light of dawn, the noise of morning garbage trucks, the smell of morning coffee—anything that might tip off a subject about the correct time. Furthermore, each TIC is built on springs to prevent subjects from feeling vibrations given off by the rest of the hospital and thereby guessing the approximate time.

It is complete isolation from the outside world, a "timeless chamber" in any real-world sense.

The growing field of chronobiology is the study of how time affects behavior and health. According to Dr. Peter Whybrow, a colleague of Dinges, "the field of chronobiology has gained much momentum in the last ten years. The natural cycles influence people in ways that are not always realized."[2] He adds that there is a growing realization that many mental illnesses, such as manic depression and schizophrenia, may be related to disruptions in natural cycles.[2] By altering the circadian (day–night) cycle in TICs, clinicians theorize that they may be able to treat a patient whose system has somehow become disjointed. They do this through a therapy process of resynchronizing the patient with the real world.

THE WEIGHT ratio of your body to your brain is about forty to one. In dinosaurs, the ratio was much greater. For example, in the apatosaurus, the ratio was 377,000 to one.

Besides the circadian cycle, the lunar (monthly) cycle and the circannual (yearly) cycle are also being studied in investigations at the University of Pennsylvania Hospital. The changing of the seasons and the effects (if any) of the gravitational pull of the Moon on health and behavior are receiving research attention.

Dinges argues that this research is particularly timely as the postindustrial world is rapidly moving toward a twenty-four-hour society. Whereas once most human activity stopped at night, today many businesses, factories, stores, and even the world's stock markets operate around the clock. What will be the effect of these changes on the human body?

Dinges estimates that one quarter of all workers in industrial nations now work occasionally on the night shift. He observes that "although there is no way to stop the coming of the 24-hour society since it is cheaper for most industries to operate 24 hours a day, we have to understand people's biological limits. And we have to use this knowledge to minimize the

YOUR BRAIN tissue under a microscope is the color of pink cotton candy.

disruptions to people."[1] He notes, "in truth, the 24-hour society is already here."[3]

Dinges says that many companies rotate the roster of workers once a week. Often, this switching of workers from the afternoon to the morning shift, and then to the night shift, seriously disrupts people's biological cycles, causing stress, reduced productivity, and accidents. He believes that we must understand far more about this process. His own work aims at learning how to better identify the people who are most susceptible to accidents late at night. For example, if a test could be developed, it might be possible to screen out airline pilots or nuclear power plant operators who would be most prone to falling asleep on the job.

And as Dinges observes, increased knowledge about the circadian cycle is already proving helpful in telling us what time of day patients should receive medications in order to maximize their effectiveness.

And as to what other new insights the TICs research may reveal about human behavior and health, Dinges believes, only time will tell.

Dr. Ron Grunstein, a Sydney sleep disorder specialist, says that temporal isolation chambers "are very useful as research tools." However, he adds that so far, there are no hard data to substantiate claims that TICs will cure such conditions as schizophrenia. Such conclusions would come only after a great deal of rigorous research and over a long period of time.[4]

CAN WE LEARN UNDER ANESTHESIA?

There is strong evidence that perception and some form of learning occur even when a person is clinically unconscious. Perhaps this means that consciousness is not essential to the learning process. Does the human brain "sleep on a problem"? Consider this from University of Sheffield psychologist Dr. Jackie Andrade:

A patient undergoing surgery with general anesthesia can reasonably expect to remember nothing about the operation on recovery. Cases of direct recall of intraoperative events have been reported, but these are rare and are nearly always attributable to faulty anesthetic technique or apparatus failure. However, a study by Levinson in 1965 alerted people to the possibility that information processes may continue despite clinically adequate anesthesia. In this study, he subjected 10 dental surgery patients to a mock crisis in which, mid-operation, the anesthetist exclaimed, "Stop the operation, I don't like the patient's color. His/her lips are much too blue. I'm going to give a little oxygen." Subsequently, patients had no recall for the "crisis." However, under hypnosis one month later, four of them repeated verbatim the anesthetist's exclamation and four showed evidence of partial recall.[5, 6]

NEURODEGENERATIVE DISEASE: ALL IN THE FAMILY

When parents pass on the wrong genes, a tragic neurode-generative disease can occur. Flawed genes result in defi-ciencies of specific enzymes. The lack of those enzymes allows toxins to build up in the blood. These toxins grad-ually accumulate in the liver, spleen, bones, and—most destructively—the brain. For example, a neurodegenera-tive disease such as Tay–Sachs disease can destroy a healthy-looking infant. The child will lapse into a coma and die within a few years, and nothing can be done.[7]

Chapter 34
The **Traumatized Brain**

Research reveals that a single instance of overwhelming terror can alter the chemistry of the brain. Such terror can make people more sensitive to adrenaline surges, which can have a debilitating effect that can last for decades.[1]

Scientists have observed for some time that sensitivity to adrenaline surges is a major factor in posttraumatic stress disorder (PTSD). In PTSD a person can experience normal events as repetitions of the original trauma. PTSD affects disaster survivors, combat veterans, crime victims, and millions of others around the world.

Now, there is direct evidence that PTSD has a biological basis.

Several studies suggest that specific sites in the brain undergo these changes. And some scientists think that these latest findings may open the door for the development of medications to blunt the biological changes in PTSD.

One of these scientists is Dr. Dennis Charney at Yale University. He notes,

> *Victims of a devastating trauma may never be the same biologically. It does not matter if it was the incessant terror of combat, torture, or repeated abuse in childhood, or a one-time experience, like being trapped in a hurricane or almost dying in an auto accident. All uncontrollable stress can have the same biological impact.*[2]

Charney adds that people usually have to experience catastrophic stress in order for the brain changes to occur. Such stress would have to be an overwhelming threat to life or safety and one over which they have no control. Interestingly, less severe stress, such as that caused by financial problems or even the natural death of a loved one, does not seem to trigger the biological changes.

In general, the more intense the trauma and the longer it lasts, the more likely it is to result in PTSD. However, researchers are still puzzled about why some people exposed to a catastrophe develop symptoms of PTSD, whereas others exposed to the identical event do not. And another puzzle is why symptoms can last forty years or longer in some people, but in others they clear up either spontaneously or through therapy.

According to Charney, evidence for the biological changes has been growing since the mid-1980s. He cites laboratory experiments on animals subjected to stress. Notwithstanding the ethical considerations, such experiments often involve electric shocks that the animals cannot escape, while their brain activity is calmly studied.

The main changes observed have been in the way in which and rate at which the brain secretes chemicals it normally produces under stress. Changes occur in three ways. First, change occurs in the locus caeruleus. This is a structure that regulates the brain's secretion of two chemicals called catecholamines. Both are hormones that mobilize the body for an emergency. In a sense, the locus caeruleus becomes hyperactive and secretes too much of the hormones, even in situations that hold little or no threat.

Second, change occurs in the form of increases in the secretion of corticotropin-releasing factor. This is another hormone that mobilizes the body to meet an emergency. It is regulated by the brain circuitry linking the pituitary gland with the hypothalamus (a structure in the brain's emotional center). Again, the increased secretions alert the body for emergencies that, in the case of PTSD, just are not there.

Third, change occurs in the opioid system of the brain, making it hyperactive as well. This can have the effect of blunting pain. Indeed, this brain change may account for the emotional numbing symptom so often reported in people with PTSD. Ironically, such emotional numbing means that the sufferer may have an impaired ability to experience tender feelings.[2]

Dr. Matthew Friedman believes that such findings may hold a promise of relief for those with PTSD. He notes that "understanding the brain as the basis of post-traumatic stress can help us design a medication that reverses these changes."[3]

As Dr. Lennis Echterling says, "Being the victim . . . is not a single point in time; it is an on-going condition that goes on for months and even years after the disaster."[4]

Research suggests that it is not only the immediate survivors of PTSD who suffer psychological damage.

Primary survivors (those who escape death) often have physical injuries such as burns, broken bones, bleeding, and shock. It is common for such injuries to cause later psychological problems, especially if they result in disfigurement or continual pain.

Primary survivors often experience serious psychological trauma, with many developing persistent and profound psychological disorders, even if they suffered no physical injuries at all. Hysteria, anxiety, anger, depression, and guilt are common in primary survivors. In fact, research demonstrating this reaction goes back at least to 1944 with the classic Lindemann study concerning the survivors of the famous 1942 Coconut Grove nightclub fire in Boston, in which 491 people died.[5]

Nevertheless, serious psychological trauma can also be suffered by people nowhere near the disaster site. Secondary survivors (bereaved families and friends of those killed) are very much disaster victims. Much recent research verifies this.

A team of Minnesota researchers summarized much of the research on secondary survivors. They claim that the sudden and violent nature of disasters, particularly airplane crashes, intensifies risks to the survivor's psychological health:

> *Those who are exposed to air disasters may be especially vulnerable because of the sudden and violent nature of the event. . . . [And] there is evidence that sudden, unanticipated death is more acutely stressful and disruptive than death that is expected. The very suddenness of air disaster deaths thus increases the risk of psychological injury for the families and close friends of victims.[6]*

Furthermore, the researchers point out that the initial death notification is often harsh, impersonal, and shattering, worsening the psychological scarring. It is "often made by telephone, as anxious relatives call seeking information about their loved ones. Families and friends may present themselves at the accident scene, seeking information and displaying a variety of stress or grief reactions."[6]

In addition, the researchers add that the timing of disasters, so often bitterly tragic, worsens the survivor's trauma: "Timing is sometimes cruel as when an air disaster occurs during a holiday season and expectations of joyful reunions are destroyed in seconds."[6] For example, when a U.S. Army charter flight crashed near Gander, Newfoundland just before Christmas 1985, killing all 256 on board, families received the news in a large hall where they had assembled for a "welcome home" holiday celebration. The room was filled with colorful banners, decorations, and excited children. A study from the Walter Reed Army Institute of Research showed that this setting "contributed to an intensified sense of shock, disbelief, and sense of loss that still persists in the cases of certain next-of-kin."[7]

For several years now, behavioral studies have highlighted the fact that disaster workers are also at significant psychological risk. Primary responders (firefighters, police officers, ambulance personnel, doctors, nurses, and morgue staff) are exposed to profoundly disturbing stimuli—gruesome sights, sounds, and smells—that often remain all their lives. Studies show that this is exacerbated when, first, workers see themselves as similar to the victims and form a personal identification with them and, second, workers continue to toil long beyond their normal endurance limits (a common occurrence in disasters).

According to the Minnesota researchers, air crashes often

result in badly mutilated and fragmented bodies scattered over a wide area. For instance, in the Gander crash, only three of the 256 recovered bodies were intact enough to be viewed by relatives, and many body parts were never found at all. "Such circumstances prolong the body recovery and identification operations for workers, increasing their exposure to traumatic stimuli."[6]

Secondary responders (those providing subsequent assistance to primary or secondary survivors) are also very much at psychological risk. For example, in the aftermath of the 1977 Granville train disaster in Sydney, a team of researchers discovered that depression, feelings of helplessness, and disorientation were reported in workers whose function was to provide emotional support to bereaved families.[8]

After the 1983 Ash Wednesday bush fires in Adelaide, researchers discovered that intense and intimate involvement between helpers and victims increased sleep disturbances, fatigue, and even muscle tension. In fact, this was particularly so for those providing emotional support and counseling.[9]

Moreover, the Minnesota researchers report that in a study of rescue workers involved in the 1985 Dallas–Fort Worth plane crash, perhaps surprisingly, "those who worked primarily with families of victims displayed more symptoms than any other group."[6]

Dr. Beverley Raphael, author of *When Disaster Strikes*,[10] argues that there are three primary sources of stress for disasters helpers:

The close encounter with death, reminding helpers of their own vulnerability.

The sharing of the anguish of victims and their families, which often results in a close empathic identification.

The role ambiguity and role conflict.[10]

There are other psychological victims of disasters. These include leaders of response teams, community leaders, and, in the case of air crashes, airline staff and airport personnel.[10]

The Minnesota researchers report numerous examples. After one major air disaster that took more than two hundred lives, an airline official had to walk through a temporary morgue to get to the only available telephone. The horrific sight of body parts of women and children was so terrible that the official needed mental health therapy afterwards.

A ticket clerk still remembers the faces of the mother and her two young children whom he squeezed aboard a flight at the last minute—a flight that later crashed, killing all 275 passengers.[6]

Ironically, research shows that even the behavioral scientists who study disasters have not been immune to such psychological traumas.[6]

The victims of disasters are many.[11, 12]

Another form of psychological trauma to the brain comes as a result of long-term imprisonment suffered by one who does not deserve it, such as a political prisoner or a prisoner of war (POW).

For example, in the extraordinary event that prisoners of war are held against their will for decades, such prisoners are likely to suffer great emotional trauma. This trauma probably would persist for the remainder of the person's life. Indeed, it is almost impossible to imagine an imprisonment more shattering to the human psyche.

Research shows that when one is a POW for even a short period of time, the psychological damage is massive and long-lasting.

Among U.S. soldiers taken captive during the Korean War,

as many as nine out of ten survivors suffered from PTSD and other mental health problems more than thirty-five years after their release. This was the finding of New Orleans researchers.[13, 14] Their research continued with returnees from the Gulf War.[15]

IN 1938, AN Italian psychiatrist by the name of Ugo Certry performed the first electric shock treatment. The patient spoke incoherently in nonsense syllables before the treatment. After the first wave of electricity, the patient burst into song. After the second shock, the patient clearly spoke: "Stop! Are you trying to kill me?" Certry concluded that the treatment should cease, the patient was cured, and a new mental health therapy was born.

Surviving U.S. POWs released by North Korea in the early 1950s numbered about 3,200. While imprisoned, these men faced brutal conditions, including random killings, torture, forced marches, solitary confinement for months, near starvation, and frequent hostile interrogations.

The New Orleans researchers intensively studied twenty-two of these former POWs many years after release. The team concluded that such "intense, prolonged stress may cause remarkably long-lasting psychiatric disorders in almost anyone, regardless of their initial psychological health."[13]

The persistent symptoms of PTSD and other mental health problems experienced by the POWs included recurring memories and dreams of wartime traumas, emotional detachment from loved ones, extreme suspicion of others, difficulty concentrating, anxiety disorders such as panic attacks, and severe depression.

Their experiences of captivity rendered many former POWs incapable of simple functioning as normal human beings. In what is as ironic as it is tragic, upon their return to freedom, some had to be confined yet again—this time for their own safety—in psychiatric facilities.

The Korean War POWs that the New Orleans researchers studied had spent an average of only twenty-eight months in captivity. Most were psychologically scarred despite their relatively brief imprisonment.

By contrast, any Vietnam War POWs imprisoned for twenty to thirty years seem to have survived a profoundly worse situation. However, the degree to which they have been psychologically scarred and their chances for recovery are open to speculation because studies are lacking on people confined in this way for so long.

Nevertheless, several factors indicate that these POWs are at much greater risk of permanent psychological damage than either those experiencing a shorter POW confinement or those serving a normal twenty- to thirty-year sentence in a prison in their own country.

Soldiers are trained to fight. They are not trained to be captured. Thus, upon being taken as a POW, the soldier is left without norms to guide behavior. Nearly a century of behavioral science research tells us that the longest periods of "normlessness" place the greatest stress on the individual. Does one resist and risk death? Does one collaborate to survive, even at the risk cowardice? How does one come to terms with being continually under threat of death, seemingly unendingly? How does one cope without rights, without a useful role, without loved ones, without country, without means of communication, without hope?[13]

The Vietnam POWs would have experienced an almost unprecedented length of time enduring maximum at-risk status.

Behavioral science also tells us that if one wants to destroy another's mind and spirit, merely confining them apart from their fellows usually does the job. Humans are social beings. Total denial of our social needs, cutting us off from our own kind, is perhaps the greatest nonphysical form of torture known. One can endure pain but never loneliness. This is why solitary confinement is such a feared punishment for prisoners already in prison. This is also why fundamental values can be altered and madness provoked in those interned alone. Testimony to this is Arthur Koestler's *Darkness at Noon* (1941) and even Aleksandr Solzhenitsyn's *One Day in the Life of Ivan Denisovich* (1962). On the other side of this, a primary message of Agnes Newton Keith's *Three Came Home* (1946) is that, despite the physical horrors of a Japanese POW camp, it was endurable because one shared the horrors with others.

Prolonged imprisonment without knowledge as to when the confinement will end causes the person to lose all normal perspective. Hard labor, a harsh climate, meager dwellings, poor food, foreign surroundings, and lack of a sense of time are defeating and, over twenty or thirty years, devastating.

For the Vietnam War POWs, it will be a long road back.[16]

COMPASSION FATIGUE

The study of traumatic stress has usually focused on the PTSD afflicting people affected by a shocking event. Secondary PTSD occurs in those who suffer traumatic stress from providing help for those with PTSD. This would include disaster relief workers, firefighters, police rescue workers, Red Cross workers, doctors, nurses, ambulance personnel, and crisis and trauma counselors. Another term for secondary PTSD is *compassion fatigue,* that which is suffered by those who treat the traumatized.[17]

THE PROGNOSIS HAS IMPROVED FOR THOSE WITH SPINAL CORD INJURIES

The spinal cord carries messages from the brain to the entire body. Damage to the spinal cord, from an auto accident or a sports injury, for instance, can cause paralysis and impair many body processes and functions. Spinal cord injuries cause patients to suffer severe urinary tract infections, respiratory problems, pneumonia, and so on. In previous decades the prognosis was poor for their recovery. But today, 90 percent or more of patients admitted to hospital with spinal cord injuries eventually leave the hospital. Their life expectancy now exceeds sixty years.

The reason why the prognosis has improved for those with spinal cord injuries is that doctors now administer drugs immediately after the injury. For example, studies show that when one steroid drug, methylprednisolone, is given within eight hours after the injury, patients are three times more likely to recover body functions than those not receiving the drug.

Researchers are now experimenting with ways to repair and regrow damaged nerve cells. In 1996, Swedish neurologists successfully reconnected the spinal cords of rats, using a chemical "glue" and cells from the rats' chests, with the result that the rats could move their legs again.[18]

ELECTROCONVULSIVE THERAPY

Do you think electric shocks are a thing of the past for psychiatric patients? Think again. More than 100,000 people receive electroconvulsive therapy (ECT), otherwise known as electric shock treatment, every day in the United States alone.[19]

Chapter 35
The **TV Brain**

R esearch suggests that excessive amounts of TV watching
physically shape the child's brain.

This finding is causing real concern among child development experts. They worry about the subtle effects of heavy TV
watching on the child's ability to learn. Experts are wondering
whether too much time spent watching TV might crowd out
time in the child's life needed for the vital activities of thinking, reflection, reading, conversation, self-generated play, and
human interaction. Their warning is clear: In a child's life, TV
is to learning what junk food is to health.

How is the TV brain created? According to noted learning
specialist Dr. Jane Healy,[1] the child's growing brain can be
physically shaped by TV just as the brain is shaped by other
repeated experiences. The idea here is that the growing brain

interacts with the environment in determining which sets of the brain's synaptic
connections are strengthened and preserved and which are weakened or lost
altogether.

TV programs artificially manipulate
the brain into paying attention through the
use of frequent visual and auditory
changes. Healy claims that TV programs
and advertisements, including those
designed specifically for children, "are
planned to capitalize on the brain's involuntary response to
zooms, pans, loud noises, and bright colors, keeping it unnatu-
rally alerted—but at a responding level rather than at a thinking level."[1]

The cumulative effect of this TV manipulation produces
the TV brain, a brain geared to television but possibly little else.

The TV brain is created in much the same way as lazy eye
can result in blindness. If a child suffers from lazy eye (ambly-
opia), for a time a patch is worn over the good eye to force the
lazy eye to work normally. Otherwise, the work of both eyes
will be done by only one. If that happens, the brain eventually
regards the lazy eye as useless. The brain may then shut it
down, and blindness in that eye could result.

According to Healy,

*The neurological foundations for reading comprehension,
analytic thinking, utilization of "literate" syntax, sustained
attention, and problem-solving thus depend on certain types
of experiences in the everyday environment. Because this
"plasticity" of the brain appears to extend even into adoles-*

cence, we must question the quality of stimulation available to young people in our fast-paced media age.[1]

Healy agrees that research also has found that extensive television viewing may reduce a child's attention span:

Studies in which children watch fast-paced programs and then perform tasks such as reading or solving complex puzzles show reduced ability to stick with the task. Sustained problem-solving, planning, organizing ideas, and reading comprehension, especially may be affected over the long term.[1]

Moreover, Healy contends that research demonstrates that TV requires no active problem–solving or language expression:

The effects on the human brain of this receptive medium may be most apparent in language development. While TV adds some vocabulary knowledge and information, it does not develop syntactic skills, speaking and writing skills, or the ability to organize the bits of information gained.[1]

Healy also warns that TV

may have hypnotic and possibly neurologically addictive effects. Television may change the frequency of electrical impulses in the brain to block active mental processing by producing a preponderance of slow (alpha) waves, classically associated with lack of mental activity. No one has investigated whether persistent viewing invariably changes brain patterns, but we know that alpha levels can be altered by training. Moreover, the longer a look at TV continues, the greater the probability it will be maintained. Thus, if children get "glued" to the set during a program, they are more likely to remain fixated when the scene breaks to a commercial.[1]

If Healy and others are correct, then they have found a possible explanation for an increasingly common observation of teachers (an observation also backed up by the findings of researchers): Compared with students in previous decades, students today do not think as well. They seem to have shorter attention spans, diminished capacity to stick with a problem, reduced comprehension of the complexities of language, faltering oral expression, and lowered listening abilities. However, at the same time, TV and video watching and video game playing by children have increased.

By the age of five, the height of the brain's critical period for cognitive and language development, the average Australian child watches approximately twenty-eight hours per week of TV and videos. Primary school students see about twenty-five hours, and high school students see about twenty-eight.

Although their view is controversial, Healy and others are convinced that poorer thinking is caused by more TV watching. They stress that the development of the TV brain begins in early childhood. Thus, if we are going to do something about it, we had better do it early.

Animal studies tend to back the claims of Healy and others. Anatomist Marian Diamond argues that "the brain's 'hardwiring' is affected by different types of stimulation."[2] Diamond's research on the brains of rats (not far removed from kids as a species, some parents would say) shows that a lack of healthy stimulation limits the growth of a rat's cerebral cortex.

Diamond's laboratory experiments involved separating a

family of rats, placing one group in an isolated cage while keeping a larger group in a cage with stimulating toys. It was found that the stimulated rats had larger cortices, larger nerve cell bodies, and larger blood vessels in the brain.

Diamond does not draw direct parallels between her rat experiments and experiments of children watching TV. She points out that she tried moving the cage of isolated rats closer to the cage with the stim

> YOUR BRAIN cells move information very, very fast. However, today's computer switches typically transmit data 100,000 times faster than do brain neurons.

ulated rats, "where they could watch but not participate." The result: still no additional cortex growth for the isolated rats.[2]

How can we protect our children from developing a TV brain?

Turning off the TV set is one solution. Healy suggests another:

> *Children's mental habits are changing at least partially because of television and video screens. Simply to lament these changes and wish for "the good old days" is useless. Because growing brains are still malleable during school years, schools must adapt to their students' needs with well-planned educational programs, including those in "visual literacy," that focus on language and listening skills, mental organization, and analytic thinking.*[1]

When trying to overcome the scourge of the TV brain, as with the breaking of any habit, it could be a case of mind over matter.[3]

DO SUBLIMINAL MESSAGES SINK IN?

Can Big Brother infiltrate our TV sets with subliminal messages? Can advertisers drive us to blindly buy their products? "No." At least this is according to researchers from the University of Washington. They've found that subliminal messages can affect the way we think, but they are so fleeting that they are highly unlikely to influence behavior. They conducted an experiment in which 481 subjects had to rapidly classify simple words shown on a screen that had been preceded by an additional word flashed on the screen subliminally. Some subliminally flashed words helped the subject in the classification task, others did not. It was discovered that the subliminally flashed word influenced correct responses only for about one tenth of a second. After that time, the subjects had to classify from scratch, and any effect disappeared. It was as if they had not seen the word at all. The researchers describe this as "the response window." When it comes to subliminal messages, it seems that this window is almost entirely shut.[4, 5]

THE BRAIN TUNER

Cerebrex is the brainchild of Yoshiro NakaMats, a Tokyo inventor. NakaMats starts each day by sitting in his invention for twenty to thirty minutes. Special short-frequency waves are transmitted through his feet, causing blood to rush to his head, which in turn brings more oxygen to the brain, giving a relaxed, euphoric feeling. After being caressed at the same time with alpha waves and the gentle trickling sound of a stream, NakaMats says his brain feels as if he had just awakened from eight hours of sleep. All of this is supposed to erase fatigue, help you think better, prevent Alzheimer's disease, and increase memory, creativity, and sexual potency. Already available in Japan, Cerebrex is found in offices or in "brain-tuning" centers, where several of the chairs are lined up as in a beauty parlor.[6]

Afterword:
The Deal's Still On

We hope you liked *The Odd Brain*. It's the latest in the series of "Odd Books" by Dr. Stephen Juan. The first was *The Odd Body*, also published by Andrews McMeel. The "Odd Books" prove that just about anything can get published these days! If you enjoy these books, let Andrews McMeel know.

Some of you may have read *The Odd Body* and remembered the deal offered in the back of that book. The response to the deal was very gratifying. Letters and e-mails came from all over the world and continue to come. Well, the deal's still on. If you have an OBQ—Odd Body Question—that you'd like answered (or artfully dodged), send it to us. Send in more than one if you wish. We'd love to try to answer all of them. If you are the first reader we receive the question from and if your question is chosen for inclusion in the next book, your name will be included at the bottom of the question as it appears in the book. We'll even send you a free copy of the book to express our thanks. If you are the second, third, or subsequent reader we receive the question from, we'll at least acknowledge you in the Acknowledgments at the front of the book. Just think: immortality in print!

We also write a weekly international syndicated newspaper column. Let your local newspaper know. You can then read Odd Body Questions answered every week.

Send your OBQs to

Dr. Stephen Juan
Faculty of Education and Social Work
University of Sydney
New South Wales 2006 Australia
E-mail: s.juan@edfac.usyd.edu.au

Notes

Chapter 1: The Antiseptic Brain

1   M. Diamond, A. Scheibel, G. Murphy, and T. Harvey, "On the brain of a scientist: Albert Einstein," *Experimental Neurology*, 1985, vol. 88, pp. 198–204. (Dr. Marian Diamond is an anatomist at the University of California at Berkeley. Dr. Arnold Scheibel is a psychiatrist at the University of California at Los Angeles.)

2   S. Juan, "Einstein's brain was doing the washing," *The Sydney Morning Herald*, February 8, 1990, p. 12.

3   J. Herbst, *Bioamazing: A Casebook of Unsolved Human Mysteries*, Atheneum, New York, 1985, p. 12.

4   P. Whitfield, *The Human Body Explained*, Henry Holt, New York, 1995, p. 73. (Dr. Philip Whitfield is an expert in natural science at King's College, University of London.)

5   Interview with L. Squire, February 14, 1997. (Dr. Larry Squire is a neuroscientist at the University of California at San Diego.)

6   J. Newberger, "New brain development research," *Young Children*, May 1997, pp. 4–9.

Chapter 2: Asperger's Disorder

1   S. Baron-Cohen, "An assessment of violence in a young man with Asperger's syndrome," *Journal of Child Psychology and Psychiatry*, 1988, vol. 29, no. 3, pp. 351–360. (Dr. Simon Baron-Cohen is a psychiatrist at the St. Mary's Hospital Medical School in London.)

2   E. Susman, "How to tell Asperger's from autism," *The Brown University Child and Adolescent Behavior Letter*, January 1996, pp. 1, 6. (Dr. Edward Susman is a psychologist at the Bradley Hospital in Providence, Rhode Island.)

3   I. Everall and A. LeCouteur, "Firesetting in an adolescent boy with Asperger's syndrome," *British Journal of Psychiatry*, 1990, vol. 157, pp. 284–287. (Dr. I. Everall and Dr. A. LeCouteur are psychiatrists at the Institute of Psychiatry in London.)

4   S. Davies, D. Bishop, A. Manstead, and D. Tantam, "Face perception in children with autism and Asperger's syndrome," *Journal of Child Psychology and Psychiatry*, 1994, vol. 35, pp. 1033–1057. (Dr. S. Davies and colleagues are from the University of Manchester.)

5   J. McKelvey, R. Lambert, L. Mottron, and M. Shevell, "Right hemi-
     sphere dysfunction in Asperger's syndrome," *Journal of Child Neurology*,
     1995, vol. 10, pp. 310–314. (Dr. J. R. McKelvey and colleagues are from
     the Department of Neurology and Neurosurgery at McGill University.)

6   I. Fukunishi, "Social desirability and alexithymia," *Psychological Reports*,
     1994, vol. 75, pp. 835–838. (Dr. Isao Fukunishi is a psychiatrist at the
     Tokyo Institute of Psychiatry.)

7   S. Juan, "Why John bashed Betty," *Australian DR Weekly*, August 31,
     1990, p. 25.

8   Dr. David Rosenhan is a psychiatrist at Stanford University.

9   H. Eysenck and M. Eysenck, *Mindwatching: Why We Behave the Way We
     Do*, Multimedia Books, London, 1994, pp. 67–68.

Chapter 3: Body Dysmorphic Disorder

1   K. Phillips, "Body dysmorphic disorder: The distress of imagined ugli-
     ness," *American Journal of Psychiatry*, 1991, vol. 148, pp. 1138–1149. (Dr.
     Katharine Phillips is a psychiatrist at the Harvard Medical School.)

2   K. Phillips, "Body dysmorphic disorder: Diagnosis and treatment of
     imagined ugliness," *Journal of Clinical Psychiatry*, 1996, vol. 57, suppl. 8,
     pp. 61–65.

3   O. Brawman-Mintzer, R. Lydiard, K. Phillips, A. Morton, V. Czepowicz,
     N. Emmanuel, G. Villareal, M. Johnson, and J. Ballenger, "Body dysmor-
     phic disorder in patients with anxiety disorders and major depression: A
     comorbidity study," *American Journal of Psychiatry*, 1995, vol. 152, pp.
     1665–1667. (Dr. O. Brawman-Mintzer is from the Medical University
     of South Carolina in Charleston.)

4   K. Phillips and S. Taub, "Skin picking as a symptom of body dysmorphic
     disorder," *Psychopharmacological Bulletin*, 1995, vol. 31, pp. 279–288.

5   N. Schmidt and P. Harrington, "Cognitive–behavioral treatment of
     body dysmorphic disorder: A case report," *Journal of Behavioral Therapy
     and Experimental Psychiatry*, 1995, vol. 26, pp. 161–167. (Dr. N. B.
     Schmidt and Dr. P. Harrington are psychiatrists from the Uniformed
     Services University of the Health Sciences in Bethesda, Maryland.)

6   Interview with E. Hollander cited in B. Bower, "Deceptive appearances:
     Imagined physical defects take an ugly personal toll," *Science News*, July
     15, 1995, pp. 40–41. (Dr. Eric Hollander is a psychiatrist from Mount
     Sinai Hospital in New York.)

7   S. Juan, "When beauty sees a beast," *The Sydney Morning Herald*, April 23, 1992, p. 16.

8   H. Marano, "What killed Margaux Hemingway?," *Psychology Today*, December 1996, pp. 48–51, 75, 78.

9   B. McEwen and H. Schmeck, *The Hostage Brain*, Rockefeller University Press, New York, 1994, pp. 6–7. (Dr. Bruce McEwen is the head of the Hatch Laboratory of Neuroendocrinology at Rockefeller University in New York. Harold Schmeck is the former national science correspondent for *The New York Times*.)

10   Interview with by M. Merzenich cited in E. Ubell, "Secrets of the brain," *Parade*, February 9, 1997, pp. 20–22. (Dr. Michael Merzenich is a neurologist at the University of California at San Francisco.)

Chapter 4: The Brain of the Vampire

1   Interview with D. Dolphin, July 10, 1997. (Dr. David Dolphin is a professor of biochemistry at the University of British Columbia in Vancouver.)

2   D. Dolphin, "Porphyria, vampires, and werewolves: The aetiology of European metamorphosis legends," paper presented to the meeting of the American Association for the Advancement of Science, Washington, D.C., 1985, pp. 1–9.

3   H. Sandvik and A. Baerheim, "Does garlic protect against vampires? An experimental study," *Tidsskrift for den Norske Laegeforening*, 1994, vol. 114, no. 30, pp. 3583–3586. (Dr. H. Sandvik and Dr. A. Baerheim are from the School of Medicine at the University of Bergen.)

4   S. Juan, *Only Human: Why We React, How We Behave, What We Feel*, Random House Australia, Sydney, 1990, pp. 117–119.

5   R. Gottlieb, "The legend of the European vampire. Object loss and corporeal preservation," *Psychoanalytic Study of the Child*, 1994, vol. 49, pp. 465–480. (Dr. R. M. Gottlieb is a psychiatrist at the New York Psychoanalytic Institute.)

6   P. Jaffe and F. DiCataldo, "Clinical vampirism: Blending myth and reality," *Bulletin of the American Academy of Psychiatry and the Law*, 1994, vol. 22, no. 4, pp. 533–544. (Dr. P. D. Jaffe and Dr. F. DiCataldo are psychiatrists from the University of Geneva.)

7   R. McCully, "Vampirism: Historical perspective and underlying process in relation to a case of auto-vampirism," *Journal of Nervous and Mental Disease*, 1964, vol. 139, pp. 440–452.

8   M. Newton, "Written in blood: A history of human sacrifice," *Journal of Psychohistory*, 1996, vol. 24, no. 2, pp. 104–131.

9   J. Raines, L. Raines, and M. Singer, "Dracula. Disorders of the self and borderline personality organization," *Psychiatric Clinics of North America*, 1994, vol. 17, pp. 811–826. (Dr. J. M. Raines and colleagues are psychiatrists from the Psychiatric Institute of Pennsylvania in Philadelphia.)

10   American Psychiatric Association, *Diagnostic and Statistical Manual of Mental Disorders*, 4th ed., American Psychiatric Association, Washington, D.C., 1994, p. 654.

Chapter 5: The Brain of the Werewolf

1   C. Jung, *Collected Works*, vol. 17, Routledge and Kegan Paul, London, 1954.

2   K. Jaspers, *General Psychopathology*, 7th ed., Manchester University Press, Manchester, 1959.

3   P. Coll, G. O'Sullivan, and P. Browne, "Lycanthropy lives on," *British Journal of Psychiatry*, 1985, vol. 147, pp. 201–202. (Dr. Patrick Coll and colleagues are psychiatrists from the Cork Regional Hospital in Wilton, Ireland.)

4   P. Keck, H. Pope, J. Hudson, S. McElroy, and A. Kulick, "Lycanthropy: Alive and well in the twentieth century," *Psychological Medicine*, 1988, vol. 18, pp. 113–120. (Dr. Paul Keck and colleagues are psychiatrists from the Harvard Medical School.)

5   K. Koehler, H. Ebel, and D. Vatzopoulos, "Lycanthropy and demonomania: Some psychopathological issues," *Psychological Medicine*, 1990, vol. 20, pp. 629–633. (Dr. K. Koehler and colleagues are from the University Psychiatric Clinic at the University of Bonn.)

6   P. Sirota and K. Schild, "Animal metamorphosis (lycanthropy) still exists," *Harefuah*, 1994, vol. 126, suppl. 2, pp. 88–91.

7   S. Juan, "Lycanthropy: It brings out the animal in you," *The Sydney Morning Herald*, July 9, 1992, p. 10.

8   K. Creed, "Werewolves Anonymous," *Weekly World News,* October 22, 1996, p. 38.

9   D. Radin and D. Ferrari, "Effects of consciousness on the fall of the dice: A meta-analysis," *Journal of Scientific Exploration*, 1991, vol. 5, no. 1, pp. 61–65.

10   Research by D. Radin and D. Ferrari cited in W. Corliss, *Science Frontiers*, The Source Book Project Press, Glen Arm, Maryland, 1994. (Dean Radin and Diane Ferrari are psychometric researchers from New York University.)

Chapter 6: Cacodemonomania

1   W. Davis, *Dojo: Magic and Exorcism in Modern Japan*, Stanford University Press, Stanford, 1980.

2   E. Casper and M. Philippus, "Fifteen cases of embrujada: Combining medication and suggestion in treatment," *Hospital Community Psychiatry*, 1975, vol. 26, pp. 271–274.

3   L. De Heusch, *Le Rwanda et la Civilisation Interlacustre*, Institut de Sociologie de l'Université Libre, Brussels, 1966.

4   F. Goodman, *How About Demons? Possession and Exorcism in the Modern World*, Indiana University Press, Indianapolis, 1988.

5   J. Bozzuto, "Cinematic neurosis following 'The Exorcist,'" *Journal of Nervous and Mental Disease*, 1975, vol. 161, no. 1, pp. 43–48.

6   J. Lister, "The dangers of exorcism," *The New England Journal of Medicine*, 1975, vol. 292, pp. 1391–1393.

7   R. Mackarness, "Occultism in psychiatry," *The Practitioner*, 1974, vol. 212, pp. 363–366. (Dr. Richard Mackarness is from the Park Prewett Hospital in Basingstoke, Hampshire.)

8   S. Cappannari, B. Rau, H. Abram, and D. Buchanan, "Voodoo in the general hospital," *Journal of the American Medical Association*, 1975, vol. 232, no. 9, pp. 938–940.

9   S. Freud, "A seventeenth century demonological neurosis (1923)," in J. Strachey (ed.), *The Standard Edition of the Complete Works of Sigmund Freud*, vol. 19, Hogarth Press, London, 1953, pp. 69–105.

10   S. Hill and J. Goodwin, "Demonic possession as a consequence of childhood," *Journal of Psychohistory*, 1993, vol. 20, no. 4, pp. 399–411. (Dr. Sally Hill and Dr. Jean Goodwin are psychiatrists from the U.S. National Institute of Mental Health in Washington, D.C.)

11   Research by E. Schendel and R.-F. Kournoy cited in R. Noll, *Vampires, Werewolves, and Demons: Twentieth Century Reports in the Psychiatric Literature*, Brunner/Mazel, New York, 1992. (Dr. Eric Schendel and Dr. Ronald-Frederic Kournoy are from the Vanderbilt University Medical Center in Nashville, Tennessee.)

12   S. Juan, "Dealing with old demons," *The Sydney Morning Herald*, August 18, 1993, p. 10.

13   Research by J. Wolpaw cited in S. Brewer, "'Talking' with brain waves," *Longevity*, June 1995, p. 10. (Dr. Jonathan Wolpaw is from the New York State Department of Mental Health's Wadsworth Center in Albany.)

14   Research by S. Zeki cited in A. Motluk, "Blind brain 'sees' rapid move-
      ment," *New Scientist*, September 21, 1996, p. 13. (Dr. Semir Zeki is a
      neurobiologist at the University College, London.)

Chapter 7: Capgras's Syndrome

1   J. Capgras and J. Reboul-Lachaux, "L'illusion des 'sosies' dans un délire
      systématisé," *Bulletin de la Société Clinique de Médecine Mentale*, 1923, vol.
      11, pp. 6–16. (Dr. Joseph Capgras and Dr. Jean Reboul-Lachaux were
      both psychiatrists in Paris.)

2   S. Signer, "Capgras' syndrome: The delusion of substitution," *Journal of
      Clinical Psychiatry*, 1987, vol. 48, pp. 147–150. (Dr. Stephen Signer is a
      psychiatrist at the University of California at Los Angeles.)

3   R. Jackson, M. Naylor, B. Shain, and C. King, "Capgras syndrome in
      adolescence," *Journal of the American Academy of Child and Adolescent Psy-
      chiatry*, 1992, vol. 31, pp. 977–983. (Dr. Richard Jackson and colleagues
      are from the Department of Psychiatry at the University of Michigan.)

4   S. Frazer and J. Roberts, "Three cases of Capgras' syndrome," *British Jour-
      nal of Psychiatry*, 1994, vol. 164, pp. 557–559. (Dr. S. J. Frazer and Dr. J.
      M. Roberts are psychiatrists at the Wonford House Hospital in Exeter.)

5   G. Casu, N. Cascella, and C. Maggini, "Homicide in Capgras syn-
      drome," *Psychopathology*, 1994, vol. 27, pp. 281–284. (Dr. G. Casu and
      colleagues are from the Dipartimento di Salute Mentale at the Univer-
      sity of Parma.)

6   O. De Leon, "The Capgras syndrome: A clinical study of 9 cases,"
      Revista Medico Panama, 1993, vol. 18, pp. 128–139. (Dr. O. A. De Leon is
      a psychiatrist at the Centro Medico Paitilla in Panama City.)

7   J. Luaute and E. Bidault, "Capgras syndrome: Agnosia of identification
      and delusion of reduplication," *Psychopathology*, 1994, vol. 27, pp.
      186–193. (Dr. J. P. Luaute and Dr. E. Bidault are psychiatrists at the Cen-
      tre Hospitalier de Romans in France.)

8   S. Juan, "Capgras syndrome: Finding a cure for double trouble," *The
      Sydney Morning Herald*, September 1, 1993, p. 14.

9   A. Motluk, "When half a brain is better than one," *New Scientist*, April
      20, 1996, p. 16.

10   K. Sabbagh, "Late bloomer," *Scientific American*, February 1997, pp.
      23–24.

11   D. Dobkin, "The shrinking deficit," *Discover*, February 1996, pp. 34–36.

Chapter 8: Cotard's Syndrome

1   J. Cotard, *Maladies Cérébrales et Mentales,* Baillière, Paris, 1891.

2   E. Anderson, *Psychiatry*, Baillière, Tindall and Cox, London, 1964.

3   M. Enoch and W. Trethowan, *Uncommon Psychiatric Syndromes*, 2nd ed., John Wright and Sons, Bristol, 1979, pp. 116–133. (Dr. M. David Enoch is a former professor of psychiatry at the University of Liverpool. Dr. William H. Trethowan is former professor of psychiatry at the University of Birmingham.)

4   A. Joseph and D. O'Leary, "Brain atrophy and interhemispheric fissure enlargement in Cotard's syndrome," *Journal of Clinical Psychiatry*, 1986, vol. 47, no. 10, pp. 518–520. (Dr. Anthony Joseph and Dr. Daniel O'Leary are psychiatrists from the McLean Hospital in Belmont, Massachusetts.)

5   S. Matsukura, H. Yoshimi, S. Sueoka, K. Chihara, T. Fujita, and K. Tanimoto, "Endorphins in Cotard's syndrome," *The Lancet*, 1981, vol. 1, pp. 162–163. (Dr. S. Matsukura and colleagues are from Kobe University.)

6   S. Campbell, M. Volow, and J. Cavenar, "Cotard's syndrome and the psychiatric manifestations of typhoid fever," *American Journal of Psychiatry*, 1981, vol. 138, no. 10, pp. 1377–1378. (Dr. Susan Campbell and colleagues are psychiatrists at the Duke University Medical Center.)

7   H. Chiu, "Cotard's syndrome in psychogeriatric patients in Hong Kong," *General Hospital Psychiatry*, 1995, vol. 17, pp. 54–55. (Dr. H. F. Chiu is a psychiatrist from the Prince of Wales Hospital in Shatin, Hong Kong.)

8   G. Berrios and R. Luque, "Cotard's syndrome analysis of 100 cases," *Acta Psychiatrica Scandinavia*, 1995, vol. 91, pp. 185–188. (Dr. G. E. Berrios and Dr. R. Luque are psychiatrists at Cambridge University.)

9   S. Juan, "People who get worked up over nothing," *The Sydney Morning Herald*, January 4, 1990, p. 10.

10   Research by O. John and R. Robins cited in B. Bower, "I gotta love me," *Science News*, April 5, 1997, p. 212. (Dr. Oliver John is a psychologist at the University of California at Berkeley. Dr. Richard Robins is a psychologist at the University of California at Davis.)

11   Interview with O. John, May 25, 1997.

12   Time-Life, *Mysteries of the Human Body*, Time-Life Books, Alexandria, Virginia, 1990, p. 12.

13   Research by L. Bode cited in K. Fackelmann, "Is mental illness infectious?," *Science News*, August 17, 1996, p. 107. (Dr. Liv Bode and colleagues are from the Department of Virology at the Robert Koch Institute in Berlin.)

Chapter 9: The Craving Brain

1   M. McCutcheon, *The Compass in Your Nose and Other Astonishing Facts About Humans*, Schwartz and Wilkinson, Melbourne, 1989, p. 53.

2   Research by M. Liebowitz and D. Klein cited in S. Boynton, *Chocolate: The Consuming Passion,* Workman, New York, 1982. (Dr. Michael Liebowitz and Dr. Donald Klein are psychiatrists from Columbia University. Dr. Sandra Boynton is a psychologist from Chicago.)

3   R. Ornstein and D. Sobel, *Healthy Pleasures,* Addison-Wesley, New York, 1989, pp. 202–203. (Dr. Robert Ornstein and Dr. David Sobel are behavioral medicine specialists from Stanford University.)

4   Research by M. Schuman and colleagues cited in P. McCarthy, "Sweets for the jilted," *American Health,* June 1988, p. 98. (Dr. Marjorie Schuman and colleagues are psychologists from the University of California at Los Angeles.)

5   Research by S. Diamond and J. Blau cited in L. Troiano, "Migraine triggers?," *American Health,* November 1987, p. 128. (Dr. Seymour Diamond is from the Diamond Migraine Clinic in Chicago. Dr. J. Nathan Blau is from the City of London Migraine Clinic.)

6   J. Margaretten-Ohring, "Are you chocolate-impaired?," *University of California at Berkeley Wellness Letter*, November 1996, p. 8.

7   S. Juan, "Love in a foil wrapper," *The Sydney Morning Herald*, April 12, 1990, p. 15.

8   Editors of Time-Life, *Mysteries of the Human Body*, Time-Life Books, Alexandria, Virginia, 1990, pp. 32–33.

9   Research by D. Van Essen cited in S. Blakeslee, "How the brain's cerebral cortex gets wrinkles," *The New York Times*, February 1, 1997, p. A8. (Dr. David Van Essen is from the Washington University School of Medicine in St. Louis.)

10 Research by N. Sadato and colleagues cited in S. Menon, "Twenty-twenty fingers," *Discover*, July 1996, pp. 27–28. (Dr. Norihiro Sadato and colleagues are from the Fukui Medical School in Fukui, Japan.)

Chapter 10: The Criminal Brain

1   A. Raine, P. Venables, and M. Williams, "Relationships between central and autonomic measures of arousal at age 15 years and criminality at age 24 years," *Archives of General Psychiatry*, 1990, vol. 47, pp. 1003–1007. (Dr. Adrian Raine and colleagues are from the Department of Psychology at the University of Southern California in Los Angeles.)

2   A. Raine, P. Brennan, B. Mednick, and S. Mednick, "High rates of vio-
    lence, crime, academic problems, and behavioral problems in males with
    both early neuromotor deficits and unstable family environments,"
    Archives of General Psychiatry, 1996, vol. 53, pp. 544–549.

3   Research by A. Raine and colleagues cited in G. Celente, "Natural born
    killers?," *Psychology Today*, January–February 1995, p. 10.

4   Research by A. Raine and colleagues cited in L. Degliantoni, "The best
    crime buster," *Psychology Today*, May–June 1996, p. 24.

5   Research by A. Raine and colleagues cited in B. Bower, "Biology and
    family, partners in crime," *Science News*, July 6, 1996, p. 11.

6   R. Pihl and F. Ervin, "Lead and cadmium levels in violent criminals,"
    Psychological Reports, 1990, vol. 66, pp. 839–844. (Dr. R. O. Pihl and Dr.
    F. Ervin are from the Department of Psychology at McGill University
    in Montreal.)

7   S. Juan, "Life of crime may lead to high times," *The Sydney Morning Her-
    ald*, March 14, 1991, p. 14.

8   Associated Press, "Car antenna pierces man's brain," June 13, 1996.

9   D. Wallechinsky and A. Wallace, *The Book of Lists: The '90s Edition*, Lit-
    tle, Brown and Company, Boston, 1993, pp. 108–109.

10 Research by C. Shatz and colleagues cited in B. Vobejda, "Child's brain
    mostly formed by age 3, scientists say," *The San Francisco Chronicle*, April
    18, 1997, p. A8. (Dr. Carla Shatz and colleagues are neurobiologists at
    the University of California at Berkeley.)

11 Research by E. Balaban cited in A. Harding, "Brain researcher makes a
    quail act like a chicken," *The San Francisco Chronicle*, March 5, 1997, p.
    A4. (Dr. Evan Balaban is a neuroscientist from the Neurosciences Insti-
    tute in La Jolla, California.)

Chapter 11: The Euphoric Brain

1   R. Siegel, *Intoxication: Life in Pursuit of Artificial Paradise*, E.P. Dutton,
    New York, 1989. (Dr. Ronald Siegel is a professor of psychopharmacol-
    ogy at the University of California at Los Angeles.)

2   S. Juan, "Getting high: Our animal passion," *The Sydney Morning Herald*,
    September 29, 1992, p. 14.

3   S. Paul, "Chicago woman has 3 brains," *Weekly World News*, November
    12, 1996, p. 35.

4   Research by D. Van Essen cited in S. Blakeslee, "How the brain's cere-

bral cortex gets wrinkles," *The New York Times*, February 1, 1997, p. A8. (Dr. David Van Essen is a neuroscientist at the Washington University School of Medicine in St. Louis.)

Chapter 12: The Fearful Brain

1   A. Furnham, "Lay beliefs about phobia," *Journal of Clinical Psychology*, 1995, vol. 51, pp. 518–525.

2   B. Carducci and P. Zimbardo, "The shy brain," *Psychology Today*, November–December 1995, p. 40.

3   J. Boyd, D. Rae, J. Thompson, B. Burns, K. Bourdon, B. Locke, and D. Regier, "Phobia: Prevalence and risk factors," *Social Psychiatry and Psychiatric Epidemiology*, 1990, vol. 25, pp. 314–323.

4   S. Cohen, "Phobic disorders and benzodiazepines in the elderly," *British Journal of Psychiatry*, 1992, vol. 160, p. 135.

5   D. Hunt, *No More Fears*, Thorsons, London, 1989. (Dr. Douglas Hunt is a psychiatrist in London.)

6   Anxiety Disorders Association of America, "16 drug-free ways to fight phobias," *Your Health*, December 29, 1992, pp. 47–48.

7   S. Juan, "Fight the fright," *The Sydney Morning Herald*, April 13, 1993, p. 10.

8   A. May and H. Bauchner, "Fever phobia: The pediatrician's contribution," *Pediatrics*, 1992, vol. 90, pp. 851–854.

9   For a full list of phobias see D. Hunt, *No More Fears*, Thorsons, London, 1989, pp. 323–326.

10 Research by D. Schacter and colleagues cited in B. Bower, "Brain region linked to conscious memories," *Science News*, January 20, 1996, p. 37. (Dr. Daniel Schacter is a psychologist at Harvard University.)

11 Research by L. Ewing-Cobbs and colleagues cited in J. Neimark, "The blast that lasts," *Psychology Today*, May–June 1995, p. 22. (Dr. Linda Ewing-Cobbs is from the University of Texas Health Sciences Center in Houston.)

Chapter 13: The Gluttonous Brain

1   Interview with G. Stanley, June 24, 1997. See also D. Clarke, "The brain of a glutton," *Discover*, June 1992, pp. 14–15. (Dr. Glenn Stanley is a neurologist from the University of California at Riverside.)

2   P. Jaret, "The new diet pills," *Health*, January–February 1995, p. 58.

3   K. Flodin, "Bitter pills," *American Health*, July–August 1991, pp. 64–67.

4   S. Juan, "A pill to tame the gluttonous brain," *The Sydney Morning Herald*, July 16, 1992, p. 12.

5   Research by G. Schwartz and colleagues cited in J. Raloff, "How the brain knows when eating must stop," *Science News*, November 30, 1996, p. 343. (Dr. Gary Schwartz and colleagues are psychologists at Johns Hopkins University.)

6   Research by T. Landis and M. Regard cited in W. Carlsen, "Brain lesions can spark cravings for fine food," *The San Francisco Chronicle*, May 20, 1997, pp. A1–A15. (Dr. Theodor Landis is a neurologist in Geneva, and Dr. Marianne Regard is a neurologist in Zurich.)

7   Research by W. Rodriquez cited in P. Doskoch, "Ah, sweet memories," *Psychology Today*, November–December 1996, p. 20. (Dr. Ward Rodriquez is a psychologist at California State University at Hayward.)

8   Research by S. Kish and colleagues cited in B. Wallace, "'Speed' abusers need more and more," *The San Francisco Chronicle*, May 31, 1996, p. A2. (Dr. Stephen Kish and colleagues are from the Department of Psychiatry at the University of Toronto.)

9   Research by M. Graziano and colleagues cited in A. Motluk, "Neurons for lovers," *New Scientist*, July 19, 1997, p. 16. (Dr. Michael Graziano and colleagues are neurologists from Princeton University.)

Chapter 14: The Hallucinating Brain

1   R. Teunisse, R. Cruysberg, W. Hoefnagels, A. Verbeek, and F. Zitman, "Visual hallucinations in psychologically normal people: Charles Bonnet's syndrome," *The Lancet*, 1996, vol. 347, pp. 794–797. (Dr. R. J. Teunisse and colleagues are psychiatrists at the University Hospital Nijmegen in the Netherlands.)

2   G. Fenelon, S. Marie, J. Ferroir, and A. Guillard, "Musical hallucinations: 7 cases," *Revue Neurologie* (Paris), 1993, vol. 149, nos. 8–9, pp. 462–467. (Dr. G. Fenelon and colleagues are from the Hospital Tenon in Paris.)

3   N. Nagaratnam, S. Virk, and O. Brdarevic, "Musical hallucinations associated with recurrence of a right occipital meningioma," *British Journal of Clinical Practice*, 1996, vol. 50, no. 1, pp. 56–57.

4   M. Stephane and L. Hsu, "Musical hallucinations: Interplay of degenerative brain disease, psychoses, and culture in a Chinese woman," *Journal of Nervous Mental Disease*, 1996, vol. 184, no. 1, pp. 59–61.

5   R. Siegel (ed.), *Hallucinations: Behavior, Experience, and Theory*, Wiley, New York, 1975.

6   H. Walter, I. Podreka, M. Steiner, and E. Suess, "A contribution to classification of hallucinations," *Psychopathology*, 1990, vol. 23, no. 2, pp. 97–105. (Dr. H. Walter and colleagues are psychiatrists at the University of Vienna.)

7   P. Shulman, "Seeing things," *Discover*, July 1996, p. 30.

8   S. Juan, "Seeing something that is not there," *The Sydney Morning Herald*, October 17, 1991, p. 12.

9   Research by W. Randall and S. Randall cited in W. Corliss, "The solar wind and hallucinations," *Science Frontiers*, September–October 1994, p. 4. (Dr. W. Randall and Dr. S. Randall are psychologists at the University of Iowa.)

10   "A fish smarter than a man," *Scientific American*, October 1996, p. 28.

Chapter 15: The Happy Brain

1   P. Kramer, *Listening to Prozac*, Viking Press, New York, 1993.

2   S. Fisher and R. Greenberg, "Prescription for happiness?," *Psychology Today*, September–October 1995, pp. 32–37.

3   S. Juan, "Carroll's dream or Huxley's nightmare?," *The Sydney Morning Herald*, November 10, 1993, p. 13.

4   Research by M. Miserandino cited in M. Hettinger, "The power of positive thinking," *Your Health*, September 3, 1996, p. 18. (Dr. Marianne Miserandino is a psychologist at the Oregon Health Sciences University in Portland.)

5   D. Chalmers, "The puzzle of conscious experience," *Scientific American*, December 1995, pp. 80–86. (Dr. David Chalmers is a professor of philosophy at the University of California at Santa Cruz and author of *The Conscious Mind*, published by Oxford University Press in 1996.)

6   Research by H. Damasio and A. Damasio cited in T. Monmaney, "Study on brain paths a surprise," *The Los Angeles Times*, April 11, 1996, p. 1. (Dr. Hanna Damasio and Dr. Antonio Damasio are from the University of Iowa College of Medicine.)

Chapter 16: The Hypnotic Brain I

1   W. Poundstone, *Biggest Secrets*, William Morrow, New York, 1993, pp. 159–161, 193–199.

2   S. Juan, "Rabbits are not the only ones kept in the dark," *The Sydney Morning Herald*, November 3, 1993, p. 13.

3   J. Williams, "Stimulation of breast growth by hypnosis," *Journal of Sex Research*, 1974, vol. 10, no. 4, pp. 316–326. (Dr. James Williams was a psychologist at the University of North Carolina at Chapel Hill.)

4   R. Willard, "Breast enlargement through visual imagery and hypnosis," *American Journal of Clinical Hypnosis*, 1977, vol. 19, no. 4, pp. 195–200. (Dr. Richard Willard is a psychiatrist at the Institute of Behavioral and Mind Sciences in Fort Wayne, Indiana.)

5   S. Juan, "Bigger breasts? Just give it some thought," *The Sydney Morning Herald*, October 20, 1988, p. 20.

6   H. Klawans, *Life, Death, and In Between: Tales of Clinical Neurology*, Paragon House, New York, 1992, p. 139.

7   Research by S. Weiss cited in J. Glausiusz, "Brain, heal thyself," *Discover*, August 1996, pp. 28–29. (Dr. Samuel Weiss is a neuroscientist at the University of Calgary.)

Chapter 17: The Hypnotic Brain 2

1   W. Whitehouse, D. Dinges, E. Carota Orne, and M. Orne, "Hypnotic hypermnesia: Enhanced memory accessibility or report bias?," *Journal of Abnormal Psychology*, 1988, vol. 97, no. 3, pp. 289–295. (Dr. Wayne Whitehouse and colleagues are psychiatrists from the Unit for Experimental Psychiatry at the University of Pennsylvania in Philadelphia.)

2   S. Juan, "Going back in time can be harder than you think," *The Sydney Morning Herald*, April 6, 1989, p. 13.

3   M. Nash, "What, if anything, is regressed about hypnotic age regression? A review of the empirical literature," *Psychological Bulletin*, 1987, vol. 102, no. 1, pp. 42–52. (Dr. Michael Nash is from the Department of Psychology at the University of Tennessee at Knoxville.)

4   P. Young, "Is rapport an essential characteristic of hypnosis?," *Journal of Abnormal and Social Psychology*, 1927, vol. 22, pp. 130–139.

5   P. Young, "The nature of hypnosis: As indicated by the presence or absence of posthypnotic amnesia and rapport," *Journal of Abnormal and Social Psychology*, 1928, vol. 22, pp. 372–382.

6   W. Wells, "Ability to resist artificially induced dissociation," *Journal of Abnormal and Social Psychology*, 1940, vol. 35, pp. 261–272.

7   E. Hilgard, "Ability to resist suggestions within the hypnotic state: Responsiveness to conflicting communications," *Psychological Reports*, 1963, vol. 12, pp. 3–13.

8   E. Baker and E. Levitt, "The hypnotic relationship: An investigation of compliance and resistance," *International Journal of Clinical and Experimental Hypnosis*, 1989, vol. 37, pp. 145–153.

9   S. Lynn, J. Rhue, and J. Weekes, "Hypnotic involuntariness: A social cognitive analysis," *Psychological Review*, 1990, vol. 97, no. 2, pp. 169–184. (Dr. Steven Lynn and colleagues are from the Department of Psychology at Ohio University.)

10   S. Juan, "A suggestive little theory on hypnosis," *The Sydney Morning Herald*, October 4, 1990, p. 16.

11   O. Sacks, *The Island of the Colour Blind*, Picador, Sydney, 1996.

12   J. Glausiusz, "Brain, heal thyself," *Discover*, August 1996, pp. 28–29.

Chapter 18: Kleptomania

1   S. McElroy, H. Pope, J. Hudson, P. Keck, and K. White, "Kleptomania: A report of 20 cases," *American Journal of Psychiatry*, 1991, vol. 148, pp. 652–657. (Dr. Susan McElroy and colleagues are psychiatrists at Harvard University.)

2   S. McElroy, P. Keck, and K. Phillips, "Kleptomania, compulsive buying, and binge-eating disorder," *Journal of Clinical Psychiatry*, 1995, vol. 56, suppl. 4, pp. 14–26.

3   S. Chong and B. Low, "Treatment of kleptomania with fluvoxamine," *Acta Psychiatrica Scandinavia*, 1996, vol. 93, no. 4, pp. 314–315. (Dr. S. A. Chong and Dr. B. L. Low are psychiatrists from the Institute of Mental Health in Singapore.)

4   S. Juan, "Kleptomania," *The Sydney Morning Herald*, September 19, 1991, p. 12.

5   H. Gossling and J. Rosin, "Kleptomania before and after spontaneous subarachnoid hemorrhage: A neuropsychodynamic case report," *Fortschritt der Neurologie-Psychiatrie*, 1994, vol. 62, no. 5, pp. 164–168. (Dr. H. W. Gossling and Dr. J. Rosin are psychiatrists from the Hannover State Clinic for Psychiatry and Psychotherapy.)

6   Research by M. Foster and colleagues cited in J. Raloff, "Radicals linked to aging via the brain," *Science News*, May 18, 1996, p. 311. (Dr. Michael Foster and colleagues are from the University of North Texas Medical Science Center in Fort Worth.)

7   C. Clayman, *The Human Body*, Dorling Kindersley, New York, 1995, p. 83.

8   H. Klawans, *Toscanini's Fumble and Other Tales of Clinical Neurology*, Bantam

Books, New York, 1988, p. 74. (Dr. Harold Klawans is a neurologist from the Rush-Presbyterian–St. Luke's Medical Center in Chicago.)

Chapter 19: The Mercurial Brain

1   P. Spargo and C. Pounds, "Newton's 'derangement of the intellect': A new light on an old problem," *Notes and Records of the Royal Society of London*, 1979, vol. 34, pp. 11–32.

2   H. Klawans, *Newton's Madness: Further Tales of Clinical Neurology*, Harper and Row, New York, 1990, pp. 30–39.

3   Interview with M. Inouye, July 1, 1991, cited in S. Juan, "Sir Isaac was ripe for 'Mad Hatters' malady," *The Sydney Morning Herald*, July 25, 1991, p. 12.

4   S. Emond, "Mercury: Still a hazard after all these years," *The Harvard Medical Letter*, November 1990, pp. 7–8.

5   T. Clarkson, "Mercury: Major issues in environmental health," *Environmental Health Perspectives*, 1993, vol. 100, pp. 31–38. (Dr. Thomas W. Clarkson is from the University of Rochester School of Medicine.)

6   E. Kang-Yum and S. Oransky, "Chinese patent medicine as a potential source of mercury poisoning," *Veterinary and Human Toxicology*, 1992, vol. 34, pp. 235–238.

7   U.S. Centers for Disease Control and Prevention, "Mercury poisoning associated with beauty cream: Texas, New Mexico, and California," *MMWR Morbidity and Mortality Weekly Report*, 1996, vol. 45, pp. 400–403.

8   S. Saxe, D. Snowdon, M. Wekstein, R. Henry, F. Grant, S. Donegan, and D. Wekstein, "Dental amalgam and cognitive function in older women: Findings from the nun study," *Journal of the American Dental Association*, 1995, vol. 126, pp. 1495–1501. (Dr. S. Saxe and colleagues are from the Geriatric Oral Health Program, College of Dentistry, Chandler Medical Center at the University of Kentucky.)

9   W. Corliss, "Fungal phantasms," *Science Frontiers*, November–December 1995, p. 4.

10   Research by A. Holdcroft and colleagues cited in P. Moore, "Pregnant women get that shrinking feeling," *New Scientist*, January 11, 1997, p. 5. (Dr. Anita Holdcroft and colleagues are from the Royal Postgraduate Medical School in London.)

Chapter 20: The Murderous Brain I

1   D. Hellman and N. Blackman, "Enuresis, firesetting and cruelty to animals: A triad predictive of adult crime," *American Journal of Psychiatry*, 1966, vol. 122, no. 6, pp. 1431–1435. (Dr. Daniel Hellman and Dr. Nathan Blackman are psychiatrists at the Malcolm Bliss Mental Health Center in St. Louis.)

2   B. Justice, R. Justice, and I. Kraft, "Early-warning signs of violence: Is a triad enough?," *American Journal of Psychiatry*, 1974, vol. 131, no. 4, pp. 457–459. (Dr. Blair Justice and colleagues are from the School of Public Health at the University of Texas at Houston.)

3   D. Lewis, S. Shanok, M. Grant, and E. Ritvo, "Homicidally aggressive young children: Neuropsychiatric and experimental correlates," *American Journal of Psychiatry*, 1983, vol. 140, no. 2, pp. 148–153. (Dr. Dorothy Lewis and colleagues are psychiatrists from the New York University Medical Center.)

4   S. Kellert and A. Felthous, "Childhood cruelty toward animals among criminals and noncriminals," *Human Relations*, 1985, vol. 38, no. 12, pp. 1113–1129. (Dr. Stephen Kellert is from Yale University and Dr. Alan Felthous is from the University of Texas at Galveston.)

5   J. Kelso and M. Stewart, "Factors which predict the persistence of aggressive conduct disorder," *Journal of Child Psychology and Psychiatry*, 1986, vol. 27, no. 1, pp. 77–86. (Dr. Jane Kelso and Dr. Mark Stewart are from the Department of Psychiatry at the University of Iowa.)

6   A. Labelle, J. Bradford, D. Bourget, B. Jones, and M. Carmichael, "Adolescent murderers," *Canadian Journal of Psychiatry*, 1991, vol. 36, pp. 583–587. (Dr. Alain Labelle and colleagues are psychiatrists at the Royal Ottawa Hospital and the University of Ottawa.)

7   S. Juan, "Childhood can hold the clues to homicidal behaviour," *The Times on Sunday*, April 26, 1987, pp. 21–22.

8   S. Juan, "Deadly reasons why kids become killers," *The Sydney Morning Herald*, April 9, 1992, p. 12.

9   K. Kleiner, "Seizures may have triggered murders," *New Scientist*, February 24, 1996, p. 11.

10 Research by A. Arieli and colleagues cited in C. Eboch, "Seeing is deceiving," *Psychology Today*, March–April 1996, p. 24. (Dr. Amos Arieli and colleagues are from the Weitzmann Institute of Science in Rehovot, Israel.)

Chapter 21: The Murderous Brain 2

1   J. Achenbach, "Exploding myths of serial killers," *The Washington Post*, April 22, 1991, pp. C3, C5.

2   R. Ressler and T. Shachtman, *Whoever Fights Monsters: My Twenty Years Hunting Serial Killers for the FBI*, St. Martin's Press, New York, 1992. (Tom Shachtman is a journalist from New York City.)

3   J. Ullman, "I carried it too far, that's for sure," *Psychology Today*, May–June 1992, pp. 28–31.

4   S. Juan, "Serial killer: From loveless home to grisly fantasy world," *The Sydney Morning Herald*, September 3, 1992, p. 15.

5   J. Neimark, "The cinema in your head," *Psychology Today*, May–June 1995, p. 22.

6   M. Andrews, "1 inch from death," *Weekly World News*, March 26, 1996, p. 15.

Chapter 22: Obsessive–Compulsive Disorder

1   J. Rapoport, *The Boy Who Couldn't Stop Washing: The Experience and Treatment of Obsessive–Compulsive Disorder*, E.P. Dutton, New York, 1989.

2   S. Juan, *The Odd Body*, Andrews McMeel, Kansas City, 2004, pp. 142–145.

3   M. Feldman and C. Ford, *Patient or Pretender: Inside the Strange World of Factitious Disorders*, John Wiley, Brisbane, 1994.

4   J. Weatherup and D. Scatena, "Ten personal pointers to Jacko," *The Daily Telegraph* (Sydney), November 13, 1996, p. 5.

5   R. Miller, "Fatal obsession," *The Australian Magazine*, July 29–30, 1989, pp. 8–12, 15–16.

6   C. Wilson, *The Misfits: A Study of Sexual Outsiders*, Grafton, Sydney, 1989.

7   H. Schmeck, "Researchers link region in brain to obsessive disorder," *The New York Times*, March 8, 1988, pp. Y15, Y18.

8   J. Lucey, D. Costa, T. Blanes, G. Busatto, L. Pilowsky, N. Takei, I. Marks, P. Ell, and R. Kerwin, "Regional cerebral blood flow in obsessive–compulsive disordered patients at rest. Differential correlates with obsessive–compulsive and anxious–avoidant dimensions," *British Journal of Psychiatry*, 1995, vol. 167, pp. 629–634.

9   M. Jenike, H. Breiter, L. Baer, D. Kennedy, C. Savage, M. Olivares, R. O'Sullivan, D. Shera, S. Rauch, N. Keuthen, B. Rosen, V. Caviness, and

P. Filipek, "Cerebral structural abnormalities in obsessive–compulsive disorder: A quantitative morphometric magnetic resonance imaging study," *Archives of General Psychiatry*, 1996, vol. 53, pp. 625–632. (Dr. M. Jenike and colleagues are from the Massachusetts General Hospital in Boston.)

10 F. Toates, *Obsessional Thoughts and Behaviour: Help for Obsessive Compulsive Disorder*, Thorsons, Sydney, 1990. (Dr. Frederick Toates is a psychobiologist at the Open University in London.)

11 K. Koran, M. Theineman, and R. Davenport, "Quality of life for patients with obsessive–compulsive disorder," *American Journal of Psychiatry*, 1996, vol. 153, pp. 783–788.

12 D. Bolton, M. Luckie, and D. Steinberg, "Long-term course of obsessive–compulsive disorder treated in adolescence," *Journal of the American Academy of Child and Adolescent Psychiatry*, 1995, vol. 34, pp. 1441–1450.

13 E. Hollander, J. Kwon, D. Stein, J. Broatch, C. Rowland, and C. Himelein, "Obsessive–compulsive and spectrum disorders: Overview and quality of life issues," *Journal of Clinical Psychiatry*, 1996, vol. 57, suppl. 8, pp. 3–6.

14 J. Glausiusz, "The chemistry of obsession," *Discover*, June 1996, p. 36.

15 T. Broder, "Hooked on water," *Weekly World News*, March 26, 1996, p. 3.

Chapter 23: The Phobic Brain

1 Research by W. Sherwood cited in S. Juan, "AIDS adds to fear of blood and needles," *The Sydney Morning Herald*, June 4, 1992, p. 12. (Dr. William Sherwood is vice president for biomedical services at the American Red Cross in Washington, D.C.)

2 L. Ost, "Blood and injection phobia: Background and cognitive physiological, and behavioral variables," *Journal of Abnormal Psychology*, 1992, vol. 101, pp. 68–74. (Dr. Lars-Goran Ost is a psychiatrist from the Ulleraker Hospital and the University of Uppsala in Sweden.)

3 L. Maltin, *Leonard Maltin's 1996 Movie and Video Guide*, Signet, New York, 1995, p. 54.

4 P. DeJong, H. Merckelbach, A. Arntz, and H. Nijman, "Covariation detection in treated and untreated spider phobics," *Journal of Abnormal Psychology*, 1992, vol. 101, pp. 724–727.

5 K. Kirkby, R. Menzies, B. Daniels, and K. Smith, "Aetiology of spider phobia: Classificatory differences between two origins instruments," *Behavior Research and Therapy*, 1995, vol. 33, pp. 955–958.

6   R. Francis and G. Stanley, "Estimating the prevalence of dental phobia,"
    Australian Dental Journal, 1990, vol. 35, pp. 449–453.

7   Interview with J. G. Rubin cited in P. Avery, "Good news for dental
    phobics," *American Health*, May 1989, pp. 46, 48. (Dr. J. Gordon Rubin
    is a dentist at the Mount Sinai Dental Phobia Clinic in New York.)

8   E. Walker, P. Milgrom, P. Weinstein, T. Getz, and R. Richardson, "Assess-
    ing abuse and neglect and dental fear in women," *Journal of the American
    Dental Association*, 1996, vol. 127, no. 4, pp. 485–490. (Dr. E. A. Walker
    and colleagues are from the Department of Psychiatry and Behavioral
    Sciences at the University of Washington in Seattle.)

9   P. Gross, "Is pain sensitivity associated with dental avoidance?," *Behavior
    Research and Therapy*, 1992, vol. 30, no. 1, pp. 7–13. (Dr. P. R. Gross is
    from the National Police Research Unit in Marsden, South Australia.)

10 A. de Jongh, P. Muris, G. ter Horst, F. van Zuuren, N. Schoenmakers,
    and P. Makkes, "One-session cognitive treatment of dental phobia:
    Preparing dental phobics for treatment by restructuring negative out-
    comes," *Behavior Research and Therapy*, 1995, vol. 33, no. 8, pp. 947–954.
    (Dr. A. de Jongh and colleagues are from the Academic Centre for Den-
    tistry in Amsterdam.)

11 Interview with T. Getz, July 17, 1997. (Dr. Tracy Getz is a psychiatrist
    from the Department of Psychiatry and Behavioral Sciences at the Uni-
    versity of Washington in Seattle.)

12 S. Juan, "Dentist? Give me the pliers," *The Sydney Morning Herald*,
    August 10, 1989, p. 13.

13 See also the American Psychiatric Association's *Diagnostic and Statistical
    Manual of Mental Disorders*, 4th ed., American Psychiatric Association,
    Washington, D.C., 1994. Standards for Australia are set by the interna-
    tional conventions of the DSM-IV.

14 R. Epstein, "Why shrinks have so many problems," *Psychology Today*,
    July–August 1997, pp. 58–60, 62, 74, 76, 78; p. 59.

15 C. Wilks, "Treatment of a dental phobic with pronounced aversion to
    rubber gloves by swallowing relaxation in two appointments," *British
    Dental Journal*, 1993, vol. 175, no. 3, pp. 88–89.

16 Research by E. Kandel cited in I. Wickelgren, "Protein switch may
    unlock the secrets of long-term memory," *The New York Times*, Decem-
    ber 10, 1996, p. 1. (Dr. Eric Kandel is a neurobiologist from Columbia
    University in New York.)

17 H. Klawans, *Toscanini's Fumble and Other Tales of Clinical Neurology*, Bantam Books, New York, 1988, pp. 24–25.

18 Research by P. Cochrane cited in M. Ward, "End of the road for brain evolution," *New Scientist*, January 25, 1997, p. 14. (Dr. Peter Cochrane is from the BT Laboratories in London.)

19 J. May, *The Book of Curious Facts*, Collins and Brown, London, 1993, pp. 18–19.

Chapter 24: Prosopagnosia

1 G. Carlesimo and C. Caltagirone, "Components in the visual processing of known and unknown faces," *Journal of Clinical and Experimental Neurology*, 1995, vol. 17, pp. 691–705.

2 R. Bauer, "Autonomic recognition of names and faces in prosopagnosia: A neuropsychological application of the guilty knowledge test," *Neuropsychologia*, 1984, vol. 22, pp. 457–469.

3 D. Tranel and A. Damasio, "Knowledge without awareness: An autonomic index of facial recognition by prosopagnosics," *Science*, 1985, vol. 228, pp. 1453–1454.

4 B. Renault, J. Signoret, B. Debruille, F. Brepon, and F. Bolger, "Brain potentials reveal covert facial recognition in prosopagnosia," *Neuropsychologia*, 1989, vol. 27, pp. 905–912.

5 A. Damasio, "Neuropsychological applications of the GKT," *Proceedings of the Society for Neuroscience*, 1989, vol. 7, pp. 38–47. (Dr. Antonio Damasio is a neuropsychologist from the College of Medicine at the University of Iowa.)

6 D. Macrae and E. Trolle, "The defect of function in visual agnosia," *Brain*, 1956, vol. 79, pp. 94–110.

7 J. McNeil and E. Warrington, "Prosopagnosia: A face-specific disorder," *Quarterly Journal of Experimental Psychology (A) Human Experimental Psychology*, 1993, vol. 46, pp. 1–10.

8 J. Evans, A. Heggs, N. Antoun, and J. Hodges, "Progressive prosopagnosia associated with selective right temporal lobe atrophy. A new syndrome?," *Brain*, 1995, vol. 118, pp. 1–13.

9 S. Juan, "Prosopagnosia," *The Sydney Morning Herald*, January 31, 1991, p. 12.

10 O. Sacks, *The Man Who Mistook His Wife for a Hat*, Picador, London, 1985, p. 12.

11   *Mysteries of the Human Body*, Time-Life Books, Alexandria, Virginia, 1990, p. 13.

12   Reuters, "China brain," October 14, 1996.

Chapter 25: The Remembering Brain

1   I. Rosenfield, *The Invention of Memory: A New View of the Brain*, Basic Books, New York, 1988.

2   S. Juan, "An elephant never um, eh . . .," *The Sydney Morning Herald*, June 22, 1989, p. 19.

3   Research by E. Tulving and colleagues cited in B. Bower, "Brain scans show two-sided memory flow," *Science News*, March 26, 1994, p. 199. (Dr. Endel Tulving and colleagues are from the Department of Psychology at the University of Toronto.)

4   Research by G. Fink and colleagues cited in B. Bower, "Right brain takes memories personally," *Science News*, July 6, 1996, p. 5. (Dr. Gereon Fink and colleagues are from the Institute of Neurology in London.)

5   H. Sno and D. Linszen, "The deja vu experience: Remembrance of things past?," *American Journal of Psychiatry*, 1990, vol. 147, pp. 1587–1595. (Dr. Herman Sno and Dr. Don Linszen are psychiatrists from the University of Amsterdam.)

6   G. Berrios, "Deja vu in France during the 19th century: A conceptual history," *Comparative Psychiatry*, 1995, vol. 36, no. 2, pp. 123–129.

7   H. Sno and D. Draaisma, "An early Dutch study of deja vu experiences," *Psychological Medicine*, 1993, vol. 23, no. 1, pp. 17–26.

8   J. Bancaud, F. Brunet-Bourgin, P. Chauvel, and H. Halgren, "Anatomical origin of deja vu and vivid 'memories' in human temporal lobe epilepsy," *Brain*, 1994, vol. 117, no. 1, pp. 71–90. (Dr. J. Bancaud and colleagues are neurologists at the Paul Broca Centre in Paris.)

9   H. Levitan, "The depersonalizing process," *Psychoanalytic Quarterly*, 1969, vol. 38, pp. 97–109.

10   S. Juan, "Deja vu and you," *The Sydney Morning Herald*, September 17, 1991, p. 12.

11   M. Weinand, B. Hermann, A. Wyler, L. Carter, K. Oommen, D. Labiner, G. Ahern, and A. Herring, "Long-term subdural strip electrocorticographic monitoring of ictal deja vu," *Epilepsia*, 1994, vol. 35, no. 5, pp. 1054–1059. (Dr. M. Weinand and colleagues are at the Department of Surgery, University of Arizona College of Medicine in Tucson.)

12 K. Andrews, L. Murphy, R. Munday, and C. Littlewood, "Misdiagnosis of the vegetative state: A retrospective study in a rehabilitation unit," *British Medical Journal*, 1996, vol. 313, pp. 13–16. (Dr. Keith Andrews and colleagues are neurologists at the Royal Hospital for Neurodisability in London.)

13 T. Monmaney, "A surprising study about gravely sick," *The Los Angeles Times*, July 6, 1996, p. 2.

14 Research by S. Roberts and colleagues cited in B. Beale, "Just think, coma patients may be able to contact us," *The Sydney Morning Herald*, September 12, 1996, p. 3. (Steve Roberts and colleagues are from the Imperial College of Science and Technology in London.)

Chapter 26: Savant Syndrome

1 L. Franzini and J. Grossberg, *Eccentric and Bizarre Behaviors*, John Wiley, Brisbane, 1995, p. 194.

2 A. Tredgold, *Mental Deficiency*, William Wood, New York, 1914.

3 D. Wallechinsky and A. Wallace, *The Book of Lists: The '90s Edition*. Little, Brown and Company, Boston, 1993, pp. 439–440.

4 E. Podolsky, *Encyclopedia of Aberrations*, The Citadel, New York, 1953.

5 O. Lindsley, "Can deficiency produce specific superiority: The challenge of the idiot savant," *Exceptional Child*, 1965, vol. 31, pp. 225–232.

6 L. Mottron and S. Belleville, "Perspective production in a savant autistic draughtsman," *Psychological Medicine*, 1995, vol. 25, pp. 639–648. (Dr. L. Mottron and Dr. S. Belleville are psychiatrists at the Sainte Justine Hospital in Montreal.)

7 S. Juan, "Savants: The super talents of the subnormal," *The Medical Observer*, August 2, 1996, p. 68.

8 D. Treffert, *Extraordinary People: Understanding "Idiot Savants,"* Harper and Row, New York, 1989. (Dr. Darold Treffert is a psychiatrist in Fond du Lac, Wisconsin.)

9 S. Juan, "'Imbeciles,' but with the talent of a genius," *The Sydney Morning Herald*, November 24, 1988, p. 20.

10 Research by J. Wilding and E. Valentine cited in W. Corliss, "The untapped human mind," *Science Frontiers*, May–June 1995, p. 4. (Dr. J. Wilding and Dr. E. Valentine are psychologists at the University of London.)

11 Research by A. Shimamura and colleagues cited in M. Barasch, "The busy brain," *Psychology Today*, March–April 1995, p. 24. (Dr. Arthur

Shimamura and colleagues are from the Department of Psychology at the University of California at Berkeley.)

Chapter 27: The Schizophrenic Brain

1   G. Lewis, A. David, S. Andreasson, and P. Allebeck, "Schizophrenia and city life," *The Lancet*, 1992, vol. 340, pp. 137–140. (Dr. Glyn Lewis and colleagues are psychiatrists from the Institute of Psychiatry in London.)

2   P. Barta, G. Pearlson, R. Powers, S. Richards, and L. Tune, "Auditory hallucinations and smaller superior temporal gyral volume in schizophrenia," *American Journal of Psychiatry*, 1990, vol. 147, pp. 1457–1462. (Dr. Patrick Barta and colleagues are from the Johns Hopkins University Medical School in Baltimore.)

3   N. Ainger, "Study on schizophrenics: Why they hear voices," *The New York Times*, September 22, 1993, p. 1.

4   M. Shenton, R. Kikins, F. Jolesz, S. Pollak, M. LeMay, C. Wible, H. Hokama, J. Martin, D. Metcalf, M. Coleman, and R. McCarley, "Abnormalities of the left temporal lobe and thought disorder in schizophrenia," *The New England Journal of Medicine*, 1992, vol. 327, pp. 604–612. (Dr. Martha Shenton and colleagues are from the Harvard Medical School.)

5   M. Flaum and N. Andreasen, "The reliability of distinguishing primary versus secondary negative symptoms [in schizophrenia]," *Comparative Psychiatry*, 1995, vol. 36, no. 6, pp. 421–427. (Dr. Martin Flaum and Dr. Nancy Andreasen are psychiatrists from the University of Iowa Hospitals and Clinics in Iowa City.)

6   Interview with P. McGuire cited in B. Bower, "Brain scans seek roots of imagined voices," *Science News*, September 9, 1995, p. 166. (Dr. Philip McGuire is a psychiatrist from the Institute of Psychiatry in London.)

7   B. Bower, "Faulty circuit may trigger schizophrenia," *Science News*, September 14, 1996, p. 164.

8   J. Eagles, "Are polioviruses a cause of schizophrenia?," *British Journal of Psychiatry*, 1992, vol. 160, pp. 598–600. (Dr. John Eagles is a psychiatrist from the Royal Cornhill Hospital in Aberdeen.)

9   Research by D. Silbersweig and E. Stern cited in K. Leutwyler, "Schizophrenia revisited," *Scientific American*, February 1996, pp. 22–23. (Dr. David Silbersweig and Dr. Emily Stern are from the New York Hospital–Cornell University Medical Center.)

10   Research by P. Goldman-Rakic cited in C. Conway, "A matter of mem-

ory," *Psychology Today*, January–February 1995, p. 11. (Dr. Patricia Gold-man-Rakic is a neuroscientist at Yale University.)

11   S. Juan, "Schizophrenia: An abundance of theories," *The Sydney Morning Herald*, October 15, 1992, p. 14.

12   Research by J. Megginson Hollister and colleagues cited in B. Bower, "New culprits cited for schizophrenia," *Science News*, February 3, 1996, p. 68. (Dr. J. Megginson Hollister and colleagues are psychologists from the University of Pennsylvania.)

13   "Making memories," *Scientific American*, August 1996, p. 20.

Chapter 28: The Self-Mutilating Brain

1   B. Hills, "Deadly dilemma of Australia's most unwanted man," *The Sydney Morning Herald*, May 5, 1990, pp. 67, 69.

2   A. Favazza, *Bodies Under Siege: Self-Mutilation in Culture and Psychiatry*, Johns Hopkins University Press, Baltimore, 1987. (Dr. Anthony Favazza is a psychiatrist from the School of Medicine at the University of Missouri at Columbia.)

3   N. Scheper-Hughes, "Bodies under siege: Self-mutilation in culture and psychiatry (Armando R. Favazza)," *Medical Anthropology Quarterly*, 1989, vol. 3, no. 3, pp. 312–315. (Dr. Nancy Scheper-Hughes is an anthropologist at the University of California at Berkeley.)

4   F. Basaglia, *Psychiatry Inside Out: Selected Writings of Franco Basaglia*, Columbia University Press, New York, 1987.

5   S. Juan, "Self-mutilation: The first cut is not the deepest," *The Sydney Morning Herald*, May 11, 1990, p. 11.

6   C. Krasucki, R. Kemp, and A. David, "A case study of female genital self-mutilation in schizophrenia," *British Journal of Medical Psychology*, 1995, vol. 68, no. 2, pp. 179–186. (Dr. C. Krasucki and colleagues are psychiatrists at the Institute of Psychiatry in London.)

7   Research by A. Raps and colleagues cited in W. Corliss, "Solar radiation and mental illness," *Science Frontiers*, January–February 1994, p. 4. (Dr. Avi Raps and colleagues are psychologists from the University of Tel Aviv.)

8   D. Wallechinsky and A. Wallace, *The Book of Lists: The '90s Edition*, Little, Brown and Company, Boston, 1993, p. 109.

9   M. Goldwyn, *How a Fly Walks Upside Down . . . and Other Curious Facts*, Wing Books, Avenel, New Jersey, 1995, p. 224.

Chapter 29: The Shrinking Brain

1   G. Stix, "Listening to culture," *Scientific American*, January 1996, pp. 16, 21.

2   J. Levy, R. Neutra, and D. Parker, *Hand Trembling, Frenzy Witchcraft, and Moth Madness: A Study of Navajo Seizure Disorders*, University of Arizona Press, Tucson, 1987. (Dr. Jerrold Levy and colleagues are from the Department of Anthropology at the University of Arizona.)

3   P. Yap, "Koro: A culture-bound depersonalization syndrome," *British Journal of Psychiatry*, 1965, vol. 111, pp. 43–50.

4   J. Edwards, "Indigenous koro, a genital retraction syndrome of insular Southeast Asia: A critical review," *Culture, Medicine and Psychiatry*, 1984, vol. 8, pp. 1–24.

5   M. Scher, "Koro in a native born citizen of the U.S.," *International Journal of Social Psychiatry*, 1987, vol. 33, no. 1, pp. 42–45. (Dr. Maryonda Scher is a psychiatrist from the Department of Psychiatry and Behavioral Sciences at the University of Washington in Seattle.)

6   S. Juan, *Only Human: Why We React, How We Behave, What We Feel*, Random House Australia, Sydney, 1990, pp. 117–119.

7   M. Teicher, *Windigo Psychosis*, University of Washington Press, Seattle, 1960.

8   A. Rubel, C. O'Nell, and R. Collado-Ardon, *Susto, A Folk Illness*, University of California Press, Berkeley, 1984. (Dr. Arthur Rubel and colleagues are from the Department of Anthropology at the University of California at Irvine.)

9   S. Juan, "Taboos and mental illness," *The Sydney Morning Herald*, June 15, 1994, p. 15.

10 S. Johnson, "Psychiatric manual to list cultural woes," *The San Jose Mercury News*, April 23, 1994, pp. 1A–2A.

11 C. Lindner, "You must remember this," *Men's Health*, September 1995, p. 112.

12 J. Heilman, "The good news about Alzheimer's," *Parade*, August 13, 1995, pp. 12–13.

13 S. Richardson, "The besieged brain," *Discover*, September 1996, pp. 30–31.

Chapter 30: The Shy Brain

1   B. Carducci and P. Zimbardo, "Are you shy?," *Psychology Today*, November–December 1995, pp. 34–41.

2   A. McGarry, "Professionals warned on social phobia," *The Weekend Australian*, July 6–7, 1996, p. 47.

3   I. Marks, "The classification of phobic disorders," *British Journal of Psychiatry*, 1970, vol. 116, pp. 377–386.

4   S. Turner, D. Beidel, and K. Larkin, "Situational determinants of social anxiety in clinic and non-clinic samples: Physiological and cognitive correlates," *Journal of Abnormal Psychology*, 1986, vol. 95, pp. 389–394. (Dr. Samuel Turner and colleagues are from the University of Pittsburgh School of Medicine.)

5   J. Kagan, J. Reznick, and N. Snidman, "Biological bases of shyness," *Science*, 1988, vol. 240, pp. 167–171. (Dr. Jerome Kagan and colleagues are from the Department of Psychology at Harvard University.)

6   R. Heimberg, C. Dodge, D. Hope, and R. Becker, "DSM-III-R subtypes of social phobia," *Journal of Nervous and Mental Disease*, 1989, vol. 178, pp. 172–179. (Dr. Richard G. Heimberg and colleagues are from the State University of New York at Albany.)

7   S. Turner, D. Beidel, and R. Townsley, "Social phobia: Relationship to shyness," *Behavior Research and Therapy*, 1990, vol. 28, no. 6, pp. 497–505.

8   H. Juster and R. Heimberg, "Social phobia. Longitudinal course and long-term outcome of cognitive–behavioral treatment," *Psychiatric Clinics of North America*, 1995, vol. 18, suppl. 4, pp. 821–842.

9   S. Reiter, M. Pollack, J. Rosenbaum, and L. Cohen, "Clonazepam for the treatment of social phobia," *Journal of Clinical Psychiatry*, 1990, vol. 51, no. 11, pp. 470–472. (Dr. Steward Reiter and colleagues are from the Harvard University School of Medicine.)

10 J. Jefferson, "Social phobia: Everyone's disorder," *Journal of Clinical Psychiatry*, 1996, vol. 57, suppl. 6, pp. 28–32. (Dr. James W. Jefferson is a psychiatrist at the Foundation for Health, Research and Education in Madison, Wisconsin.)

11 S. Juan, "Too shy to speak," *The Sydney Morning Herald*, May 30, 1991, p. 14.

12 B. Black and T. Uhde, "Elective mutism as a variant of social phobia," *Journal of the American Academy of Child and Adolescent Psychiatry*, 1992, vol. 31, pp. 1090–1094. (Dr. B. Black and Dr. T. Uhde are from the U.S. National Institute of Mental Health in Bethesda, Maryland.)

13 M. Stein, A. Baird, and J. Walker, "Social phobia in adults with stuttering," *American Journal of Psychiatry*, 1996, vol. 153, pp. 278–280. (Dr. M.

Stein and colleagues are from the St. Boniface General Hospital in Winnipeg and the University of Manitoba.)

14　Research by L. Nyberg cited in K. Fackelmann, "The brain's memory helpers," *Science News*, October 5, 1996, p. 218. (Dr. Lars Nyberg is from Umea University in Sweden.)

15　Research by F. Sirois cited in R. McFarland, "War hysteria and group fantasy in Colorado," *The Journal of Psychohistory*, 1991, vol. 19, no. 1, pp. 35–51.

Chapter 31: The Suicidal Brain

1　E. Coccaro, L. Siever, H. Klar, G. Maurer, K. Cochrane, T. Cooper, R. Mohs, and K. Davis, "Serotonergic studies in patients with affective and personality disorders," *Archives of General Psychiatry*, 1989, vol. 46, pp. 587–599. (Dr. Emil Coccaro and colleagues are from the Eastern Pennsylvania Psychiatric Institute of the Medical College of Pennsylvania in Philadelphia.)

2　A. Roy, I. De Jong, and M. Linnoila, "Cerebrospinal fluid monoamine metabolites and suicidal behavior in depressed patients: A 5-year follow-up study," *Archives of General Psychiatry*, 1989, vol. 46, pp. 609–612. (Dr. Alec Roy and colleagues are from the U.S. National Institute on Alcohol Abuse and Alcoholism in Bethesda, Maryland.)

3　K. Dillon, R. Gross-Isseroff, M. Israeli, and A. Biegon, "Autoradiographic analysis of serotonin 5-HT1A receptor binding in the human brain postmortem: Effects of age and alcohol," *Brain Research*, 1991, vol. 554, pp. 56–64. (Dr. Kathryn Dillon and Dr. Anat Biegon are psychiatrists from the New York University Medical Center. Dr. Ruth Gross-Isseroff and Dr. Malka Israeli are neurologists from the Weizmann Institute of Science in Rehovot, Israel.)

4　Interview with D. Baron, March 22, 1993. (Dr. David Baron is the deputy clinical director of intramural research at the U.S. National Institute of Mental Health in Washington, D.C.)

5　Interview with A. Biegon, March 21, 1993.

6　Research by G. Pandey and colleagues cited in K. Vergoth, "The end of suicide," *Psychology Today*, November–December 1995, p. 20. (Dr. Ghanshyam Pandey and colleagues are psychiatrists at the University of Illinois.)

7　M. Maes, P. Cosyns, H. Meltzer, F. De Meyer, and D. Peeters, "Seasonal-ity in violent suicide but not in nonviolent suicide or homicide," *American Journal of Psychiatry*, 1993, vol. 150, pp. 1380–1385.

8   C. Mills, "Suicides and homicides in their relation to weather changes," *American Journal of Psychiatry*, 1934, vol. 91, p. 669.

9   W. Fenton and T. McGlashan, "Antecedents, symptom progression, and long-term outcome of the deficit syndrome in schizophrenia," *American Journal of Psychiatry*, 1994, vol. 151, pp. 351–356. (Dr. Wayne Fenton and Dr. Thomas McGlashan are psychiatrists from Yale University.)

10 S. Luck, E. Vogel, and K. Shapiro, "Word meanings can be accessed but not reported during the attentional blink," *Nature*, 1996, vol. 383, pp. 616–618. (Dr. Steven Luck, Dr. Edward Vogel, and Dr. Kimron Shapiro are psychologists at the University of Iowa.)

11 A. Motluk, "How the brain goes on the blink," *New Scientist*, October 19, 1996, p. 19.

12 K. Ross, "Bizarre disease makes victims jump out windows—because they think they're on fire," *Weekly World News*, July 9, 1996, p. 45.

Chapter 32: The Thrill-Seeking Brain

1   I. Bernstein, "Taboo or toy?," in J. Bruner, A. Jolly, and K. Sylva (eds.), *Play*, Penguin Books, Melbourne, 1978, pp. 194–198.

2   W. Cannon, *Bodily Changes in Pain, Hunger, Fear and Rage: An Account of Researches into the Function of Emotional Excitement*, Appleton-Century, New York, 1929.

3   M. Apter, *The Dangerous Edge: The Psychology of Excitement*, The Free Press, New York, 1992. (Dr. Michael Apter is a psychologist at the University of Chicago.)

4   S. Juan, "Why we love the thrill of danger," *The Sydney Morning Herald*, July 21, 1993, p. 12.

5   M. Persinger, "On the possibility of directly accessing every human brain by electromagnetic induction of fundamental algorithms," *Perceptual and Motor Skills*, 1995, vol. 80, pp. 791–792. (Dr. Michael A. Persinger is a neurologist from Laurentian University in Sudbury, Ontario.)

6   J. Dixit, "What makes athletes great," *Psychology Today*, November–December 1996, p. 18.

Chapter 33: The Time-Twisted Brain

1   Interview with D. Dinges, August 3, 1991, cited in S. Juan, "Time twists may help combat ills," *The Sydney Morning Herald*, August 15, 1991, p. 12. (Dr. David Dinges is a psychologist at the University of Pennsylvania Hospital in Philadelphia.)

2   Interview with P. Whybrow, August 3, 1991, cited in S. Juan, ibid. (Dr. Peter Whybrow is a psychiatrist at the University of Pennsylvania Hospital in Philadelphia.)

3   Interview with D. Dinges, July 10, 1997.

4   Interview with R. Grunstein, August 4, 1991, cited in S. Juan, ibid. (Dr. Ron Grunstein is a staff specialist at the Sleep Disorders Centre of the Royal Prince Alfred Hospital in Sydney.)

5   B. Levinson, "State of awareness during general anaesthesia," *British Journal of Anaesthesia*, 1965, vol. 37, pp. 544–546.

6   J. Andrade, "Learning during anaesthesia: A review," *British Journal of Psychology*, 1995, vol. 86, pp. 479–506.

7   R. Marion, "A deadly cry," *Discover*, December 1995, pp. 42, 44, 46.

Chapter 34: The Traumatized Brain

1   Research findings on this phenomenon were presented at an April 1994 conference on brain chemistry in Washington, D.C. sponsored by the American Psychological Association.

2   Interview with D. Charney, April 29, 1994, cited in S. Juan, "The strain of the pain stays mainly in the brain," *The Sydney Morning Herald*, May 4, 1994, p. 19. (Dr. Dennis Charney is a psychiatrist and director of clinical neuroscience at the National Center for Post-Traumatic Stress Disorder at Yale University.)

3   Interview with M. Friedman, April 28, 1994, cited in S. Juan, ibid. (Dr. Matthew Friedman is a psychiatrist at the National Center for Post-Traumatic Stress Disorder at Yale University.)

4   Research by L. Echterling cited in J. Mauro, "After the flood," *Psychology Today*, May–June 1993, p. 20. (Dr. Lennis Echterling is a psychologist at James Madison University in Virginia.)

5   E. Lindemann, "Symptomatology and management of acute grief," *American Journal of Psychiatry*, 1944, vol. 101, pp. 141–148.

6   C. Williams, S. Solomon, and P. Bartone, "Primary prevention in aircraft disasters," *American Psychologist*, 1988, vol. 43, no. 9, pp. 730–739. (Dr.

Carolyn Williams and colleagues are psychologists from the School of Public Health at the University of Minnesota.)

7   K. Wright (ed.), *Human Response to the Gander Military Air Disaster: A Summary Report*, Department of Military Psychiatry, Walter Reed Army Institute of Research, Washington, D.C., 1987.

8   B. Raphael, B. Singh, L. Bradbury, and F. Lambert, "Who helps the helpers? The effects of a disaster on the rescue workers," *Omega*, 1983–1984, vol. 14, pp. 9–20.

9   B. Berah, F. Jones, and P. Valent, "The experience of a mental health team involved in the early phase of a disaster," *Australian and New Zealand Journal of Psychiatry*, 1984, vol. 18, pp. 354–358.

10   B. Raphael, *When Disaster Strikes*, Basic Books, New York, 1986.

11   S. Juan, "The hidden impact of major disasters," *The Sydney Morning Herald*, February 9, 1989, p. 14.

12   S. Juan, "Damage done to those left behind," *The Sydney Morning Herald*, February 16, 1989, p. 13.

13   P. Sutker, D. Winstead, Z. Galina, and A. Allain, "Cognitive deficits and psychopathology among former prisoners of war and combat veterans of the Korean conflict," *American Journal Psychiatry*, 1991, vol. 148, no. 1, pp. 67–72. (Dr. Patricia Sutker and colleagues are psychiatrists from the Veterans Administration Medical Center in New Orleans.)

14   P. Sutker, A. Allain, and D. Winstead, "Psychopathology and psychiatric diagnoses of World War II Pacific theater prisoners of war survivors and combat veterans," *American Journal of Psychiatry*, 1993, vol. 150, no. 2, pp. 240–245.

15   P. Sutker, J. Davis, M. Uddo, and S. Ditta, "War zone stress, personal resources, and PTSD in Persian Gulf War returnees," *Journal of Abnormal Psychology*, 1995, vol. 104, no. 3, pp. 444–452.

16   S. Juan, "Survivors face a life sentence of trauma," *The Sydney Morning Herald*, June 18, 1992, p. 6.

17   C. Figley (ed.), *Compassion Fatigue*, Brunner/Mazel, New York, 1995.

18   E. Ubell, "Secrets of the brain," *Parade*, February 9, 1997, pp. 20–22.

19   M. Barasch, "Who knocks shocks?," *Psychology Today*, November–December 1995, p. 16.

Chapter 35: The TV Brain

1   Interview with J. Healy, November 12, 1992, cited in S. Juan, "The 'TV brain': What it switches off," *The Sydney Morning Herald*, November 26, 1992, p. 14. (Dr. Jane Healy is a psychologist at the Vail Mountain School in Cleveland, Ohio and at Cleveland State University. Dr. Healy is the author of *Your Child's Growing Mind*, Doubleday, New York, 1989, and *Endangered Minds: Why Children Don't Think and What We Can Do About It*, Simon and Schuster, New York, 1991.)

2   S. Covington, "TV may stunt kids' brains, experts warn," *The San Jose Mercury News*, October 3, 1992, p. 4.

3   Interview with J. Healy, July 11, 1997.

4   A. Greenwald, S. Draine, and R. Abrams, "Three cognitive markers of unconscious semantic activation," *Science*, 1996, vol. 273, pp. 1699–1702. (Dr. Anthony Greenwald and colleagues are from the Department of Psychology at the University of Washington in Seattle.)

5   A. Motluk, "Mind control ads 'don't sink in,'" *New Scientist*, September 28, 1996, p. 20.

6   M. Abrams and H. Bernstein, "Soon you'll curl up with an electronic book," *The San Francisco Chronicle*, June 1, 1992, pp. B1, B4.

Index

Note: Page numbers in italics
indicate boxed text.

index

index

index

index

index

About the Author

Dr. Stephen Juan is an anthropologist, educator, journalist, and author, often called Australia's "Wizard of Odds." His various "Odd Books" have been translated into numerous languages, with *The Odd Body* being translated into nineteen languages. A combined behavioral and biological scientist by training and one of the world's best communicators of human research, Dr. Juan was born in the Napa Valley in California. He received his B.A., M.A., and Ph.D. from the University of California at Berkeley and has taught at the University of Sydney for twenty-seven years. Currently he divides his time between homes in Sydney, Canberra, and California. A lively and popular speaker, Dr. Juan appears regularly on Australian news, current affairs, and lifestyle television and radio programs. His comments frequently appear in the Australian, Canadian, and U.S. press. Dr. Juan addresses any and all topics having to do with being a human being: body, brain, behavior, and the future of the human race. In his diverse career, Dr. Juan has been a pioneer in the field of developmental anthropology, a leader in science education, and the founding editor of the award-winning Australian magazine *Better Parenting*. Dr. Juan was also trained as a TV reporter and commentator by the Seven Television Network in Sydney. As a professional speaker, Dr. Juan has given numerous after-dinner talks and convention addresses around the world. He has been honored in Australia and overseas for his writing and other public education work. The American Medical Association and the U.S. National

Association of Physician Broadcasters are among the international organizations honoring him. His syndicated weekly column appears in newspapers around the world. Dr. Juan likes to think of himself as an explainer of all things human. Dr. Juan has a lively sense of humor and never takes himself or life too seriously.